Civil Society in Africa

Civil Society in Africa: The Role of a Catholic Parish in a Kenyan Slum

By

Christine Bodewes

CAMBRIDGE
SCHOLARS
PUBLISHING

Civil Society in Africa: The Role of a Catholic Parish in a Kenyan Slum
By Christine Bodewes

This book first published 2013

Cambridge Scholars Publishing

12 Back Chapman Street, Newcastle upon Tyne, NE6 2XX, UK

British Library Cataloguing in Publication Data
A catalogue record for this book is available from the British Library

ISBN (10): 1-4438-5234-1, ISBN (13): 978-1-4438-5234-0

TABLE OF CONTENTS

Preface and Acknowledgements vii

List of Abbreviations x

Maps of Kenya xii

Chapter One: The Civil Society Debate 1

Historical Evolution of Civil Society 2
The Advocates 6
The Critics 13
Kenyan Civil Society Analyzed 16

Chapter Two: The Slum Crisis in Kenya 25

Kenya and the Creation of a Neo-Patrimonial State 25
The Historical Evolution of the Slums 31
Kibera Slum 45
Christ the King Catholic Church 56

Chapter Three: The Civic Education Program 61

Civil Society's Historical Role Providing Civic Education 62
The OHR's Development of a Civic Education Program 67
Civic Education prior to the 2002 Election 70
The 2003 Program 79
The 2004 Program 83
The 2005 Program 85
The Impact of Civic Education 88
Conclusion 99

Chapter Four: The Campaign against Chang'aa 101

The Issue of Chang'aa prior to the Social Analysis 102
The OHR's Campaign against Chang'aa 110
Chang'aa as the Priority Issue of the Soweto Sub-Parish 122
Conclusion 133

Chapter Five: Slum Upgrading 135

The Government's Plan to Upgrade Soweto Village 136
The Creation of the Settlement Executive Committee 159
The Councilor Co-Opts the Upgrade 165
Civil Society's Response 167
Conclusion 171

Chapter Six: Forced Evictions 173

The Government's Threat of Evictions 174
Efforts to Secure a Permanent Moratorium 196
Conclusion 208

Chapter Seven: Conclusion 211

Summation 211
Summary Analysis 213
Impediments within Kibera's Environment 219
Impediments within the Local Church and Parish 227

Bibliography 237

Index 255

PREFACE AND ACKNOWLEDGEMENTS

In this book, I test the theory of scholars who argue that civil society plays a key role in promoting democracy, human rights and the rule of law in Africa. It investigates what, if anything, the Office of Human Rights (OHR), a ministry of a Catholic parish located in Kibera slum in Nairobi, Kenya, contributed to the consolidation of democracy. I argue that the civil society advocates are only partially correct in their claims. On one hand, the OHR was able to inculcate a small percentage of parishioners with democratic values, behavior and skills. However, apart from a small number of parishioners, the OHR was not able to mobilize parishioners to hold local government officials in Kibera to account for their corruption and abuse of power. The reality of Kibera's social, economic and political environment, as well as the internal functioning of the local Catholic Church and the parish, inhibited the vast majority of parishioners from exposing and confronting the human rights abuses perpetrated by government officials.

My personal history provides the background for this study. In 1997, after practicing as a lawyer for seven years, I joined Maryknoll Lay Missioners, a Catholic lay mission group based in the United States of America. In 1998 I was assigned to Nairobi, Kenya, and worked as a full-time volunteer lawyer at a local non-governmental organization (NGO), the Kituo cha Sheria (KCS) (Legal Aid Center). From 1998 through 2001, I worked with a team of Kenyan lawyers providing legal advice to slum dwellers faced with evictions and other land and housing crises. I also participated in the Land Caucus, the Pamoja Trust and the Muungano wana Vijiji, civil society organizations that feature in this study. In 2002 I was invited by a Guadalupe missionary priest to start a human rights ministry in the parish of Christ the King located in Kibera slum. I was the coordinator of the OHR until February 2006 when I turned over the office to a team of Kenyan lawyers.

This book examines the major activities of the OHR during my tenure as coordinator. It is primarily an analysis of events in which I was intimately involved. The study also involved considerable fieldwork because I returned to Kenya in 2008 to interview people concerned. I spoke to numerous informants including parishioners, the OHR staff, priests, sisters, brothers and laypersons, church personnel, human rights lawyers, activists and community organizers. My interviews also included missionaries, aid workers and human rights activists involved in these activities who are no longer in Kenya. In the body of this book I make reference to these interviews by the date on which they occurred. However, because most interviews were conducted in confidentiality, the names of the interviewees are withheld by mutual agreement. I am grateful for their insights, but the study is my personal interpretation of events in which I was actively involved in the light of substantial academic literature. I was often perplexed by the tension between the claims being made for civil society organizations such as those in which I worked and helped found, and my personal experience. As someone who worked for over eight years at the grass-roots level in both NGOs and faith-based organizations (FBOs) promoting human rights in the slums of Nairobi, my study provides a unique insight into the reality of civil society in Africa.

Chapter one sets out the two distinct perspectives concerning the role of civil society in the democratization process; the advocates who celebrate the potential of civil society to deepen democracy and the critics who argue that the transformative potential of civil society has been overstated. It also explains the civil society debate in Kenya and considers the views of several scholars who argue that although Kenyan civil society has not promoted democracy and human rights in the way it was anticipated in the 1990s, a few sectors have made a modest contribution to the democracy-building process in the 2000s.

Chapter two describes the context for my study. It first describes the historical evolution of a neo-patrimonial state in Kenya and civil society's efforts to introduce multi-party democracy. It also explains the emergence of the urban slum phenomenon in Nairobi as well as efforts by a number of Catholic missionaries and local human rights activists to respond to the slum crisis in the mid to late-1990s. It then looks at the locale of my research, Kibera slum, and highlights its particular social, economic and political dynamic. I end with a brief introduction to the Catholic parish of Christ the King and its basic structures including the OHR.

Chapter three examines efforts by the OHR to inculcate democratic values, beliefs and skills in parishioners through civic education classes taught in numerous parish groups. This chapter focuses on the dynamics within the Kibera community and the parish that affected its efforts. It also assesses whether the parishioners' new knowledge empowered them to pursue the common interests of the Kibera community in the civic and political arena.

Chapter four examines whether the OHR was able to mobilize parishioners to expose the corruption and abuse of power by government functionaries involved in the distribution and sale of chang'aa, a toxic and illegal brew that is widely sold and drunk in Kibera, and which parishioners identified as the biggest problem in the community. This chapter focuses on the campaign against chang'aa instigated by the OHR, and it challenges the assumption of civil society advocates that the grass roots has the ability to confront local officials in a repressive and corrupt environment like Kibera.

Chapter five looks at the efforts of the OHR to respond to a broad spectrum of corruption, malfeasance and abuse of power that emerged in connection with the government's decision to upgrade one of Kibera's villages. It examines the response not only of the parishioners, but also of other local civil society actors, and assesses whether the response was consistent with the expectations of civil society advocates.

Chapter six analyzes the OHR's response to the government's planned large-scale, forced evictions in the slums of Nairobi as well as the response of other civil society actors. This chapter also considers the particular attributes of expatriate missionaries, particularly their international networks, which allowed them to play a distinctive role in responding to the eviction threat.

The concluding chapter answers a number of questions relative to the civil society debate, namely, whether a local Catholic parish has the ability to socialize and mobilize its membership to promote democracy. It also describes how the expectations of the civil society advocates take little account of the reality in Kibera. The social, economic and political environment as well as the internal functioning of both the local Catholic Church and the parish was not conducive to ordinary Catholics holding local officials to account for their corruption and abuse of power.

A large portion of the manuscript for this book was completed while I was a doctoral student in African Christianity at the School of Oriental and African Studies in London. I wish to thank my thesis supervisor, Professor Paul Gifford, for his unfailing guidance and counsel throughout the entire project. I am especially grateful to him for sharing his vast knowledge of Africa, his rigorous standards and his humor. I would also like to thank my family and friends who have supported me in this process, especially my mother and father for their witness and example. I thank in a very special way Teddy Bodewes, Christine Holevas and Marleen Loos for their help and support on the manuscript and everyone at Sanctuary Farm for their encouragement and hospitality. Finally, I thank the staff from the Office of Human Rights in Kibera, the volunteer lawyers and the parishioners at Christ the King who have shared their ideas, hopes and insights and helped me in so many ways.

LIST OF ABBREVIATIONS

AIC	African Independent (Instituted) Church
AMECEA	Association of Member Episcopal Conferences in Eastern Africa
ANPPCAN	African Network for the Prevention and Protection against Child Abuse and Neglect
CJPC	Catholic Justice and Peace Commission
CKRC	Constitution of Kenya Review Commission
COHRE	Center for Housing Rights and Evictions
COT	Community Organization Training
CRS	Catholic Relief Services
DELTA	Development Education Leadership Teams in Action
DO	District Officer
FBO	Faith-Based Organization
GBM	Green Belt Movement
IJM	International Justice Mission
IFC	International Finance Corporation
IPPG	Inter-Parties Parliamentary Group
JPC	Justice and Peace Commission
KANU	Kenya African National Union
KCS	Kituo cha Sheria
KEC	Kenya Episcopal Conference
KENSUP	Kenya Slum Upgrading Program
KPLC	Kenya Power and Light Company
KRC	Kenya Railways Corporation
Ksh	Kenya Shilling (exchange rate during 2000-2005 approximately 1US$ = Ksh 80)
LSK	Law Society of Kenya
NARC	National Alliance Rainbow Coalition
NCC	Nairobi City Council
NCCK	National Council of Churches of Kenya
NCEC	National Convention Executive Council
NCEP	National Civic Education Program
NDP	National Development Party

NHC	National Housing Corporation
OHR	Office of Human Rights
PA	Provincial Administration
PC	Provincial Commissioner
PPC	Parish Pastoral Council
SCC	Small Christian Community
SEC	Settlement Executive Committee
UN-Habitat	United Nations Human Settlements Program

MAPS OF KENYA

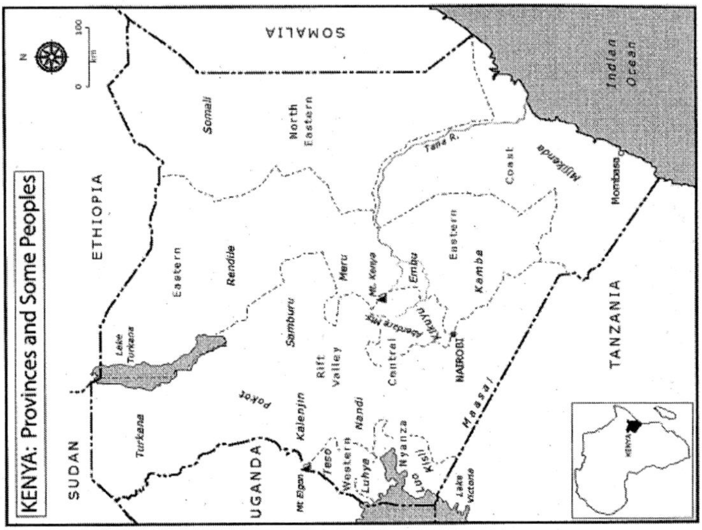

Christianity, Politics and Public Life in Kenya by Paul Gifford

CHAPTER ONE

THE CIVIL SOCIETY DEBATE

After the fall of the Berlin Wall in 1989, civil society was catapulted onto the global stage in the wake of widespread democratic transitions that started in Eastern Europe and spread throughout the world. In less than five years, the African continent found itself in a sea change of political transformation as the majority of states in sub-Sahara Africa took their first steps to remove the neo-patrimonial, authoritarian governments that had taken root since independence.[1] The impetus to push for political liberalization has been attributed to the growth and political activity of civil society across the African continent.[2] Voluntary and associational groups composed of organized labor, students, intellectuals, journalists, professional associations and grass-roots movements, frequently led by Christian churches, joined together to advocate political reform and multi-party elections.[3] This political transition toward democratization is often called Africa's Second Liberation.

There are several explanations given for Africa's Second Liberation. Most scholars agree that in addition to external pressure following the collapse of the Soviet Union and the release of Nelson Mandela, many African despots recognized that they could no longer rule without a modicum of legitimacy. There was also growing pressure from citizens

---

[1] African transitions in the 1990s led to divergent outcomes and in most cases political liberalisation did not result in liberal democracies. However, significant shifts in African political life did occur. For example, in 1989, 39 of 45 sub-Saharan countries had authoritarian forms of rule. Five years later, 31 had conducted democratic presidential or parliamentary elections and not a single *de jure* one-party state remained. Susan Dicklitch, *The Elusive Problem of NGOs in Africa: Lessons from Uganda* (New York: St. Martin's Press, 1998), 1.

[2] Stephen N. Ndegwa, *The Two Faces of Civil Society: NGOs and Politics in Africa* (West Hartford, CT: Kumarian Press, 1992), 2.

[3] For a full account of the role played by Christian churches, see Paul Gifford, *African Christianity: Its Public Role* (London: Hurst & Co., 1998); Paul Gifford, ed., *The Christian Churches and the Democratisation of Africa* (Leiden: E.J. Brill, 1995) and John W. de Gruchy, *Christianity and Democracy: A Theology for a Just World Order* (Cambridge: Cambridge University Press, 1995).

and grass-roots movements within civil society who, fed up with poverty, economic mismanagement and authoritarianism, initiated vocal demands for democracy and good governance. Moreover, as African nations began to lose their strategic political and military status in the post-Cold War era, foreign donors started requiring evidence of demonstrated progress toward good governance, multi-party elections and market-centered economies before resuming aid and investment in Africa.

With the emergence of democratization and the goal of improved governance, civil society became the central focus of analyzing the relationship between the state and society in Africa. This analysis sparked what has become an ongoing debate over the role of civil society in opposing undemocratic governments and furthering democratic consolidation in Africa. There are two opposing sides to this debate. Commonly referred to as the advocates, a number of Africanist scholars maintain that civil society is a significant, even essential, component to sustained democratic reform in Africa including the promotion of the rule of law and human rights. For the advocates, civil society has played and continues to play the central role in making African states more democratic, transparent and accountable.

On the other side of the debate are a growing number of scholars less sanguine in their views on civil society. As more empirical evidence has become available and analyzed, the critics have identified a broad scope of objections to treating civil society as the panacea for solving Africa's long-term political problems. Some critics reject outright the notion as a naive ideal. Others argue that civil society organizations are simply being asked to do too much with too little on a continent overrun with poverty, corruption and neo-patrimonial structures.

Historical Evolution of Civil Society

The definition of civil society is highly contested in contemporary African discourse. As Bebbington and Riddell note, "Civil society is a notoriously slippery concept … . It is used in different ways by different people and those uses are not always consistent."[4] Several factors account for its nebulous character. Civil society has a long and rich history in Europe's political philosophy dating from Hegel and Marx through to

[4] Anthony Bebbington, and Roger Riddell, "Heavy Hands, Hidden Hands, Holding Hands? Donors, Intermediary NGOs and Civil Society Organizations," in *NGOs, States and Donors: Too Close for Comfort*?' ed. David Hulme, and Michael Edwards (New York: St. Martin's Press, 1997), 108-09.

Hobbes and Locke.[5] Its uses and meaning have materially changed as academic scholarship has emphasized different political and ideological dimensions of the concept depending on the political and social context of the era. Notwithstanding the lack of consensus on its meaning, most scholars agree that it is an important concept central to the contemporary debates on African democratization.[6]

According to Ernest Gellner, civil society is a simple notion that has been tangled up by its roots in Hegelo-Marxist metaphysics.[7] Before turning to the civil society debate, a brief overview of its origin and evolution will highlight the definitions and meanings given to civil society in its modern lexicon. In classical political thought, from Aristotle to Rousseau, civil society was indistinguishable from the state. In the 18th century, a fundamental shift in the thinking about civil society occurred when liberal philosophers began to view civil society as a buffer against the state. Alexis de Tocqueville asserted that autonomous associations guarantee that the state will be unable to arrogate more power than an active citizenry is willing to grant.[8] In addition to limiting tyranny by the majority, de Tocqueville believed that civil society also plays a key role in teaching civic virtues and likened it to "large free schools, where all the members of the community go to learn the general theory of association."[9]

It was Hegel who first drew a clear philosophical distinction between the state and civil society locating civil society as an intermediate stage of social organization between the family and the state that allowed for the expression and protection of private interests.[10] In recognition that interests within civil society might overwhelm the public good, Hegel asserted that the state would guide and override civil society when

---

[5] For the history of civil society, see John Keane, *Civil Society and the State: New European Perspectives* (London: Verso, 1988).

[6] Some scholars, however, argue that civil society is a uniquely Western concept that is difficult, if not impossible, to apply to Africa. See David Lewis, "Civil Society in African Contexts: Reflections on the Usefulness of a Concept," *Development and Change* 33, no. 4 (2002): 569-86 and Victor Azarya, "Civil Society and Disengagement in Africa," in *Civil Society and the State in Africa*, ed. John W. Harbeson, Donald S. Rothchild, and Naomi Chazan (Boulder, CO: L. Reinner Publishers, 1994), 87-88.

[7] Ernest Gellner, *Conditions of Liberty, Civil Society and its Rivals* (London: Penguin Press, 1996), 11.

[8] See Alexis de Tocqueville, *Democracy in America*, ed. Phillips Bradley, trans. Henry Reene (New York: Alfred Knopf, 1945), 115-20.

[9] Ibid., 117.

[10] See G.W.F. Hegel, *Philosophy of Right*, trans. T. M. Knox (Oxford: Clarendon Press, 1942), 148.

necessary to preserve the greater public well-being.[11] In contrast to Hegel, Karl Marx viewed the state as subordinate in its relations with civil society.[12] In Marx's view, civil society was another instrument for furthering the interests of the dominant class under capitalism. In a similar vein, Antonio Gramsci described civil society as an array of educational, religious and associational institutions that guaranteed the ideological hegemony of the ruling class.[13] Although both Marx and Gramsci perceived civil society to be a non-state sphere of domination by the bourgeoisie, Gramsci placed it alongside the state, not at its base.[14]

Robert Putnam has also made a significant contribution to the corpus of literature on civil society regarding the role of social capital and the value of voluntary associations in nurturing trust and cooperation based on his study of associational life in Italy and the United States.[15] For Putnam, the most important virtue of civil association lies in its capacity to socialize participants into horizontal networks of reciprocity and collective action as opposed to vertical networks of patron-client arrangements.

The definition of civil society that I use for purposes of my research is the one put forth by Larry Diamond and adopted by many Africanist scholars. Commonly referred to as the "conventional view;" Diamond defines civil society, "as the realm of organized social life that is voluntary, self-generating, (largely) self-supporting, autonomous from the state and bound by a legal order or set of shared rules."[16] Civil society relates to public and not private interests that "involve citizens acting collectively in a public sphere to express their interests, passions, and ideas, exchange information, achieve mutual goals, make demands on the state, and hold state officials accountable."[17] It is composed of a vast array of formal and informal organizations including groups that are: (1)

---

[11] Ibid., 152.

[12] Karl Marx, *Critique of 'Philosophy of Right,'* ed. Joseph O'Malley (Cambridge: University Press, 1970), 5-6.

[13] Antonio Gramsci, *Selections from the Prison Notebooks*, ed. and trans. Quintin Hoare, and Geoffrey Nowell Smith (New York: International Publishers, 1971), 12.

[14] See Stephen Orvis, "Civil Society in Africa or African Civil Society?" *African and Asian Studies* 36, no.1 (2001): 19-20.

[15] See Robert D. Putnam, *Bowling Alone: The Collapse and Revival of American Community* (New York: Simon & Schuster, 2000) and Robert D. Putnam, Robert Leonardi, and Raffaella Nanetii, *Making Democracy Work: Civic Traditions in Modern Italy* (Princeton: Princeton University Press, 1993).

[16] Larry Diamond, "Toward Democratic Consolidation," *Journal of Democracy* 5, no.3 (1994): 5.

[17] Ibid.

economic, (2) cultural and religious, (3) informational and educational, (4) interest-based, (5) developmental, and (6) issue and civic-orientated.[18] In addition, civil society includes organizations that are part of the ideological marketplace such as the media, universities, think tanks and publishing houses.[19]

According to the conventional view, because civil society is distinct from society and acts as an intermediary between the private sphere and the state, civil society excludes individual and family life, inward-looking group activity such as recreation, entertainment and spirituality, profit-making enterprises and political efforts to take control of the state.[20] Diamond also excludes revolutionaries, religious fundamentalists and ethnically chauvinistic organizations on the grounds that their attempt to monopolize political space is contradictory to the pluralistic notions of civil society. The conventional view also holds that if an organization is to promote democracy, it must function democratically in its internal processes. This definition therefore excludes organizations deemed undemocratic, uncivil or that act outside the constraints of the law.[21]

Civil society advocates generally agree on the fundamental elements contained in Diamond's definition, but some have added and subtracted from it in varying degrees with regard to the level of antagonism between the state and civil society. Diamond, who is closely aligned to the de Tocqueville view, asserts that civil society "must be autonomous from the state, but not alienated from it. It must be watchful but respectful of state authority."[22] In contrast, Jean François Bayart claims that at its core, civil society is always in confrontation with the state.[23] Michael Bratton argues for a neutral definition that avoids judging the nature of the state-society relations; it is a relationship that ebbs and flows as the state and social actors engage with one another.[24]

---

[18] Ibid., 6.
[19] Ibid.
[20] Ibid., 5.
[21] Axel Hadenius, and Frederick Uggla, "Making Civil Society Work, Promoting Democratic Development: What Can Donors Do?" *World Development* 24, no. 10 (1996): 10-11.
[22] Ibid., 15.
[23] Jean François Bayart, "Civil Society in Africa," in *Political Domination in Africa: Reflections on the Limits of Power*, ed. Patrick Chabal (Cambridge: Cambridge University Press, 1986), 111.
[24] Michael Bratton, "Beyond the State: Civil Society and Associational Life in Africa," *World Politics* (1988): 415.

The Advocates

The civil society advocates argue that civil society is not only a positive force; it also plays the most important and critical role in democratization. For example, Diamond claims that civil society is "the cutting edge of the effort to build a viable democratic order."[25] In his view:

> Civil society is a crucially important factor at every stage of democratization. The greater the number, size, autonomy, resourcefulness, variety and democratic orientation of popular organizations in civil society, the greater will be the prospects for some kind of movement from rigid authoritarianism, and for subsequent movement toward semi-democracy and democracy.[26]

Harbeson agrees. He argues that civil society is the:

> Hitherto missing key to sustained political reform, legitimate states and governments, improved governance, viable state-society and state-economy relationships, and prevention of the kind of political decay that undermined new African governments a decade ago.[27]

Chazan also holds to this view claiming, "The nurturing of civil society is … the most effective means of controlling repeated abuses of state power, holding rulers accountable to their citizens, and establishing the foundations for durable democratic government."[28]

Enthusiasm for civil society is not limited to academics and theorists. The development and donor communities have taken an even stronger position in support of civil society, particularly NGOs, as the possible solution to the economic and governance woes of Africa. Adopting the New Policy Agenda of the post-Cold War era, donors reduced the amount of official aid given directly to states and substituted NGOs as the new

---

[25] Larry Diamond, Juan Linz, and Seymour Lipset, Democracy in Developing Countries (Boulder, CO: L. Reinner Publishers, 1988), 26.
[26] Larry Diamond, "Beyond Autocracy: Prospect for Democracy in Africa," (Paper presented at Inaugural Seminar of the Governance Program, Carter Centre, Emory University, Atlanta, 1989), 25.
[27] John W. Harbeson, "Civil Society and Political Renaissance in Africa," in *Civil Society and the State in Africa*, ed. John W. Harbeson, Donald S. Rothchild, and Naomi Chazan (Boulder, CO: L. Reinner Publishers, 1994), 1-2.
[28] Naomi Chazan, "Africa's Democratic Challenge," *World Policy Journal* 9, no. 2 (1992): 282.

channel for providing traditional welfare services.[29] Although NGOs (especially churches) had a long history of providing services such as health care and education in the developing world, under the New Policy Agenda, NGOs were identified as the preferred channel for social welfare because they were perceived to be more cost effective, less bureaucratic, and better able to target the poor and promote grass-roots participation.[30] As aid was made more available in the 1990s, there was an explosion in the number of service-provision NGOs often referred to as the "global NGO revolution."[31]

In addition to providing social services, NGOs are also seen as the ideal vehicle for building democracy and a stronger civil society which are, in turn, essential for economic growth under the New Policy Agenda.[32] NGOs are "supposed to act as a counterweight to state power by opening up channels of communication and participation, providing training grounds for activists promoting pluralism and by protecting human rights."[33] The notion that a stronger civil society is critical for democratization caught fire throughout Africa. By the mid-1990s, a plethora of a new kind of organization evolved–the human rights/advocacy NGO; organizations dedicated exclusively to advocacy, civic education, voter education and election monitoring.[34]

According to civil society advocates, civil society organizations have the potential to advance democracy in two general ways: (1) by helping generate a transition away from authoritarian rule to electoral democracy and (2) by deepening and consolidating democracy once it is established.[35]

---

[29] The New Policy Agenda replaced the outdated development logic of the 1970s; at its centre is the reliance placed on markets and the private sector as the most effective mechanisms for achieving economic growth and providing services to citizens. See David Hulme, and Michael Edwards, ed., *NGOs, States and Donors: Too Close for Comfort?* (New York: St. Martin's Press, 1997), 5-6 and Julie Hearn, "The 'Invisible' NGO: US Evangelical Missions in Kenya," *Journal of Religions in Africa* 32, no. 1 (2002): 46.

[30] Hulme, and Edwards, *NGOs, States*, 6.

[31] Jim Igoe, and Tim Kelsall, *Between a Rock and a Hard Place: African NGOs, Donors and the State* (Durham, NC: Carolina Academic Press, 2005), 27.

[32] Hulme, and Edwards, *NGOs, States*, 6.

[33] Ibid.

[34] Marina Ottaway, Thomas Carothers, and the Carnegie Endowment for International Peace, ed., *Funding Virtue: Civil Society Aid and Democracy Promotion* (Washington, D.C.: Carnegie Endowment For International Peace, 2000), 80-82.

[35] Larry Diamond, *Developing Democracy: Toward Consolidation* (Baltimore: Johns Hopkins University Press, 1999), 233.

Democratization requires not only a regime change from authoritarian rule, but also the creation and operation of democratic institutions and the exercise of democratic citizenship that protects human rights and promotes the rule of law.[36] As a consequence, civil society's role in promoting democracy does not end after the first competitive multi-party election takes place; rather, its role significantly increases in scope and importance. In Diamond's view:

> It is one thing to get to democracy. It is quite another thing, and often much more difficult, to keep it, to consolidate it, to breathe real life and meaning into it, to make it endure. Many of the countries that have made transitions to democracy…are in grave political crisis now because democracy is simply not working to deliver the broad developmental progress, honest and decent government, protection for human rights, and political and social tranquility, that people want.[37]

In a post-authoritarian context, the most important task in the consolidation process is restoring the primacy of the rule of law because in its absence, violence, thuggery and lawlessness are the routine methods of political action.[38] The rule of law means that all citizens are equal before the law and that the "laws themselves are clear, publicly known, universal, stable, non-retroactive, and fairly and consistently applied to all citizens by an independent judiciary."[39] For democracy to become grounded, the consolidation process must also strengthen the right to inalienable human rights, constitutionalism and institutional structures such as political parties, the legislature and the judicial system in order to ensure political rights, civil liberties and mechanisms of accountability.[40] Democratic consolidation also requires citizenry to inculcate democratic principles and methods both on a behavioral and attitudinal level. This involves what is termed the "habituation" of democracy where the norms and procedures of democracy become so internalized that citizens instinctively follow the

---

[36] Antonio F. Moreno, *Church, State, and Civil Society in Postauthoritarian Philippines: Narratives of Engaged Citizenship* (Manila: Ateneo de Manila University Press, 2006), 112.

[37] Larry Diamond, and the Centre for Democratic Studies, *Globalization of Democracy: Trends, Types, Causes and Prospects* (Abuja, Nigeria: C.D.S. Occasional Publications, 1992), 46.

[38] Moreno, *Church, State*, 175.

[39] Ibid., xiv.

[40] David Beetham, *Democracy and Human Rights* (Cambridge: Polity Press in association with Blackwell, 1999), 92.

rules of the game.[41] It also involves the development of a political culture where values like moderation, tolerance, civility, knowledge and participation are fully integrated and adopted by the majority of society.[42] Because values and attitudes do not change quickly, the consolidation of democracy is a long-term process that can take several decades.[43]

Civil society organizations tend to be far less active when they are needed most in consolidating and strengthening an already existing democracy. During the transition, "all sorts of organizations, movements, and networks push not only for their narrow functional or ideological interests but for democracy and civil liberties."[44] After the transition, the group's systemic concern for democracy tends to be overtaken by the ensuing interplay of competing interests within the group.[45] Moreover, the post-authoritarian phase is a difficult time, a period of substantial challenges, both large and small, in the realm of politics and policy.[46] The long-term struggle to make democracy work is much less exciting than the moral crusade to rid the country of a despotic ruler.

Larry Diamond, one of the leading civil society advocates, has identified a number of particular functions that civil society is able to perform to help deepen and consolidate democracy. The most fundamental function of civil society is to limit and contain the power of the government.[47] Once a transition has occurred, civil society can support the democratization process by holding the state to greater accountability to both the law and public expectations of responsible government through a process of checks and monitoring. Civil society organizations typically perform this watchdog function by holding the government to public scrutiny and exposing the abuses of state power. While the exposure alone does not guarantee a popular reaction, punishment or deterrence, it can galvanize civil society to take further action.[48]

---

[41] Diamond, *Developing Democracy*, 65.
[42] Ibid., 163.
[43] Michael Bratton, and Nicolas van de Walle, *Democratic Experiments in Africa: Regime Transitions in Comparative Perspective* (Cambridge: Cambridge University Press, 1997), 6-8.
[44] Diamond, "Civil Society," 7-8.
[45] Ibid.
[46] Larry Diamond, *The Democratic Revolution: Struggle for Freedom and Pluralism in the Development World, Perspectives on Freedom* (New York: Freedom House, 1992), 16.
[47] Diamond, "Toward Democratic," 7.
[48] Diamond, *Developing Democracy*, 240.

A second democracy-building function performed by civil society is to supplement the role of political parties by stimulating political participation, increasing political efficacy and skills of citizens, and promoting an understanding of the rights and obligations of democratic citizenship. In this role, civil society organizations provide training grounds for citizens to gain practical experience in democracy. Civil society organizations become what de Tocqueville refers to as "large free schools" where the community learns the art of association, participatory habits and the skills of democratic citizenship including communication and political skills.[49] For example, leaders within civil society associations generally learn how to organize people, debate issues, mediate conflicts, develop consensus, manage finances and build coalitions. They also learn to be accountable to their members, in turn; the membership learns how to hold their leaders accountable.[50] As a result, in addition to learning skills beneficial to improving the welfare of their own organizations, individuals also learn skills that are readily transferable to the political sphere.

Third, many civil society organizations have adopted democracy education as an explicit project in order to socialize adults and young people to the values of a democratic political culture. Democracy theorists agree that democracy requires a distinctive set of political values, orientations and beliefs that include:

> Tolerance for opposing political beliefs and positions and also more generally for social and cultural differences; pragmatism and flexibility, as opposed to a rigid and ideological approach to politics; trust in other political actors and in the social environment; a willingness to compromise, springing from a belief in the necessity and desirability of compromise; and civility of political discourse and respect for other views.[51]

Efforts to inculcate democratic values are usually attempted through civic education and human rights training. According to Diamond, the best way for citizens to learn about democracy is not receiving instruction in a classroom.

> Citizens learn by doing, by groping together for solutions in extensive workshops, by meeting frequently to discuss issues and hear the views of others, by teaching these principles to others, by repeatedly listening to

[49] Ibid, 11.
[50] Dicklitch, *The Elusive Promise*, 12.
[51] Diamond, Linz, and Lipset, *Democracy in Developing*, 26.

> civilized and substantive debates of the issues, by keeping actively informed, by creating new organizations of their own.[52]

Even though civic education can be slow and difficult because it involves intensive, small group work, it is the central function of civil society organizations committed to the democratization process.[53]

A fourth way civil society supports democracy is to create alternate channels, apart from political parties, for citizens to articulate and represent their interests. It is in this advocacy role that civil society organizations mobilize the community to channel their demands directly to the government. In addition to empowering citizens to voice their concerns, civil society also facilitates citizens to take direct action to achieve their ends. Civil society organizations compete with each other to influence government officials to adopt positions supporting their members and to follow formal rules, a process that in turn facilitates open, free and fair political debate. In this way, civil society helps build organizations that can act independently to confront the government either by holding it to account, influencing a policy or offering alternate policy ideas.

Fifth, civil society is able to gather and disseminate information that helps empower the community in their collective defense and pursuit of their mutual interests. Providing independent and accurate information about what the government is actually doing versus what it says it is doing and the impact it has on citizens at a local level is considered an invaluable function of civil society. "While civil society groups may sometimes prevail temporarily by dint of raw numbers (e.g., in strikes and demonstrations) they generally cannot be effective in contesting government policies or defending their interests unless they are well-informed."[54] That is why the ability to gather and disseminate accurate information is a vital technique used by human rights organizations that want to overcome government cover-ups typical of repressive regimes.[55]

A sixth function of civil society is to recruit and train new political leaders. For most civil society theorists, the recruitment and training of leaders is a long-term byproduct of the successful functioning of civil society organizations. Leaders in civil society organizations learn "how to organize and motivate people, debate issues, raise and account for funds, craft budgets, publicize programs, administer staff, canvass for support,

---

[52] Diamond, *The Democratic Revolution,* 17.
[53] Ibid.
[54] Diamond, "Toward Democratic," 10.
[55] Ibid.

negotiate agreements, and build coalitions."[56] This kind of experience gives leaders and activists within an organization both the skills and self-confidence that qualify them for service in government and party politics.

A seventh democracy-building function of civil society is the generation of "a wide range of interests that may cross-cut, and so mitigate, the principal polarities of political conflict."[57] The issue-based groups bring together people from different ethnic, religious and regional groups. The joint pursuit of democracy and related issues can help dissipate historical divisions and narrow interests. The more organizations that a person can join, the more he or she will associate with different types of people who hold different political views, which will give that person a more sophisticated political outlook and enhance his or her tolerance and readiness to compromise.

Eighth, civil society organizations are able to enhance democracy by undertaking conflict resolution and mediation. This is especially true for civil society organizations generated out of religious and human rights communities. "When a wide range of political actors come to trust these organizations–the organizations gain a 'reserve of influence' that can be drawn on in a political crisis."[58]

Ninth, civil society can deepen democracy by helping local communities break the cycle of patron-client relationships whereby local authorities such as chiefs and land owners purchase deference and control of the citizenry through the dispensation of material rewards.[59] If civil society is able to eliminate the fear of outside intervention or punishment, it can sever "the psychological and structural bonds of clientelism that have historically locked them in a dependent and subordinated status, isolated from one another and unable to rally around their common material or cultural interests."[60]

A final, overarching function of civil society is derived from the combined success of the above functions.[61] "By enhancing the accountability, responsiveness, inclusiveness, effectiveness, and hence legitimacy of the political system, a vigorous civil society gives citizens

---

[56] Ibid., 9.
[57] Ibid.
[58] Diamond, *Developing Democracy*, 248.
[59] Ibid., 244.
[60] Ibid.
[61] Diamond identifies three additional functions not addressed in this thesis: (1) election monitoring, (2) community development and (3) economic reform.

respect for the state," which can improve the state's ability to garner deference and obedience from its citizens.[62]

For purposes of this study, I reduce Diamond's list of function to two general categories typically identified by civil society advocates.[63] First, a civil society organization has the power to socialize its members with participatory norms and a sense of efficacy in social and political life. By inculcating democratic values and habits among its members, a civil society organization can build a culture that supports democracy. Second, a civil society organization has the power to mobilize its members to resist a tyrannical regime. By building an organization that can act independently and is willing to confront the state, a civil society organization has the power to hold the government to account and influence policy.

The Critics

A substantial number of Africanist scholars do not agree that civil society is central to sustained democratic reform in Africa. The fundamental criticism of these scholars is that the advocates' "vision is based on a flawed conception of social realities."[64] For example, Patrick Chabal and Jean-Pascal Daloz assert that civil society is just another structure that Africans use to make a profit within a neo-patrimonial state.[65] In their view:

> The explosion of NGOs is not a reflection of the flowering of civil society in the sense in which it is usually understood in the west. It is in reality (rather than fiction) evidence of the adaptation by African political actors to the changing complexion of the international aid game.[66]

Others like Robert Fatton, an outspoken opponent of what he calls the "reveling and exaggerated celebrations" of the advocates, argue that

---

[62] Diamond, *Developing Democracy*, 240.

[63] See Michael Foley, and Bob Edwards, "The Paradox of Civil Society," *Journal of Democracy* 7, no. 3 (1996): 39 and Nelson Kasfir, "Civil Society, the State and Democracy in Africa," in *Civil Society and Democracy in Africa: Critical Perspectives*, ed. Nelson Kasfir (London: Frank Cass, 1998), 128.

[64] Peter Von Doepp, "Liberal Visions and Actual Power in Grassroots Civil Society: Local Churches and Women's Empowerment in Rural Malawi," *Journal of Modern African Studies* 40, no. 2 (2002): 276.

[65] Patrick Chabal, and Jean-Pascal Daloz, *Africa Works: Disorder as Political Instrument* (Oxford: James Currey, 1999), 22.

[66] Ibid., 23.

African civil society mirrors African political society.[67] For Fatton, civil society is composed of ethnic particularisms, class interests, individual egotism and all types of religious and secular fundamentalisms.

> Civil society in Africa is conflict-ridden and prone to Hobbesian wars of all against all. It is the prime repository of 'invented' ethnic hierarchies, conflicting class visions, patriarchal domination and irredentist identities fueling deadly conflicts in many areas of the continent.[68]

As a result, African civil society amounts to no more than a "disorganized plurality of mutually exclusive projects fragmented by the contradictory historical alternatives of competing social actors, institutions and beliefs."[69]

Nelson Kasfir also objects to the advocates' claims. In his analysis of African civil society, Kasfir concludes that the advocates have mistakenly exported idealized notions of Western democracy and foisted them on Africa without understanding the kind of associations that exist in Africa and their relationship to the state.[70] According to Kasfir, the outdated notions of pluralism advocated by Diamond, Chazan and others cannot work in Africa. Pluralists maintain that as economic and social interests diversify, more groups will be formed to represent these interests and as these groups compete with each other to influence public policy, the government will attain more information and thus will provide more efficient solutions. Kasfir asserts that this theory works in the United States because its political system, which is based on checks and balances, allows small interest groups to affect public policy.[71] The situation in Africa is very different. Unlike in America, there is markedly unequal access to state officials, organizational skills and material resources.[72] The state is all-powerful and the only entity that changes policies. It is also much more difficult to reconcile divergent interests and organize collective action in Africa because most people live in rural areas where few uniting interests and motives for change have emerged. In Kasfir's view, "there simply is no welter of competing interests to whom an African policymaker needs to listen."[73]

---

[67] Robert Fatton, "Africa in the Age of Democratization: The Civic Limitations of Civil Society," *African Studies Review* 38, no. 2 (1995): 72.
[68] Ibid., 73.
[69] Ibid., 72.
[70] Kasfir, "Civil Society," 123-45.
[71] Ibid., 130-31.
[72] Ibid., 143.
[73] Ibid., 133.

A number of scholars and donors from the development sector are also critical of the argument that civil society, particularly NGOs, can cure the ills of Africa. Many of these doubts emerged in the early 1990s when the NGO revolution was just beginning in earnest in Africa. Edwards and Hulme pointed out that, due to their very nature NGOs, are inherently limited by their incapacity for research, poor networking with other NGOs, and the absence of representatives from the beneficiary community and weak links with the policy sector, making any effect localized and small.[74] John Clark also warned of the innate weaknesses of NGOs. In Clark's experience, NGO leaders are often charismatic and committed but "maintain an ill-defined structure and tend to be somewhat dictatorial in decision making."[75] Accountability is also an Achilles heel for many NGOs. Frequently, to the extent NGOs are held accountable, it is usually for how the donor money is spent, not whether or not a project is effective.

The degree of criticism of NGOs varies according to the different sectors. Although there has been a modicum of support for NGOs engaged in alleviating poverty and helping marginalized communities adapt to modernization, harsh criticism has been lodged against the largest sector of African NGOs, the professional human rights/advocacy organizations that focus on promotion of democracy and good governance.[76] According to Kasfir, given that most African states depend on ethnic mobilization to maintain their positions, these newly created professional advocacy NGOs have no ability to impact the political struggle in Africa because they have no social roots in society.[77] Ottaway and Coruthers agree; in their view, these organizations are merely creations of foreign donors that reflect "free-floating political pluralism" and not the "social demands for representation and a role in policy-making" by the local communities.[78] Because they have no substantive connection to the grass roots, these kinds of organizations generally focus on broad and abstract issues and ignore the real, local concerns of the ordinary people. They tend to promote foreign objectives unrelated to ongoing political and social realities and cease to exist when the donor money dries up. As a result,

---

[74] Hulme, and Edwards, *NGOs, States*, 17.

[75] John Clark, *Democratizing Development: The Role of Voluntary Organizations* (West Harford, CT: Kumarian Press, 1991), 63-73.

[76] William Fisher, "Doing Good? The Politics and Antipolitics of NGO Practices," *Annual Review of Anthropology* 26 (1997), 440.

[77] Kasfir, "Civil Society," 142.

[78] Ottaway, and Carothers, *Funding Virtue*, 12.

many of these programs have little impact and can even have negative consequences.[79]

In their research on the relationship between donors and civil society, Ottaway and Carothers also highlight the dilemma facing civil society in Africa.[80] According to their observations, they conclude that while the professional NGOs that are favored by donors are poorly rooted in society, top-down, plagued with management problems and dependent on foreign money, they are the only organizations in Africa that are willing to engage the state and hold it to account. In their view:

> The voluntary associations that Africans have formed themselves are grassroots organizations with a proven ability to organize and survive on their own, responsive to the demands of their members and thus more representative. But in recent years they have not attempted to represent the interests of their members in the political process and as yet have played no role in promoting democratization. They are more likely to disengage from the state than seek to hold it responsible.[81]

Ottaway and Carothers also observe that donors face a dilemma. Should they continue to fund professional NGOs that are not sufficiently integrated in the society or should donors redirect their funds to the more informal grass-roots organizations with the aim of building their political and social capacity?[82]

Kenyan Civil Society Analyzed

The issues raised in the civil society debate have also been addressed in Kenya, but in a limited manner. Scholarship focuses primarily on the role played by NGOs during the country's transition to multi-party elections in the early 1990s, a period of optimism and euphoria. There are both advocates and critics of civil society, but over time the debate has become dominated by the critics. While most scholars agree that Kenyan NGOs helped topple the despotic regime of President Moi and advance the process of constitutional reform, typical of civil society in many fledgling democracies, NGOs did not make an equally substantial contribution to

---

[79] See Lisa VeneKlasen, "The Challenge of Democracy-Building: Practical Lessons on NGO Advocacy and Political Change," in *NGOs, Civil Society and the State: Building Democracy in Transitional Societies*, ed. Andrew Clayton (Oxford: INTRAC, 1996), 219.

[80] See Ottaway, and Carothers, *Funding Virtue*, 81-86.

[81] Ibid, 85.

[82] Ibid.

democracy building in Kenya beyond the authoritarian period. After nearly two decades of struggle, Kenya has achieved only minor democratic reform. It is therefore not surprising that many scholars have changed their minds about Kenyan NGOs. The NGO sector is no longer characterized as the "beacon of hope" for democracy and, instead, is frequently described as corrupt, authoritarian and elitist. Pessimism about NGOs and their ability to deepen democracy and human rights in Kenya is fueled by several fundamental weaknesses endemic in the NGO sector: (1) poor leadership; (2) undemocratic organizational structures and (3) donor dependence.

Poor Leadership

In 1996 Stephen Ndegwa was the first scholar to publish substantial empirical findings on the role of NGOs in promoting democracy in Kenya. In his study, Ndegwa analyzed two local NGOs, the Green Belt Movement (GBM) and the Undungu Society of Kenya, between 1990 and 1992 during the buildup to the first multi-party elections. He found that both NGOs were administered by well-known political reformers and yet only one, the GBM, managed to transform itself into an activist organization. In contrast, the other NGO accommodated the repressive state even in the face of numerous political opportunities and pressure by its own clients to oppose the state. Ndegwa concluded that there is "nothing inherent in civil society organizations that make them opponents of authoritarianism and proponents of democracy."[83] Most organizations are willing only to take up interests that are tied to their own institutional survival. The factor determining whether or not a well-endowed NGO is transformed into an activist organization is its leadership's willingness to commit its resources to a progressive political agenda.[84]

NGO leadership in Kenya has continued to draw a tremendous amount of criticism. In his comparison of Kenya's and Zambia's transitions to multi-party elections in the early 1990s, Shadrack Nasong'o found that Kenyan civil society made only a modest contribution to democratization because it is weak and fractured along ethnic lines.[85] One of the key reasons that Kenyan civil society is weak is poor NGO leadership. Nasong'o observed that, good intentions aside, "the nature and structure of

---

[83] Ndegwa, *The Two Faces*, 6.

[84] Ibid., 1.

[85] Shadrack W. Nasong'o, Contending Political Paradigms in Africa: Rationality and the Politics of Deomcratization in Kenya and Zambia (London: Routledge, 2005), 79.

the leadership of most of these organizations mirror that of the authoritarian state."[86] Leadership, especially in the human rights sector, is generally "drawn from the elite and middle class and hails from either the intelligentsia or more commonly, the legal profession" and, as a result, many NGO personnel share the "alignment and project of the state-based elite."[87] Many NGO leaders are motivated by self-advancement and personal accumulation; some even run their NGOs like family businesses.[88]

In 2002 Walter Oyugi corroborated this conclusion when he found that many NGOs were "'oligarchies' whose paths are determined by the founder's perception of a community's needs."[89] According to his study of 22 NGOs engaged in activities designed to promote good governance, many founders operate their NGOs as personal fiefdoms and often refuse to disclose financial information. He also concluded that numerous NGOs are an outlet for self-employment for the people who start them. A 2004 study of the NGO sector by Karuti Kanyinga is even more critical. In analyzing the NGOs' historical role in promoting democracy, Kanyinga concluded:

> The majority tends towards 'elitism,' they are formed by urban elites more often for rent-seeking purposes. They use them as instruments of accessing donor funds and as platforms for launching political careers....They have intense internal wars among themselves over either leadership or over who should proximate influential donors. Power struggles initially associated with the political elites are also now visible in this sector.[90]

Kanyinga's study also highlighted the fact that many NGOs tend to recruit personnel based on shared ethnic identity, with a result that they are not only divided along ethnic lines, they also frequently pursue patrimonial agendas tied to the country's political economy.[91]

---

[86] Ibid., 85.
[87] Ibid.
[88] Ibid., 86.
[89] Walter Oyugi, "The Role of NGOs in Fostering Development and Good Governance at the Local Level in Africa with a Focus on Kenya," *African Development* 24, no.4 (2004): 47
[90] Karuti Kanyinga, "Civil Society Formations in Kenya: A Growing Role in Development and Democracy," in *Civil Society in the Third Republic*, ed. Duncan Okello, and National Council of NGOs (Kenya) (Nairobi: National Council of NGOs, 2004), 17.
[91] Ibid., 23.

Undemocratic Organizational Structures

A number of scholars have also found that many Kenyan NGOs are inherently undemocratic in their organizational structures and operations. According to Nasong'o, NGOs "seek to democratize the African State yet they are themselves undemocratic and unaccountable. They seek to deconstruct personal rule in Africa yet at the same time, they are themselves embodiments of personal rule albeit at a microscopic level."[92] Oyugi reached a similar conclusion: "Few NGOs (have) either formal, democratic systems for choosing office bearers, or transparent mechanisms for canvassing grass-roots opinion."[93] The NGOs' failure to provide the grass roots with opportunities to participate in their projects has limited the community's efforts at self-help and created greater dependency on the NGO sector. In Oyugi's view, NGOs that frustrate the organic efforts of the grass roots undermine the only genuine civil society that exists on the ground. Ndegwa identified the NGOs' failure to empower the grass roots as the sector's single greatest failure. He also predicted that if civil society fails to mobilize the grass roots to participate at the local level, there is no hope for democracy in Africa.[94]

Donor Dependency

Conventionally, NGOs are not-for-profit organizations, but this does not mean they are in voluntary work. To the contrary, most are professional organizations that have expensive overhead costs and require large amounts of resources. Because the majority of NGOs in Kenya are not capable of sustaining themselves financially, they are reliant on foreign donors to provide their financial support and, in some instances, personnel and political opportunity.[95] The availability of donor funds to Kenyan NGOs has resulted in mixed results. On one hand, an NGO with an autonomous source of funds independent from the state may be able to avoid a traditional patron-client relationship with the government and be better placed to confront the state. On the other hand, NGO dependence on international donors can make an organization's future insecure and enable the donors to have great influence over operations causing some NGOs to

[92] Nasong'o, *Contending Political*, 85.
[93] Oyugi, "The Role of NGOs," 47.
[94] Ndegwa, *The Two Faces*, 14-15.
[95] John Makumbe, "Is there a Civil Society in Africa?" *International Affairs* 74, no. 2 (1998): 311.

shape funding proposals to fit the agendas of donors, marginalizing the needs of the intended beneficiaries.[96]

According to Nasong'o, Kenyan NGOs' reliance on Western donors has turned many of them into "programmatic appendages of international funding agencies."[97] Oyugi concurs: "NGOs are viewed as focusing their attention on their legal obligations to the donors rather than their moral obligations to their client groups" because "the poor do not have the ability to force 'accountability' on NGOs."[98] Perhaps the most negative impact of donor dependence is the competition it breeds. According to Kanyinga, competition for resources among Kenyan NGOs has dramatically undermined their potential to partner and network toward common solutions.[99]

NGOs are not the only civil society actors in Kenya that have failed to live up to the expectations of the civil society advocates. In 2002 Frederick Wanyama tested the civil society debate as it related to community-based groups (CBOs) located in rural areas of western Kenya during the country's transition to multi-party elections. The CBOs were small, voluntary self-help groups that had emerged in response to the scarcity of social and economic resources.[100] Wanyama found that the associational life made possible by the CBOs did not empower their members to participate in the process of political liberalization because they were preoccupied with their socio-economic needs, not the political reform process. Due to their historical patron-client relationships with local politicians, CBOs entered the local political arena primarily to access development resources.[101] According to Wanyama, instead of discussing public policy issues and demanding accountability by the state to its citizens, most CBOs were conspicuously absent from the reform movement; some even accepted and supported the authoritarian

---

[96] See Maina Keengwe, Fiona Percy, Orito Mageka, and Muhamud Sheik Adan, *NGO Roles And Relationships: Partnership Dilemmas for cal NGOs in Kenya* (Nairobi: International Institute for Environment and Development, 1998), 10.

[97] Shadrack W. Nasong'o, "Negotiating New Rules of the Game: Social Movements, Civil Society and the Kenyan Transition," in *Kenya: The Struggle for Democracy*, ed. Godwin R. Murunga, and Shadrack W. Nasong'o (London: Zed Books, 2007), 51.

[98] Oyugi, "The Role of NGOs," 47.

[99] Kanyinga, "Civil Society," 23.

[100] Frederick Wanyama, "The Third Sector and the Transformation of Governance in Africa: The Case of Community-Based Organizations," (Paper presented to the International Society for Third-Sector Research, University of Cape Town, South Africa, 2002), 6.

[101] Ibid., 12.

governance style of Moi in exchange for development projects in their regions. He concluded that the reality of the political environment in which the CBOs functioned was antithetical to the expectations of civil society advocates.[102]

Not all scholars agree with the level of criticism leveled against civil society in Kenya; the debate is ongoing. Recently, a small number of critics have posited a more moderate view. They assert that although civil society has not lived up to its expectations and become the "midwife of democracy" as it was anticipated in the 1990s, civil society has made a modest contribution to the democracy process in the 2000s. In their view, civil society has an important role to play in the democratization process, just not the leading role.

In 2004 Stephen Orvis undertook an empirical study of three Kenyan NGOs and one Catholic diocese's justice and peace commission, all of which provided civic education and paralegal training in rural Kenya during 1999-2000. Like other scholars, Orvis was critical of NGOs in Kenya especially human rights NGOs funded by foreign donors. He contended that these NGOs were biased toward the urban elite, had little or no domestic constituency and existed mostly to serve the interests of donors.[103] Notwithstanding his pointed criticisms, he concluded that efforts by the four organizations produced multiple benefits for the long-term prospects of democracy in Kenya.[104] People who participated in civic education had greater awareness and knowledge than those who had not. Additionally, trained paralegals learned how to negotiate legal disputes with local authorities notorious for corruption and brutality. Orvis concluded that rather than "declaring civil society either the savior of democracy or dead across Africa," scholars should focus more on its evolution.[105]

Henry Wambuii reached an even more positive conclusion in his 2006 analysis of how the AIDS pandemic in Kenya has contributed to democratic consolidation in the country.[106] In his study, he found that following the transfer of power to President Kibaki in 2002, the new government expressed a willingness to work with civil society organizations addressing AIDS-related issues. Increased cooperation

---

102 Ibid., 20.

103 Stephen Orvis, "Kenyan Civil Society: Bridging the Urban-rural Divide?" *Journal of Modern African Studies* 41, no. 2 (2003): 248.

104 Ibid., 249.

105 Ibid., 266.

106 Henry K. Wambuii, *The Politics of HIV/AIDS and Implications for Democracy in Kenya* (Lewiston, NY: Edwin Mellen Press, 2006), 8.

between the state and civil society created new opportunities for civil society to partner with the state, not only to care for people living with AIDS, but also to be involved in the policy process. The positive results of civil society's participation included increased empowerment and legal protection for people living with AIDS.[107] Wambuii concluded that the state's willingness to engage civil society actors in the policy debate, something that had been the exclusive purview of the political elite, was evidence of important democratic gains in the country and a platform for continued democratization.[108]

With respect to religious organizations, there is a significant amount of scholarly literature that presumes Christian churches in Africa are one of, if not the most, significant sector within civil society that promotes grass-roots democracy and human rights.[109] However, there is no detailed study of a particular church body's contribution to the democracy-building process. The scholarly literature which examines the role played by some Christian churches in Kenya's struggle for democracy does so through an analysis of the churches' efforts vis-à-vis its historical relationship with the state, not as a member of civil society.[110] Moreover, this literature focuses almost exclusively on efforts by high-level Christian clerics, mostly Anglicans, during the country's initial transition to democracy, not efforts by ordinary church members to consolidate democracy at the grass-

---

[107] Ibid., 35.

[108] Ibid., 37.

[109] See, e.g., Paul Gifford, "Africa's Churches and the 'Second Liberation Struggle,' of 1989-93," in *The Years 1989-90: Turning Point in European and Non-European Christian History*, ed. Klaus Koschorke (Wiesbaden: Harrassowitz Verlag, 2008), 136-55; Agnes C. Aboum, "The Churches' Involvement in the Democratisation Process in Kenya," in *Peacemaking and Democratisation in Africa*, ed. Hizkias Assefa, and George Wachira (Nairobi: East African Educational Publishers, 1996), 95-114; De Gruchy, *Christianity and Democracy*, 165-92 and Samuel P. Huntington, *The Third Wave: Democratization in the Late Twentieth Century* (Norman, OK: University of Oklahoma Press, 1991), 72-85.

[110] See Paddy Benson "Faith Engaging Politics: the Preaching of the Kingdom of God." In *Religion and Politics in Kenya* edited by Ben Knighton, 96-120. (New York: Palgrave Macmillan), 2009; Gideon G. Githiga, *The Church as the Bulwark against Authoritarianism: Development of Church and State Relations in Kenya with Particular Reference to the Years after Political Independence 1963-1992* (Oxford, Regnum, 2001) and Galia Sabar-Friedman, C*hurch, State, and Society in Kenya: From Mediation to*
Opposition, 1963-1993 (London: Frank Cass), 2002.

roots level.[111] In addition, no study has specifically addressed the role of the Catholic Church as a member of civil society.[112] The lack of scholarship is not limited to Kenya. Only three scholars have undertaken studies that address the Catholic Church's role as a member of civil society in Africa. These studies are general and do not provide an in-depth analysis of how the church functions at the grass-roots level. Nor have there been any empirical studies of a religious body working in Kenya's urban slum milieu. This case study of how a Catholic parish in Kibera slum promoted democracy and human rights is intended as a contribution to the civil society debate in a much neglected area of study.

---

[111] John Lonsdale, "Compromised Critics," and Gifford, *Christianity, Politics*, expand their analysis to the 2000s.

[112] See Von Doepp, "Liberal Visions," 280-95, in Malawi; Ronald Kassimir, "The Social Power of Religious Organisation and Civil Society: the Catholic Church in Uganda," in *Civil Society and Democracy in Africa Critical Perspectives*, ed. Nelson Kasfir (London: Frank Cass, 1998), 68-72 in Uganda and Tracy Kuperus, "Building Democracy: An Examination of Religious Associations in South Africa and Zimbabwe," *The Journal of Modern African Studies* 37, no. 4 (1999): 652-60, in South Africa and Zimbabwe.

CHAPTER TWO

THE SLUM CRISIS IN KENYA

Kenya and the Creation of a Neo-Patrimonial State

Under its first two presidents in the post-colonial era, Jomo Kenyatta (1963-1978) and Daniel arap Moi (1978-2002), Kenya evolved into a neo-patrimonial state defined by personal rule, repressive authoritarianism and clientelism. Poverty, ethnic clashes, large-scale corruption and human rights violations became Kenya's trademark characteristics. The repressive state also created a political culture of fear that turned many Kenyans into silent and passive spectators.

Jomo Kenyatta, admired as a hero of Kenyan nationalism and the country's first president, is credited with ushering in a period of relative stability and economic prosperity in the immediate post-colonial era. His government, however, was not a democracy; it was largely a personalized regime that rotated around him and an inner circle of political elite. In addition to amending the independence constitution 10 times to increase his executive powers,[1] he also eliminated opposition parties making the country a *de facto* one-party state. Kenyatta's political opponents risked harassment, imprisonment and even death.[2]

Clientelism was a key component of his regime. Kenyatta's considerable hold on key levers of governance gave him control over the state's resources, which he used to create an elaborate patronage network that favored his ethnic community, the Kikuyu, who tended to dominate the country's politics, business and civil service.[3] While Kenyatta's vice-president, Daniel arap Moi, was a Kalejin, most important cabinet and

---

[1] Kivutha Kibwana, George Kanyi Kimondo, and James Thuo Gathii, *The Citizen and the Constitution* (Nairobi: Claripress, 1996), 5.

[2] Githu Mugai, "Joma Kenyatta and the Rise of the Ethno-Nationalist State in Kenya," in *Ethnicity & Democracy in Africa*, ed. Bruce Berman, Dickson Eyoh, and Will Kymlicka (Oxford: James Currey, 2002), 212-13.

[3] Elisha Atieno-Odhiambo, "Hegemonic Enterprises and Instrumentalities of Survival: Ethnicity and Democracy in Kenya," *African Studies* 61, no. 2 (2002): 240-42.

political positions were held by Kikuyu.[4] Kenyatta's patronage system depended upon and produced massive corruption as he doled out the state's largesse. Kenyatta's patron-client networks also turned ethnicity into the primary medium of political contestation.[5] The goal of the electoral process became control of the state because it was the primary locus of wealth accumulation.[6]

Despite the authoritarian nature of the state, a large voluntary sector emerged. Coming out of colonial rule with overwhelming development problems, Kenyatta invited churches and missionaries to continue their efforts to provide the country with primary education and health care. He encouraged the rural population to form self-help groups (*harambee*) and contribute labor, materials and money to build schools, health clinics and other social infrastructure. Kenyatta also had an open-door policy for NGOs. Although Kenyatta is generally given credit for his tolerance of civil society, some scholars contend that his perceived support was due to the fact that the NGOs only provided non-controversial development and relief aid because they were prohibited from engaging in political opposition.[7]

When Kenyatta died in 1978, he was succeeded by his vice-president, Daniel arap Moi, who advanced the flawed legacy of Kenyatta even further. In order to consolidate his power, Moi either eliminated or restricted those sectors of civil society that he felt could mobilize political opposition. He banned ethnic welfare associations, stifled agrarian cooperatives, incorporated self-help groups into administrative and political structures and transformed *harambee* projects into political platforms.[8] Following a failed coup attempt in 1982, Moi turned Kenya into a *de jure* one-party state when he criminalized all opposition parties.

---

[4] There are 42 ethnic groups in Kenya; the largest groups are the Kikuyu (22%), Luhya (14%), Luo (13%), Kalejin (12%), Kamba (11%), Kisii (6%) and the Meru (6%).

[5] For details on the role of political ethnicity, see Bruce Berman, "Ethnicity, Bureaucracy & Democracy: The Politics of Trust," in *Ethnicity & Democracy in Africa*, ed. Bruce Berman, Dickson Eyoh, and Will Kymlicka (Oxford: James Currey, 2002).

[6] Adams Oloo, "The Contemporary Opposition in Kenya: Between Internal Traits and State Manipulation," in *Kenya: The Struggle for Democracy*, ed. Godwin R. Murunga, and Shadrack W. Nasong'o (London: Zed Books, 2007), 94.

[7] See Jeremiah Owiti, Otieno Aluoka, and Adams Oloo, "Civil Society in the New Dispensation: Prospects and Challenges," in *Civil Society in the Third Republic*, ed. Dunkan Okello, and National Council of NGOs (Nairobi: National Council of NGOs, 2004), 76.

[8] Kanyinga, "Civil Society,"14.

Moi transformed the ruling political party, the Kenya African National Union (KANU), into an organ of personal rule that superseded the power of parliament whose primary function was to rubber stamp Moi's proclamations including 20 amendments to the constitution that further consolidated power in the executive.[9] He also subordinated the judiciary by removing security of tenure for judges.[10] Intolerant of opposition, human rights abuses rose sharply as Moi suppressed the freedoms of the press, expression and assembly.[11] Political dissenters, especially lawyers, university lecturers and students, were frequently detained without trial, tortured and killed.[12] Arbitrary arrests, political trials and police brutality were commonplace.[13]

Like his predecessor, Moi fully embraced the patronage system; he simply redirected the distribution of state resources from the Kikuyu to the Kalejin community.[14] Corruption was rampant as the president and his allies plundered public resources. In the 1990s, government corruption cost the formal economy over $8.7 billion.[15] The redistribution of state resources for political purposes created a permanent financial crisis in the country. Under the Moi regime, Kenya's income disparity was consistently ranked in the five worst in the world; over half the country lived below the poverty line, surviving on less than $1 a day.[16]

---

[9] Jennifer A. Widner, *The Rise of a Party State in Kenya: From "Harambee!" to "Nyayo!"* (Berkley: University of California Press, 1993), 162-63.

[10] Jill Cottrell, and Yash Ghai, "Constitution Making and Democratization in Kenya (2000-2005)," *Democratization* 14, no. 1 (2007): 3.

[11] Mutuma Ruteer, and Kenya Human Rights Commission, *Shackled Messengers: The Media in Multiparty Kenya* (Nairobi: Kenyan Human Rights Commission, 1997), i-ii.

[12] Umoja wa Kupigiana Demokrasia Kenya, *Moi's Reign of Terror: A Decade of Nyayo Crimes against the People of Kenya* (London: Umoja Secretariat, 1989), 18.

[13] Mutuma Ruteer, and Kenya Human Rights Commission, *Mission to Repress: Torture, Illegal Detentions and Extra Judicial Killings by the Kenyan Police* (Nairobi: Kenyan Human Rights Commission, 1998), 1-4, 15.

[14] Owiti Okech, Kivutha Kibwana, Smokin Wanjala, and Centre for Law and Research International, *The Anatomy of Corruption in Kenya: Legal, Political and Socio-Economic Perspectives* (Nairobi: Claripress, 1996), 127.

[15] Korwa Adar, "Assessing Democratisation Trends in Kenya: A Post-mortem of the Moi Regime," *Journal of Commonwealth & Comparative Politics* 38, no. 3 (2000): 114.

[16] See Society for International Development Eastern Africa Office, *Pulling Apart: Facts and Figures in Inequality in Kenya* (Nairobi: Society for International Development Eastern Africa Office, 2004), 5.

By the mid-1980s, Moi had co-opted, suppressed or outlawed most civil society associations advocating democracy.[17] Only two sectors were able to speak out against state repression; a number of prominent Protestant clerics and Catholic bishops as well as a small group of human rights lawyers associated with the Law Society of Kenya (LSK), an organization of professional lawyers.[18] A deeply religious country, Kenya's clerics were viewed as the bastion of moral propriety and principle and commanded respect at all levels of society.[19] Using the pulpit, radio broadcasts, daily newspapers and publications, the clerics were the first actors in Kenya to place political reform and multi-party democratization on the national public agenda. They also publicly confronted the state on authoritarianism, ethnic clashes, electoral malpractices, land conflicts, corruption and election violence.[20] Moi did not hesitate to condemn the outspoken clerics, accusing them of interfering in politics, serving foreign masters and selling out to Western values, but he was not able to arrest or detain them because of their moral authority, prestigious status and access to international funds and networks.[21]

Although the Catholic bishops were slower to join the movement for reform, the impact of their intervention was significant. Unlike the Protestant clerics who were frequently accused of speaking more as individuals than as church representatives, the hierarchical nature of the

---

[17] President Moi neutralized trade unions and the women's organizations and refused to register rival parties or NGOs that threatened to challenge him.

[18] For the role played by the LSK, see Robert M. Press, *Peaceful Resistance: Advancing Human Rights and Democratic Freedoms*, *Ethics and Global Politics* (Aldershot, England: Ashgate, 2006), 112-13.

[19] The clerics were Anglican Bishops David Gitari, Henry Okullo, Alexander Muge, Catholic Bishop Ndingi Mwana a' Nzeki and Presbyterian Reverend Timothy Njoya. However, while the top leadership of the Christian churches were outspoken in their opposition to the regime, not all bishops, priests and Christians agreed. There were churches such as the African Inland Church, Legio Maria Church, Redeemed Gospel Church and the Seventh-Day Adventists that formed alliances with Moi and tried to suppress calls for change. See Mutahi Ngunyi, "Religious Institutions and Political Liberalization in Kenya," in *Markets, Civil Society and Democracy in Kenya*, ed. Peter Gibbon (Uppsala,: Nordiska Afrikainstitutet, 1995), 136.

[20] For details on the history of the churches' role, See Herve Maupeu, "The Churches and the Polls," in Out for the Count: The 1997 General Election and Prospects for Democracy in Kenya, ed. Marcel Rutten, Alamin Mazrui, and Francois Grignon (Kampala: Fountain, 2001), 50-70.

[21] Galia Sabar-Friedman, "Church and State in Kenya, 1986-1992: The Churches Involvement in the 'Game of Change,'" *African Affairs* 96 (1997): 28-30.

Catholic Church allowed the bishops to speak with a unanimous voice. United as one group under the Kenya Episcopal Conference (KEC), the Catholic bishops issued 18 pastoral letters that condemned the state's repression and called for democracy and constitutional reform. Signed by every bishop in the country, these letters were published in the national daily newspapers and read in every Catholic parish across the country.

Increasing discontent with the government's lack of accountability, corruption and human rights abuses eventually prompted foreign donors to join the struggle for political liberalization.[22] In December 1991, one month after all foreign aid was suspended; Moi capitulated to demands for reform and repealed Section 2(a) of the constitution to allow for the first multi-party election since 1966. Despite widespread unpopularity and violence, Moi won the 1992 elections. His victory was attributed to his use of coercive mechanisms and because the opposition parties were divided along ethnic lines.[23]

In the aftermath of the elections, in recognition that the country could not carry out democratic reform as long as the institutional and legal framework of a one-party state remained intact, the pro-democracy movement in Kenya started making demands for a constitutional review process.[24] Once again, the Christian churches played a prominent role; they organized meetings, workshops and seminars, issued formal letters and made public pronouncements calling for constitutional reform including a review process that would involve the entire citizenry. The issue of constitutional reform, however, did not feature prominently for most Kenyans. After 40 years of authoritarian rule, most citizens had retreated from the state and public life; overall, Kenyans had become more inward looking, less trustful and more fearful.[25]

The movement for constitutional review did not begin in earnest until a number of radicalized civil society activists under the umbrella of the National Convention Executive Council (NCEC) with strong support from

---

[22] Prior to 1990, Western countries remained relatively silent in the face of Kenya's deteriorating human rights situation because Kenya's espousal of capitalism and pro-Western alignment made it an important ally during the Cold War.

[23] Moi used tactics such as gerrymandering, stuffing ballot boxes, violent intimidation of opposition candidates, censorship and armed thugs who instigated ethnic clashes.

[24] George Kimondo, "Towards a Genuine Multi-party System in Kenya," in *The Citizen and the Constitution, Kenya: Constitutional Debate Series*, ed. Kivutha Kibwana, and George Kimondo (Nairobi: Claripress, 1996), 63.

[25] Cottrell, and Ghai, "Constitution Making," 3.

the opposition political parties and religious leaders launched a drive for constitutional reform in 1997.[26] The NCEC led thousands of disgruntled Kenyans to the streets of Nairobi to demand constitutional and election reform. Fearing an uncontrollable descent into lawlessness, the opposition parties supported by the religious leaders abandoned the civil society process and negotiated a compromise with the government. A new forum called the Inter-Parties Parliamentary Group (IPPG) was created that agreed to minimum reforms including the repeal of several laws restricting civil and political rights. Despite the minor changes, Moi won the 1997 election due to the opposition's failure to field a united slate of candidates; the election was once again marred by violence and allegations of vote rigging.

A major component of the IPPG reforms was the Constitution of Kenya Review Commission Act (the Review Act), which established a commission to review the constitution after the elections. However, following Moi's reelection, numerous disputes arose over how the Review Act should be implemented. At the center of the political wrangling was whether the review process should be a people-driven process that would include widespread public participation or a parliamentary one preferred by President Moi.[27] Frustrated with the government's refusal to expand participation to the broader public, in 1999 a number of civil society organizations led by religious leaders initiated a parallel reform process under the aegis of the Ufungamano Initiative (named for its venue). A number of religious leaders from Catholic, Protestant, Muslim and Hindu groups used churches, mosques and temples as forums for collecting views from citizens about the constitutional review process.[28] In response, the government formed a parliamentary committee to solicit views to counteract efforts by the religious leaders. For almost two years, competing constitution-writing projects were under way in Kenya.[29] It was not until March 2001 when Professor Yash Ghai, a highly-respected Kenyan lawyer appointed by Moi to chair the Constitution of Kenya Review Commission (CKRC), brokered a merger of the two groups that a

---

[26] For details, see Willy Mutunga, *Constitution-Making from the Middle: Civil Society and Transition Politics in Kenya, 1992-1997* (Nairobi: SAREAT, 1999).

[27] Gabrielle Lynch, "The Fruits of Perception: 'Ethnic Politics' and the Case of Kenya's Constitutional Referendum," *African Studies* 65, no. 2 (2006): 239.

[28] Shadrack W. Nasong'o, "Kenya: the Struggle for Democracy," in *Kenya: the Struggle for Democracy*, ed. Godwin R. Murunga, and Shadrack W. Nasong'o (London: Zed Books, 2007), 46.

[29] Orvis, "Kenyan Civil Society," 251.

process for the comprehensive review of the constitution of Kenya was finally in place.[30]

It was amidst the scenario of political repression and corruption described above that Kenya's capital city, Nairobi, became one of the most densely populated slum cities in Africa.[31] In my study I analyze a number of different interventions undertaken by the human rights ministry of a Catholic parish located in Kibera slum. Before describing the particular characteristics of Kibera, I provide a brief history of how the slums developed in Nairobi and civil society's historical response to human rights issues that emerged in the 1990s.

The Historical Evolution of the Slums

By 2002, there were over 150 slums in Nairobi housing more than 2 million people; approximately 60% of the city's population occupied less than 5% of the city's total land area. Population experts reported that Nairobi had the highest urban growth rate in Africa and projected its slum population would double by 2030.[32] The extraordinary growth of slums in Nairobi is tied to three key historical factors: (1) the country's long-standing land struggle; (2) the origin of Nairobi as a colonial capital city and (3) the lack of urban planning in the post-independence period.[33]

The squatter community first emerged with the advent of colonialism at the turn of the 20th century when the British colonial government declared vast tracts of land occupied by Africans to be Crown Land, property of the Queen of England.[34] Colonial laws also created "native reserves," blocks of land designated for each ethnic group where Africans were forced to move so the best arable land could be farmed by white

---

[30] Njuguna Nge'ethe, and M. Katumanga, "Transition and the Politics of Constitution-Making: A Comparative Study of Uganda, South Africa and Kenya," in *The Politics of Transition in Kenya: From Kanu to Narc*, ed. Walter Oyugi, Peter Wanyande, and C. Odhiambo-Mbai (Nairobi: Heinrich Boll Foundation, 2003), 334.

[31] Mike Davis, *Planet of Slums* (London: Verso, 2006), 95.

[32] African Population and Health Center, *Population and Health Dynamics in Nairobi's Informal Settlements: Report of the Nairobi Cross-Sectional Slums Survey 2000* (Nairobi: African Population and Health Research, 2002), 1.

[33] Although Kibera is referred to as both a "slum" and "informal settlement" in much of the literature, I use the term slum because it is the term most regularly used by the residents when describing their settlement.

[34] Caesar Lukudu, Catholic University of Eastern Africa, and Konrad-Adenauer-Stiftung, *Alienation of Public Land in Kenya* (Nairobi: Catholic University of Eastern Africa, 2000), 21.

settlers.[35] As settlers expropriated more and more land, colonialists rapidly displaced whole communities (particularly the Maasai and Kikuyu). At the same time, the colonial administration enacted punitive pass laws that restricted Africans' access to the city and prohibited them from purchasing urban land. From the colonials' view, the capital city was the exclusive domain of Europeans and, to a lesser extent, Asians.[36] Africans were allowed in town temporarily to work as railway workers, government clerks and domestic house help, but they were expected to return to their rural homes when their employment ended. A policy of residential segregation located African residences in the least desirable sections of Nairobi.[37] The only housing provided was in barrack-style units composed of one-room dormitories rented to single, male laborers.[38]

Since the number of barracks was few, most Africans were left to build their own homes with mud and wattle in designated "native locations" on the outskirts of Nairobi. Although the municipal authorities allowed these settlements, they provided no infrastructure or services and occasionally razed the villages, ordering the residents to return to their rural homes. The European citizenry, who viewed the slums as dens for thieves, illegal brewers and prostitutes, typically welcomed the demolitions, but since most of the urban slum dwellers did not have rural homes due to the scarcity of arable land on the reserves, the displaced built new settlements as quickly as the old ones were destroyed.

Unfortunately, the colonial government's plan to build housing for the growing African urban population, which constituted over half of Nairobi's residents by the end of World War II, was not implemented. The post-war economic boom had passed by 1954 and the housing built during

---

[35] Christopher Leo, *Land and Class in Kenya* (Toronto: University of Toronto Press, 1984), 4.

[36] The Asian population refers to the 32,000 Indian laborers who the colonial government brought from India to build the Uganda-Kenya railway. After the railway was finished, 6,700 Indians remained. Barred from purchasing rural land, most Indians managed shops and engaged in small-scale trade. See Kefa Otiso, "Colonial Urbanization and Urban Management in Kenya," in *African Urban Spaces in Historical Perspective*, ed. Steven J. Salm, and Toyin Falola (Rochester, NY: University of Rochester Press, 2005), 79.

[37] Spatial segregation was accompanied by a color bar that denied Africans access to hotels, restaurants and other private establishments. Otiso, "Colonial Urbanization," 79.

[38] Gervase Macoloo, "The State and Low-Income Urban Housing Production and Consumption in Kenya," in *Issues in Resource Management and Development in Kenya: Essays in Memory of Professor Simeon H. Ominde*, ed. Robert Obudho, and J.B. Ojwang (Nairobi: East African Educational Publishers, 2000), 251.

this period did not come close to meeting the needs; between 1948 and 1962, the urban population increased by a remarkable 174%.[39] The housing crisis worsened following independence as the removal of colonial restrictions on the movement of Africans led to a large influx of landless people who migrated to Nairobi in search of jobs.[40] Unprepared for the surging population growth, President Kenyatta urged urban migrants to return to their rural homes, even threatening to take the farms of people who left their land for the city.[41] Many, however, could not return and therefore resorted to constructing temporary shanties as their only means of shelter. Overwhelmed by the growing waves of urban migrants with nowhere to live, Kenyatta eventually acquiesced to their putting up one-room shacks on vacant public land so long as the structures were not too close to the town center.[42] Although the local area chiefs had no legal authority to allocate government land, they exploited their power and demanded that the new migrants pay a levy or bribe in exchange for "official permission" to build non-permanent structures on public land.

The mushrooming slums soon became an embarrassment to the Kenyatta government and in 1966 the new government reinstituted the colonial policy of slum eradication citing the need to promote public health.[43] The demolitions, however, did not stop the flow of urban migrants or the spread of new slum villages. Rapid population growth coupled with a scarcity of arable land led to an even higher demand for

---

[39] Kenneth Macharia, "Slum Clearance and the Informal Economy in Nairobi," *The Journal of Modern African Studies* 30, (1992): 228.

[40] Between the 1962 and 1969 censuses, the growth of Africans in Nairobi grew at an annual rate of 11% as an unprecedented number of rural migrants moved to Nairobi.

[41] Herbert H. Werlin, *Governing an African City: A Study of Nairobi* (New York: Africana Publishing Co.,1974), 117.

[42] Paul Syagga, Winnie Mitullah, and Sarah K. Gitau, *Nairobi Situation Analysis: Consultative Report* (Nairobi: Government of Kenya, and UN-Habitat, 2001), 33.

[43] The expanding slum settlements and shanty town were an eye-sore for Kenyatta's top official who wanted to promote Nairobi as the "Green City in the Sun" in order to attract tourists and their much-needed foreign exchange. The new government also wanted to prove that it could maintain law and order, especially in the capital city. Thus, justifying their actions under the Public Health Act, city officials burned down several slum areas located in the central area of the city. For the next eight years, city council authorities regularly demolished shanties located on road reserves and city council land.

urban housing.[44] Slum dwellers displaced by evictions either started new squatter villages or moved into other, already over-crowded slum areas in Mathare Valley, Kibera and Kawangware, which led to even greater congestion and worsened living conditions. Between 1965 and 1970, the number of slum dwellers grew from 40,000 to 92,000.[45]

In 1972 the Kenyatta government reversed its position on slum evictions after a study done by the International Labor Organization identified the informal sector as an important source of employment and services for the country. Although the government stopped the demolitions, it did not institute any substantive large-scale slum improvement projects, resulting in a dramatic growth of the informal sector; by 1980, there were over 310,000 slum dwellers in Nairobi.[46]

When Moi became president, he adopted a different approach to the slums from that of his predecessor. Instead of trying to eradicate the slums through demolitions, he discouraged their growth through a policy of neglect. Characterizing slum dwellers as "illegal squatters," the government deliberately denied slum dwellers access to basic infrastructure-electricity, clean water, drains, roads and sanitation-and city services such as primary schools, hospitals, clinics and recreational facilities, in the hope that the substandard living conditions would force slum dwellers to move. Moi's policy, however, did not curb the spread of slums. A combination of unprecedented population growth, rural poverty, the lure of urban life and most importantly, the potential to secure a wage-paying job led to the exponential growth of poor migrating to the capital city; an estimated 1.8 million people lived in the slums by 1995.[47]

Moi's policy of neglect had far-reaching consequences for Nairobi's slum dwellers. More than 50% of the primary school children living in slum areas do not attend school and the vast majority of children who are schooled attend one of the many informal schools that are privately administered and of inferior quality.[48] The lack of access to basic education is linked to low literacy and income levels in slum areas. In addition, city authorities' refusal to provide slum areas with basic services

---

[44] Winnie Mitullah, "Towards a Policy of Upgrading Informal Settlements and Site and Service Schemes in the City of Nairobi, Kenya," *African Urban Quarterly* 7, nos. 1 and 2 (1992): 188.

[45] Syagga, Mitullah, and Gitau, *Nairobi Situation,* 34.

[46] Ibid.

[47] Ibid., 35.

[48] See Outreach Development Services, "Participatory Urban Appraisal Study of Mashimoni, Kambi Muru, Lindi and Silanga Villages–Kibera Informal Settlement," (Report prepared for Oxfam GB, Nairobi, 2001), 22.

has led to their informal commoditization by exploitive middlemen at substandard levels.[49] For example, slum dwellers are required to purchase potable water in 20-liter jerry cans from private water vendors at prices three times more than the price charged by local authorities.[50] Since over 95% of the population do not have access to proper sanitation, people must pay to use a pit latrines typically shared by 50 to 100 people. The lack of sanitary facilities to dispose of human waste and garbage has led to high rates of morbidity and mortality caused by diseases stemming from unsanitary environmental conditions.[51]

Civil Society's Response to the Slum Crisis

Despite the repressive environment for civil society under the Moi regime, there were a small number of civil society actors including several NGOs, the National Council of Churches of Kenya (NCCK), an umbrella organization of mainline Protestant churches, and a handful of Catholic missionaries and Kenyan human rights activists who responded to the worsening conditions in the slums. Because the details of civil society's interventions are complex, I focus on the major interventions of the Catholic missionaries and NGOs during the eviction crisis in the 1990s that influenced the OHR's activities in the 2000s.[52]

The Catholic Church

Although admired for the time he devoted to pastoral responsibilities, Kenya's first Cardinal, Maurice Otunga, gave little attention to the slums throughout the 1970s and 1980s.[53] His approach reflected the general

---

[49] Marie Huchzermeyer, "Slum Upgrading Initiatives in Kenya within the Basic Services and Wider Housing Market," (COHRE Discussion Paper No.1/2006, COHRE, Geneva, 2006), 5.

[50] See Fernando da Cruz, Kerstin Sommer, and Ombretta Tempra, *Nairobi Urban Sector Profile* (Nairobi: UN-Habitat, 2006), 10.

[51] The mortality rate for under-five children is two to three times higher in the slums (151 per 1,000) than the city as a whole (62 per 1,000) and 50% higher than in the rural areas. See Harvey Herr, and Karl Guenter, "Estimating Global Slum Dwellers: Monitoring the Millennium Development Goal 7, Target 11," (Paper presented to UN-Habitat, Nairobi, 2003), 14.

[52] For the role taken by the NCCK, see National Council of Churches of Kenya, *Nairobi Demolitions, What Next?* (Nairobi: National Council of Churches of Kenya, 1991), 10-23.

[53] Interview with missionary priest C, April 13, 2008.

ambivalence felt by the official church in Rome that acknowledged the growing problems associated with rapid urban migration, but did not offer a concrete analysis of the issues or direction concerning how the church should respond to the growing slum crisis.[54]

As the number of slum dwellers grew exponentially during the 1980s, Cardinal Otunga designated the slum areas as mission territory and asked several missionary congregations from Europe and North America to build new parishes in the marginalized areas of Nairobi. Unlike the local church, the expatriate missionaries had access to international funding necessary to build new churches and supplement parishioners' weekly contributions for the upkeep of the priests and general parish maintenance. The Cardinal, however, did not want priests to live inside the slum areas because he feared that they would face untenable physical and psychological obstacles.[55] In addition to the endemic violence and security threats, the Cardinal was concerned that the priests would be unduly exposed to immoral vices such as illicit alcohol and prostitution which were commonplace.[56] It was not until 1987 that the Cardinal reluctantly consented to the requests of two missionary priests to live full-time in the slums, a Mexican Guadalupe in Kibera and an Italian Comboni in Korogocho. By that time, seven congregations had built new parishes that serviced poor and low-incomes areas.

Unfortunately, early calls for guidance and coordination about how the priests should respond pastorally to a population disorientated in a new urban milieu, exposed to the slum culture rife with disease, violent crime, illiteracy, drunkenness, drugs and prostitution, not to mention the lack of employment, housing and schools, went unanswered. In the vacuum of official guidance by the local church, the missionary congregations pursued their individual policies; the key priorities for most missionary congregations were traditional pastoral activities such as the sacramental and prayer life of Catholics and building the basic structures of a new parish which included churches, primary schools and health clinics.

Some congregations were not equipped or trained to respond the complex urban slum apostolate. Many priests applied pastoral methods designed for rural parishes to complicated urban problems, approaches that frequently did not work. For example, it was relatively easy for a priest to organize parish-based groups in the rural areas by announcing

---

[54] Francesco Pierli, "The Church and the Slums: 50 Years of a Painful and Yet Fruitful Journey," in *The Slums: A Challenge to Evangelization*, ed. Francesco Pierli, and Yago Abeledo (Nairobi: Paulines Publications Africa, 2002), 134.
[55] Interview with missionary priest C, April 13, 2008.
[56] Ibid.

meetings after mass; parishioners readily integrated with one another because they shared the same language, culture and background. Group formation in the slum areas, however, was very different. Due to the mix of ethnic identities and conflicting customs, values and traditions, parishioners were reluctant to come together even when the meeting was for their own benefit, a situation that frustrated the pastoral programs of many priests.

The situation in the slums became significantly worse in the early 1990s as the movement for multi-party democracy gained strength. Breaking from his quiet acquiescence of the slums, in November 1990 President Moi unexpectedly ordered the Nairobi City Council (NCC) to demolish two large settlements, Muoroto and Kibagare, displacing over 30,000 people.[57] The demolitions were ordered to punish the inhabitants for supporting opposition politicians and activists calling for a one-party state.[58] Moi's demolition of these two slums, originally believed to be an anomaly, initiated a decade of systematic slum eradication by the state. After the introduction of multi-party elections in 1992, the demand on President Moi to dispense resources necessary to retain key political supporters escalated. Urban public land, valuable and easily disposed of, soon became one of Moi's favored means of patronage. Since much of the public land in Nairobi was occupied by slum dwellers, political allies of Moi who were illegally allocated plots were supported by the government to remove the occupants with the use of force.[59] From the mid-1990s onward, police, chiefs and hired youth wingers regularly demolished houses, kiosks and market areas in the middle of the night without warning, displacing tens of thousands of slum dwellers. Common to all these evictions was the use of force and violence, the loss of property and sometimes life.[60]

Cardinal Otunga condemned the particularly brutal nature of the Kibagare demolition, but he did not want to engage the state in a public debate on the controversial land issue. Despite his reticence to get

---

[57] Africa Watch Committee, *Kenya, Taking Liberties, an African Watch Report* (New York: Human Rights Watch, 1991), 256.

[58] Kinuthia Macharia, "Tensions Created by the Formal and Informal Use of Urban Space: The Case of Nairobi, Kenya," *Journal of Third World Studies* 24, no. 2 (2007): 158.

[59] Jacqueline Klopp, "Pilfering the Public: The Problem of Land Grabbing in Contemporary Kenya," *Africa Today* 47, no. 1 (2000): 9-13.

[60] For details, see Christine Bodewes, and Ndaisi Kwinga, "Kenyan Perspective on Housing Rights," in *National Perspectives on Housing Rights*, ed. (The Hague: Martinus Nijhoff, 2003), 231-35.

personally involved, he did not prohibit missionaries who were working in the slums from responding to the growing crisis. For example, in 1993 a Maryknoll priest from the United States started the Slums Committee, a group of lay representatives from nine parishes that met regularly to discuss what the church could do to help slum dwellers improve their security of tenure and resist forced evictions. The Committee, however, was limited in what it could do. In addition to the risk of arrest if caught openly addressing these issues, the group had few resources and lacked the church's official public support. In that same year, a missionary priest from Italy agreed to the request of a local NGO to hold the legal title for a program to train local community organizers in the issue-based organizing techniques popularized in the Philippines during the overthrow of Marcos.[61] The human rights NGOs that were asked to host the community organization training (COT) program all refused because they did not want to risk being deregistered by the government. The Comboni Fathers agreed to sponsor the COT because, as expatriates, they faced less risk of retaliation and it was their hope that the program would facilitate slum dwellers to lobby for secure tenure and land ownership in the slums. Every year three Filipino nationals trained 10 to 15 Kenyans selected from churches, NGOs and government agencies working in Korogocho and Kibera slums as community organizers.[62]

Unlike in the Philippines, the Kenyan church did not accept the COT strategy because church leaders were afraid the confrontational style of organizing would invite retaliation by the government. The only priests who supported the program were the missionaries working in Korogocho and Kibera who sent nearly a dozen individuals from their pastoral teams to be trained as community organizers. However, only a few pastoral workers returned to the parishes after their training. The priests did not have adequate financial resources to compete with the higher salaries paid by NGOs keen to hire community organizers to set up development projects. The pastoral workers who returned lacked sufficient numbers and institutional support to organize Catholics around the dangerous and complex issue of land.

---

[61] The Kenyan chapter of African Network for the Prevention and Protection against Child Abuse and Neglect (ANPPCAN), a local NGO working with street children, was the local implementer and a Filipino NGO, Community Organizers People's Enterprises, provided the trainers to lead the program. Funding was provided by the German donor, Misereor.

[62] Interview with housing NGO community organizer E, February 8, 2009.

Human Rights NGOs

As the missionaries struggled to respond to the worsening situation, a number of human rights NGOs were also trying to promote the rights of the slum dwellers; key among them was the KCS, the oldest human rights NGO in Kenya that had provided slum dwellers with free legal services since the early 1970s. As land grabbing and forced evictions accelerated, lawyers at KCS broke ranks with most NGOs that typically met slum dwellers on an individual basis in their offices, and began visiting slum dwellers in their communities to teach them their legal rights and discuss issues related to land grabbing and forced evictions. KCS's strategy of meeting directly with the communities was laden with risk because President Moi had criminalized any gathering of five or more people without a permit. Despite the threat of arrest, the KCS lawyers clandestinely met numerous slum groups including the Slums Committee, which started a collaborative relationship between the KCS lawyers and the Catholic missionaries involved in the Slums Committee. In 1994 lawyers filed the first of many lawsuits on behalf of affected slum communities challenging the legality of the state's forced evictions and seeking judicial redress for the displaced communities.

The impact of KCS's legal interventions, however, was limited because of widespread corruption and incompetence in the judiciary. Judges frequently dismissed the cases on the grounds that slum dwellers were illegal occupants and therefore lacked standing to file a case in court. In some instances, filing the lawsuit actually provoked the evictors to demolish structures sooner in order to pre-empt legal action. Frustrated by an ineffective legal process, the KCS hired a number of community organizers to work alongside the lawyers to help communities resist evictions by means of organized protests and physical resistance. The state retaliated quickly to these tactics. Undercover police officers followed and harassed the community organizers as they moved throughout the settlements.[63] Slum dwellers who tried to hold meetings were regularly threatened, intimidated and even arrested by local chiefs. The government identified the lead Filipino trainer as a "foreign activist" and canceled her visa. In March 1995, the KCS office was fire bombed in retaliation for lawyers investigating a claim of government land grabbing; KCS property was destroyed and the office was temporarily closed.

---

[63] Interview with housing NGO community organizer A, April 17, 2008.

Collaborative Efforts

The state's heightened level of repression was the impetus for a number of civil society actors to join together to address the eviction crisis in a more coordinated fashion. In 1995 an Italian missionary priest started the Land Caucus, an informal group of missionaries, lawyers and community organizers who met regularly to strategize about specific evictions and different tactics that could be used to prevent the demolitions. The Caucus was a loose coalition that never numbered more than 10 to 15 people; apart from the KCS, none of the Caucus members had institutional support. Given the risks attendant to organizing slum dwellers, most NGOs and religious congregations were afraid to get involved because of possible arrest, imprisonment and deportation.

As more and more slum dwellers faced the threat of eviction, the Filipinos active in the Land Caucus promoted the idea of organizing a city-wide organization of slum dwellers referred to as the Muungano wana Vijiji (Federation of the Urban Poor) to lobby for a moratorium on evictions and recognition of the right to the land they occupied. In August 1996 an American missionary priest provided financial support for a community organizer to mobilize evicted slum dwellers to join village-based Muungano groups. Within a year, over 50 slum communities had active Muungano groups whose members organized thousands of slum dwellers to attend protest demonstrations, street marches, night vigils, prayer meetings and court appearances, all in an effort to resist evictions. The state's reaction was harsh; members of the Muungano were often beaten by the police or arrested.[64] During this period, some of the KCS lawyers and missionaries active in the Land Caucus offered the Muungano groups administrative, legal and strategic support.

In 1998 members of the Land Caucus submitted proposals to two international donors to fund the Muungano's activities.[65] However, none of the NGOs was willing to formally incorporate the Muungano into their programs because they feared that the state would deregister them. Facing less risk of retaliation as an expatriate priest, a missionary agreed to hold the donor funds on behalf of the Muungano. The director of KCS, with substantial input from the Land Caucus, provided strategic guidance and support for the Muungano groups. From 1998 through 2000, community organizers facilitated workshops about land and housing in over 80 slum villages.

---

[64] As an example, 75 of the 100 Muungano members who attended a prayer rally to protest the eviction of Westlands Market were arrested.

[65] The donors were Oxfam GB and Misereor.

Despite the active role and support given to the Muungano by a number of expatriate missionaries, the Muungano was not a project of the local Catholic Church. To the contrary, Cardinal Otunga's successor, Archbishop Raphael Ndingi Mwana a' Nzeki, declined to give the Muungano official support or speak publicly on the issue of evictions. His position was a surprise given that he had been a charismatic champion of human rights when he was bishop of the Diocese of Nakuru (1972-1996). Ndingi's participation in social justice issues changed after he was made the Archbishop of Nairobi. Throughout his 10-year tenure, apart from making annual pastoral visits to the slum parishes, he spent minimal time and effort addressing the particular needs of slum dwellers. According to a missionary priest who worked closely with the Archbishop:

> The slums were hot politically because of the land issue and he was not prepared to deal with it. Archbishop Ndingi moved to Nairobi from a small town where there were no slums. The slum situation in Nairobi was too complex and he did not understand what he should do.[66]

Following the lead of the Archbishop, no Kenyan priest ever responded to repeated invitations to support the Muungano or join the Land Caucus.

The impact of the Muungano's efforts to mobilize the slum dwellers to prevent evictions had mixed results in the 1990s. When evictions were at their height in the mid-1990s, the Muungano increased the slum dwellers' profile and brought the eviction issue to the attention of church leaders, NGOs, government officials, the media and international NGOs working on housing issues. They also helped four slum communities physically resist attempted evictions.[67] The more long-term impact of the Muungano's activities was less effective. The Muungano was capable of mobilizing several thousand people, but the active membership never amounted to more than several hundred people, a tiny percentage of the overall number of slum dwellers.

The greatest obstacle to the Muungano was state repression. In addition to making verbal threats and disrupting meetings, local chiefs and police periodically arrested and detained Muungano activists and community organizers. In addition, the struggle against evictions was largely driven by civil society actors; the issue was not a priority for most slum dwellers. According to a Muungano organizer, "There was a high level of complacency because most people were not directly affected by

[66] Interview with missionary priest A, September 21, 2008.

[67] They were Toi Market, Westlands Market, Mountain View Village and Chelenzi Village.

the evictions."[68] Many slum dwellers also did not have time for the Muungano activities. "People were so busy struggling that they could not volunteer time to a certain extent but not consistently; they were living in poverty and their day-to-day survival needs were too time-consuming."[69] Ethnic divisions and the competing interests of structure owners and tenants made it difficult to build a united coalition for action. Since most of the original Muungano leaders were Kikuyu structure owners, many slum dwellers perceived the movement to be for their exclusive membership.

The quality of leadership in the Muungano was also low. The original community leaders were self-selected during the height of the eviction crisis. Although some were sincerely committed to the struggle for land reform in the slums, they were the minority. Most leaders lacked the capacity to mobilize their communities and they were never given adequate leadership training or formation on the change process. As the profile of the Muungano rose and donor money became available, power struggles over the control of the funding emerged and frequently eclipsed the larger issues of land and housing reforms. A number of leaders were also increasingly resentful that NGO personnel had raised funds in their name, but retained control over how the money was spent.

The limited impact of the Muungano was also due to weaknesses within civil society. Because of the complexity and inherent risks related to the land issue in the slums, there were very few individuals, both professional NGO workers and church personnel, who were committed to the slum dwellers' struggle. In addition, there was a paucity of financial resources which restricted the scope of their effort. There were also time constraints. As the number of evictions grew, all available resources and efforts were put into fighting the demolitions. Faced with overwhelming crises, the response of the civil society actors was short-term and reactive, a situation that inhibited their ability to develop a comprehensive approach to problems in the slums. Moreover, because of the repressive political environment, an open debate on policy reform was not an option. Even if there had been a policy debate, neither the individual missionaries nor the NGO personnel had sufficient expertise and political networks to propose policy alternatives. One of the senior KCS lawyers observed:

> We had no theory as civil society in how to deal with the slums. Most of us had good intentions, but that was not enough. The Land Caucus could not change the status of the poor living in the slums because we did not

[68] Interview with community organizer A, September 26, 2008.
[69] Ibid.

> understand the invisible power and political dynamics at play in the slums. The NGOs were motivated by short-term ideals because they were there to get money. We were attracted like bees to honey to short-term projects where we could say we stopped an eviction. This gave us a very visible victory, but we were blank beyond that. We had no medium or long-term strategy.[70]

In 2000 the missionary priest holding the Muungano accounts returned to the United States and the legal responsibility for the Muungano funds was transferred to a new NGO called the Pamoja Trust (Together) that had been created by the lawyers at the KCS. The director of the KCS became the new director of the Trust and took over primary responsibility for the fundraising and implementation of the Muungano's activities. One year later, as the number of evictions declined and under pressure from its main donor, Pamoja Trust shifted the focus of the Muungano.[71] Instead of mobilizing the Muungano groups to pressure the government to issue a moratorium on slum evictions and lobby for land reform for the slums, the Trust turned the lobby groups into savings groups with the aim of collecting money for house building, a methodology popular in India.[72] The shift in methodology had far-reaching consequences. Many of the Muungano members (particularly tenants) left because they were more interested in security of tenure than home ownership. Similarly, a number of the original NGO activists who had been attracted to the movement because of their desire to effect legal reform for slum dwellers dropped out of the Muungano.

In addition, the collaboration between the Catholic missionaries and the human rights NGOs was not long lasting. In April 2002 the missionary priest who chaired the Land Caucus was reassigned to his home country. Following his departure, the eight missionaries who were involved in the Caucus met to discuss their on-going role in the group. In addition to concerns over the influence of Pamoja Trust's donor and its decision to shift the focus of the Muungano, the missionaries felt that some of the NGOs had lost their initial vision for the slum dwellers as they became increasingly entrenched in internal disputes and competition for power and resources. Some also objected to the growing corruption of certain individuals in the NGOs. A few missionaries also thought the NGOs were

---

[70] Interview with community organizer B, September 29, 2008.

[71] Interview with human rights lawyer A, September 25, 2008.

[72] For the methodology originated by Slum Dwellers International, see Sheila Patel, Sunda Burra, and Celine de'Cruz, "Shack/Slum Dwellers International: Foundations to Treetops," *Environment & Urbanization* 13, no. 1 (2001): 45-60.

not sincere in their intention to collaborate with the parishes and, instead, only wanted to use the priests' names to convince Catholic donors in Europe to finance their NGOs. The situation with the Land Caucus presented a dilemma for the missionaries. In the view of one member:

> The NGOs and parishes needed each other. The NGO sector had a certain expertise and was able to generate and disseminate information professionally. On the other hand, it was the parishes that had the moral authority and credibility on the ground; they were viewed as honest and virtuous. But the priests did not have the expertise and they were frequently blocked by the hierarchy.[73]

Although the missionaries recognized the benefits of a unified network with the NGOs, especially the advantage of their shared expertise and resources, there was agreement that their motivations and goals were at irreconcilable odds and they decided unanimously to leave the Land Caucus. Even though some people in the parishes and NGOs continued to work together on an individual basis, the formal collaborative relationship ended. Within a year, the Caucus ceased to function and there was no longer a network of civil society organizations jointly working on land and housing issues in the slums.

In an effort to maintain a collaborative network among the Catholic parishes, in 2001 several missionaries who had participated in the Land Caucus organized a new group called the Kutoka (Exodus) network made up of pastoral teams of the parishes working in slum areas. All 14 slum parishes were administered by missionaries. Recognizing their status as key stakeholders in the slums, the missionaries wanted to build a support network as well as develop an alternative way of working with slum dwellers that emphasized a long-term ministerial methodology, not the short-term project approach favored by the NGOs. According to one of the Kutoka founders:

> We wanted to put the people first. We were not there for business or salaries but because we were Catholics and shared a vision to empower people to come out of the slums. As members of pastoral teams, we were all present in the slums, shared our faith and believed that we are able to help people not just through projects, but by enhancing the humanity and dignity of the people in a manner grounded in spirituality and the teachings of the Bible.[74]

---

[73] Interview with human rights lawyer A, September 25, 2008.
[74] Interview with Kutoka network founder, September 28, 2008.

The network met four times a year to discuss ways to provide spiritual formation for slum dwellers and strategies for responding to the complex array of socio-political issues in the slums.

Kibera Slum

The specific locus of my study is Kibera slum, which has the distinction of being the largest and most densely populated slum not only in Nairobi, but all sub-Saharan Africa. Composed of 12 contiguous villages, it is located seven kilometers southeast of the city center and covers approximately 500 acres. In 2002 the NCC estimated the resident population was 600,000 people.[75] With average densities around 90,000 persons per square kilometer, the settlement occupies less than 1% of the city's total area and accommodates over 20% of its population.[76]

Kibera physically resembles the other slums in Nairobi. Most residents live in structures made of mud and wattle; on average five to six persons stay in one room that typically measures 9.3 square meters.[77] As in other slum areas, the vast majority are young; about 15% are over the age of 35 while approximately 65% are under the age of 24.[78] Education levels are very low; it is estimated that 63% of the population has finished primary school and only 37% secondary school.[79] The majority of Kiberans live in stark poverty. According to a 2004 study, Kibera reported the highest incidence of people living below the food poverty line in the Nairobi slums; around 80% of the households lived on less than 3,350 Ksh per month (the absolute poverty line was 7,350 Ksh).[80] Employment is usually found in the informal sector where wages are low and work is uncertain. Most people work as security guards, domestic maids, and food hawkers

---

[75] Burgeap, Seueca and Runji & Partners, "Kibera Urban Environmental Sanitation Project," (Report prepared for the Ministry of Local Government, and Nairobi City Council, Nairobi, 2002), 12.

[76] Daniel Biau, "Three Things We Should Know about Slums," *Habitat Debate* (March 2007), 6.

[77] Research International, "Kibera Social and Economic Mapping: Household Survey Report," (Report prepared for Government of Kenya, and UN-Habitat, Nairobi, 2005), 44.

[78] OHR, "Kibera East Baseline Survey," (Report presented to Christ the King Catholic Church, Nairobi, 2008), 15.

[79] Ibid., 18.

[80] Mugo P. Kirii, *The Nairobi Basic Needs Basket: Cost of Basic Needs Basket in Twelve Informal Settlements, Nairobi-Kenya, 2004* (Nairobi: Paulines Publications Africa, 2004), 24.

or as day laborers in factories and construction sites. In the absence of viable income activities, many resort to theft, prostitution, smuggling and illegal brewing of alcohol.

Kibera has a complex ethnic mix. Unlike most slums that generally have one or two main ethnic groups, Kibera hosts all 42 ethnic communities and many more from other African countries. Despite its melting pot culture, most Kiberans prefer to live among their shared ethnic group. Kenyans from all ethnic groups typically stay in each village, but there is generally one ethnic group that is dominant. Although there is no accurate census data, it is widely believed that Luo make up the majority of Kibera's residents.[81]

For purposes of my study, I focus on the six villages located within Christ the King parish boundaries-Soweto, Line Saba, Shilanga, Lindi, Mashimoni and Kambi Muru-home to an estimated 340,000 people. The parish also includes Highrise, a neighboring middle-class housing complex that houses several thousand people. Because of the significant variance in lifestyle and living conditions, analysis of Highrise does not feature in my study.

The village of Soweto is one of the oldest parts of Kibera.[82] First settled by Kikuyu in the 1970s, most Sowetans have lived there for two generations and are fully urbanized; very few have a home or land in their rural area. The majority of Kikuyu own the structures they live in, their small retail businesses and anywhere from one to 20 rental structures. There are also a significant number of Kamba, an ethnic group related to the Kikuyu by language and custom. They migrated to Soweto more recently in the late 1980s and 1990s from the eastern region of the country in search of jobs following the decline in agricultural productivity. Their lifestyle is similar to the Kikuyu except that most are tenants. The majority of the Kamba have homes and small plots in their rural areas and regularly return there on weekends and during planting and harvesting seasons, thereby holding dual citizenship, with one foot firmly rooted in the rural area and the other in the urban slum milieu. The neighboring village of Line Saba is newer than Soweto, but reflects a similar ethnic and economic dynamic.

In contrast, the villages of Shilanga and Kambi Muru are dominated by the Luo from western Kenya and the Luhya, a geographically contiguous community. The majority of Luo and Luhya migrated to Kibera in the late

---

81 See Johan de Smedt, "'No Raila, No Peace!' Big Man Politics and Election Violence at the Kibera Grassroots," *African Affairs* 108, no. 433 (2009): 586.

82 Following the slum upgrade project in 2003, the village of Soweto was frequently referred to as Soweto East.

1980s and 1990s in search of wage jobs in the industrial area. Most Luo and Luhya have close ties with their rural homes. In many instances, the wives and children of Luo and Luhya men remain in the rural homes while the men earn incomes in the city. Typically, people from these two communities are motivated to stay in Kibera only as long as it takes to raise funds to pay their children's school fees and build a home in the rural area where they will return to retire. Most Luhya and Luo are tenants and very few have purchased structures or started businesses. Although many can live 10 to 20 years in Kibera, they are invested financially, emotionally and culturally in their rural areas. The villages of Lindi and Mashimoni are also predominantly Luo and Luhya, but have an equal mix of Kamba and Kisii.

To understand how 600,000 people live in the sub-human conditions found in Kibera, it is helpful to understand the local social, economic and political dynamics of the community. Below I briefly outline the key factors that influenced daily life in Kibera in the early 2000s, a slum where conflict, instability and violence were pervasive.

Land Ownership

The issue of land ownership was complex and highly contested with five different groups claiming ownership of Kibera. The government claimed Kibera because the legal title of the land is vested in the Kenya Railways Corporation, a public corporation that has ownership rights over the Mombasa-Uganda railway which crosses through Kibera. The Nubian community, a small ethnic and religious minority, asserted a legal claim to the land based on its historical relationship with the colonial government. Kikuyu structure owners who were allocated plots in the 1970s and 1980s by the local chief also laid claim to Kibera. Following the lead of the area Member of Parliament (MP), the Luo tenants asserted ownership rights because of their majority occupation. To further complicate matters, it was widely believed that most, if not all, Kibera was illegally allocated to undisclosed private interests during the Moi regime.[83] The ambiguity and conflict over the ownership of Kibera has pitted different ethnic communities against one another for decades, turning it into a slum infamous for ethnic clashes and violence.

The Nubians' claim goes back to the very origin of Kibera when in 1912 the British colonial administration first settled ex-Sudanese soldiers

---

[83] Law Society of Kenya, *Report: A Mission to Kibera* (Nairobi: Law Society of Kenya Land Reform Program, 2002), 11-12.

who had served with the King's African Rifles at Buller Camp, a military reserve located in present-day Kibera.[84] The Sudanese soldiers were known as Nubians, speaking a language similar to Arabic and practicing the Muslim faith. Viewed as allies of the colonial regime, the ex-soldiers were encouraged to settle in Kibera, so they could act as an informal military reserve should the colonial government need their services on short notice. In 1932 the Kenya Land Commission denied the Nubians' claim that they be issued title deeds for Kibera and found they were "tenants of the crown."[85] Later, during the Mau Mau Emergency, in exchange for their loyalty, colonial authorities granted the Nubians permission to construct rooms to rent to the growing influx of rural migrants, turning them into the dominant class of landlords.[86]

After nearly 60 years of total domination over Kibera's commercial development, Nubian control was challenged in 1974 when the Nubians lost their seat in parliament to a Kikuyu politician. A new Kikuyu chief was also appointed to administer Kibera. Protected by the Kenyatta administration, the new chief gave Kikuyu associates an opportunity to build structures for rental incomes in exchange for unofficial bribes. The chief's actions sparked a real estate bonanza; within five years, Kibera's population tripled and the Kikuyu structure owners emerged as rivals to the Nubians.

Even though the Nubians were a small minority in the early 2000s numbering around 6,000 people, they were a well-organized group that still possessed influence because of their commercial interests (they owned 15% of the rental houses) and political networks.[87] As an example, in 1999 Nubian leaders secured the assistance of the British government to negotiate for 350 acres of Kibera but the negotiations broke down due to internal conflicts within the Nubian leadership. Recognizing that they will be displaced if the Nubians are granted ownership, other Kenyans living in Kibera viewed the Nubian community with suspicion, mistrust and even hatred.

Closely related to the dispute over the land was the on-going conflict between the structure owners and tenants. Approximately 90% of

---

[84] Timothy Parsons, "Kibra is our Blood: The Sudanese Military Legacy in Nairobi's Kibera, Location, 1902-1968," *The International Journal of African Historical Studies* 30, no. 1 (1997): 90.

[85] Kenya Colony and Protectorate, *Report of the Kenyan Lands Commission* (Nairobi: Kenya Colony and Protectorate, 1933), 171.

[86] Philip Amis, "Squatters or Tenants: The Commericalization of Unauthorized Housing in Nairobi," *World Development* 12, no. 1 (1984): 89.

[87] de Smedt, "No Raila," 585.

Kiberans were tenants who paid exorbitant rents for sub-standard housing. A highly commercialized business, during the 1980s a structure owner in Kibera generally earned a 100% return on a rental structure within nine months of his or her initial investment, quicker than in any other slum in Nairobi.[88] The vast majority of structure owners were absentee landlords who did not live in Kibera; many owned hundreds of rooms with local agents to collect rents. Because of their lucrative nature, slum rentals were an important source of political patronage; nearly 60% of the structure owners were government officials and politicians.[89] There were also small-scale residential structure owners who typically rented out anywhere from one to 20 rooms and lived in the same compound as their tenants.

Because the structure owners possessed the buildings and not the land, they were not landlords in the legal sense of the word and had no responsibility to maintain the premises or provide basic services.[90] The only relationship between the structure owners and their tenants was a commercial one. Tenants who failed to pay rent in a timely manner were frequently subjected to violence and immediate eviction. As a result, there was a long-standing struggle between structure owners and tenants over high rents and substandard services. Since nearly all the structure owners were Nubian or Kikuyu and the tenants were typically Luo, Luhya, Kamba, Kisii and Maasai, these conflicts frequently had ethnic and religious overtones. Using opposition to Nubian or Kikuyu hegemony as the rallying point, local politicians periodically used the rent issue to exploit ethnic tensions to curry political favor with their constituencies. Violent ethnic clashes related to the rent issue have erupted at least six times over the last 10 years. The most recent one occurred in December 2001; 25 people were killed and over 30,000 people were rendered homeless as Luo and Nubian youth engaged in hand-to-hand combat for two weeks.

Corrupt Local Governance Structures

Another contributing factor to the high level of unrest in Kibera was the pervasive corruption on the part of local government officials. Nairobi has a complicated and overlapping system of urban governance consisting of the Provincial Administration (the PA), an antiquated remnant of

---

[88] Ibid, 44.

[89] Paul Syagga, Winnie Mitullah, and Sarah K. Gitau, *Nairobi Situation Analysis Supplementary Study: A Rapid Appraisal of Rents in Slums and Informal Settlements* (Nairobi: Government of Kenya, and UN-Habitat, 2002), 15.

[90] Ibid., 1.

colonialism, as well as elected members of the City Council. The apex of the PA's authority is the Provincial Commissioner (PC) who is appointed by the Office of the President and oversees an established hierarchy starting with the District Officer (DO) reaching down to the chiefs and assistant chiefs.[91] In the early 2000s, Kibera had a DO who supervised three chiefs and seven assistant chiefs regionally located throughout the settlement. [92] In addition, the chiefs appointed five to 10 men from each village to assist them on a voluntary basis, commonly known as the "village elders." The DO also had a regiment of Administrative Police which is a parallel police force empowered to arrest and incarcerate people in accordance with the PA's orders.

Even though the PA had limited authority to oversee minimal administrative duties, in Kibera it operated as a shadow government wielding nearly absolute authority and was well-known for its exploitive, rent-seeking and frequently violent behavior. The chiefs' most powerful role was the illegal allocation of land to structure owners. The chiefs and elders also routinely extracted bribes for ordinary activities such as repairing a leaky roof, selling vegetables on the road or walking along the railway at night; residents who resisted or were unable to pay the bribe risked being beaten, having their structures demolished or being thrown into a cell. It was also common for the chiefs to arrest and incarcerate Kiberans in order to extort payments of additional bribes. In addition, they acted as a self-appointed judiciary resolving a wide array of complaints such as landlord/tenant disputes, domestic arguments, robberies and petty crimes. In exchange for paying a bribe, the chief or elder typically rendered judgment in favor of the party who paid the highest bribe without regard to the merits of the case. The chiefs and their assistants also controlled who could hold meetings in the community, routinely disbanding gatherings that addressed issues of a political nature or advocated for a change of the status quo. Residents who tried to organize such meetings were frequently harassed, detained and even arrested.

In addition to the PA, there were three elected councilors who represented Kiberans in the City Council. Although they were elected to

---

[91] For details on the PA, see Nick Wanjohi, *Modern Local Government in Kenya* (Nairobi: Konrad Adenauer Stiftung Agency for Development Education and Communication, 2003) and Sandra F. Joireman, *Where There is No Government: Enforcing Property Rights in Common Law Africa* (Oxford: Oxford University Press, 2011).

[92] The chiefs and assistant chiefs are employed by the government as part of the Provincial Administration and are meant to operate according to the provisions of the Chief's Act.

oversee the provision of city services such as water and sanitation, their official duties were limited because these services did not exist. Instead, the councillors' primary activities were to pursue their own political and financial interests. They were also deeply entrenched in corruption. As an example, a Kiberan who wanted to build a structure was required to seek their permission and pay a bribe or the structure would be demolished.

Political Violence

In addition to the corrupt nature of the local chiefs and their retinue, Kiberans experienced a greater degree of political interference than most other slum areas because it was the political base of the area's MP, Raila Odinga (commonly referred to as Raila). As the most powerful Luo leader in the country, Raila dominated the community's political economy. He is the son of the late Jaramogi Oginga Odinga, the nation's first vice-president under Jomo Kenyatta. After his father's death in 1994, Raila inherited the mantle of leadership of the Luo community and is expected to take it "from the political wilderness that they have been [in] nearly four decades" to the State House.[93] Raila is considered one of Kenya's most charismatic and ambitious politicians. He is also highly outspoken and controversial, frequently changing political parties, reversing his views and creating or breaking alliances with political allies and foes alike.[94]

Raila was first elected the area MP in 1992 because of the ethnic support offered by the Luo community living in Kibera and is well known for his ability to mobilize the grass-roots support of Luo, especially the youth, sometimes using unorthodox tactics. As an example, Raila provoked the deadly 2001 clashes when he unilaterally announced that rents should be reduced by half.[95] Even though Raila knew his announcement would ignite a violent confrontation with the Nubian community, he made this pronouncement to consolidate political support from his Luo constituency for the upcoming controversial merger of his opposition party with KANU.[96]

Raila has also been criticized for manipulating youth wingers to threaten voters who did not support him during elections. Employed by

---

93 Njunguna Ngunjiri, and William Ong'aro, *Raila Odinga, the Unbwogable* (Nairobi: Immediate Media Services, 2003), 14.

94 For a history of Raila Odinga, see Babafemi A. Badejo, *Raila Odinga: An Enigma in Kenyan Politics* (Lagos: Yintab Books, 2006).

95 Murithii Muriuki, "Raila Takes Tough Stand on Slum Rent," *Daily Nation*, Nairobi, December 9, 2001.

96 Law Society of Kenya, *Report: A Mission*, 7-8.

Raila's political party, the National Development Party (NDP), the youth wingers were young Luo men brought from Raila's home area to live in Kibera and pursue his political interests.[97] After Raila merged his party with KANU in March 2002, and his political profile grew at a national level, so did the power of the NDP youth wingers. By 2002 NDP youth wingers had become the most influential force in Kibera, using their extensive network of communication and threats of force to intimidate anyone perceived to be interfering with Raila's or the Luo community's interests.

Civil Society Actors

Because a full analysis of the functions of the different civil society actors in Kibera is beyond the scope of this study, I briefly identify the main sectors of civil society active during 2002-2005. How the different civil society sectors operated and collaborated with one another shall be considered in greater detail in subsequent chapters.

The development NGOs made up the largest sector; in 2004 it was estimated that there were 400 NGOs located in or near Kibera.[98] The high number of development NGOs reflected a broader phenomenon experienced throughout the country. In order to fill the widening gaps left by the state's failure to provide basic services, the number of NGOs exploded in the 1990s to help the poor cope with the perpetual lack of schools, clinics, water, latrines, drainage and refuse collection. By the mid-1990s, the NGOs and some churches extended their services to new areas of micro-finance, economic development, community organizing and capacity building.[99] Although the NGOs in Kibera covered a broad scope in terms of size, resources, expertise and impact, the vast majority had small budgets and were run by local staff that had minimal education, training and expertise. There were a handful of large international NGOs set up to address health issues, especially HIV and AIDS, that were funded by international donors and staffed by professional experts.

Apart from the OHR, there were no human rights or advocacy organizations located inside Kibera. There were two legal aid clinics located nearby, the KCS and Children's Legal Action Network (focused

---

[97] The NDP was a Luo dominated opposition party founded and headed by Raila Odinga. Although the NDP was absorbed into KANU in March 2002, the youth that worked for Raila were still commonly referred to as NDP youth wingers.

[98] Acacia Consultants, "Investigation of Actors Operating in Kibera," (Report prepared for Government of Kenya, and UN-Habitat, Nairobi, January 2004), 14.

[99] Syagga, Mitullah, and Gitau, *Nairobi Situation*, 129.

exclusively on children's cases) that offered legal services. However, since most Kiberans could not afford the filing fees for a case, few residents utilized these clinics. There were also three local development NGOs. Maji na Ufanisi (Water Aid) and ANPPCAN each employed several community organizers who worked full-time with a number of local community groups that operated small-scale water and sanitation projects. Pamoja Trust also employed a number of community organizers who worked with the Muungano savings groups in Soweto. All three NGOs had Kenyan staff, professional offices and were funded by international donors.

Religious organizations also played a very visible role in Kibera. In 2002 it was estimated that there were at least 300 churches and three mosques. The vast majority of the churches were Pentecostal and African Independent Churches (AICs).[100] The Pentecostal and AIC churches reflected the socio-economic dynamic of Kibera. Although some were affiliated with larger Pentecostal churches, most pastors came directly from Kibera and did not have formal theological training. Called in a vision or dream to take up their pastoral ministries, the majority of the pastors had full-time jobs and ministered to their flocks mostly on Sundays. Membership was small and usually numbered from 20 to 40 people; the largest churches had up to 200 members. The AIC churches were similar, but frequently held their services outdoors.

The mainline Protestant churches and the Roman Catholic Church were also present,[101] but only the Catholic and Anglican churches had parishes inside Kibera-Christ the King Catholic Church (3,000 members) and St. Jerome's Anglican Church (120 members).[102] The others built churches on the periphery of the settlement to attract a mix of slum dwellers and middle-class people; some supported daughter churches inside Kibera that had small memberships of 100 or less.[103] As products of historical missionary efforts, the pastors from the mainline Protestant churches had greater theological training than the Pentecostal and AIC

[100] For details on Pentecostal and AIC churches in Kenya, see Paul Gifford, *Christianity, Politics and Public Life in Kenya* (London: Hurst & Co., 2008), 86-108 and 109-172.

[101] The Protestant churches were the Anglican, Presbyterian, Lutheran, Friends Church, Seventh-Day Adventist and Baptist.

[102] St. Jerome's was established in Gatwikera village in the 1980s as a daughter church and became a parish in 2003. See Colin Smith, "A Missiological Study of Pentecostal Churches in an Informal Settlement in Nairobi, Kenya," (PhD diss., University of South Africa, February 2007), 207-08.

[103] Ibid., 207

pastors as well as access to financial resources from overseas church contributions and international donors. The specific attributes of the Catholic Church will be addressed in greater detail in the next section.

There were also numerous CBOs that included women's groups, welfare associations, savings and credit associations and communal self-help groups.[104] These groups were primarily concerned with subsistence matters and tended to be loosely organized, with memberships reflecting particular ethnic and/or religious identities.[105] Most women's groups functioned as informal financial organizations; typically comprised of 10 to 30 women, they were focused on saving money and, more often, borrowing money from one another. Welfare associations generally brought together people along kinship and ethnic lines for purposes of planning social and cultural events such as weddings and funerals. The communal self-help groups were formed by NGOs to assist residents generate income by selling water, cleaning toilets and collecting refuse. Although the NGOs frequently referred to these CBOs as "partners," there was generally little equality in the relationship. Lacking independent resources or expertise, most CBOs were wholly dependent on their parent NGO for their direction, funds and activities. It was not possible to determine how many CBOs existed in Kibera because most were not officially registered.

In addition to the civil society actors present inside Kibera, there were two groups that occasionally visited Kibera–the press and researchers. Since most journalists considered Kibera too dangerous to enter, the media usually came into Kibera only when there was a crisis such as ethnic clashes or political violence. Apart from those rare instances, most journalists were not willing to cover a story in Kibera unless they were paid an unofficial fee. In addition to the media, Kibera attracted more researchers, academics and observers than any other slum in Nairobi. The primary reasons for Kibera's popularity with visitors were its location and its notoriety as the largest slum in sub-Saharan Africa. Located near the city center, it provided a relatively easy and quick opportunity to view an African slum. Kibera also attracted global attention because of its proximity to the corporate offices of the United Nations Human Settlements Program (UN-Habitat), the UN agency charged with improving the world's towns and cities and host to the world's leading experts on housing and slums.

---

[104] Wanyama, "The Third Sector," 5.
[105] Syagga, Mitullah, and Gitau, *Nairobi Situation*, iv.

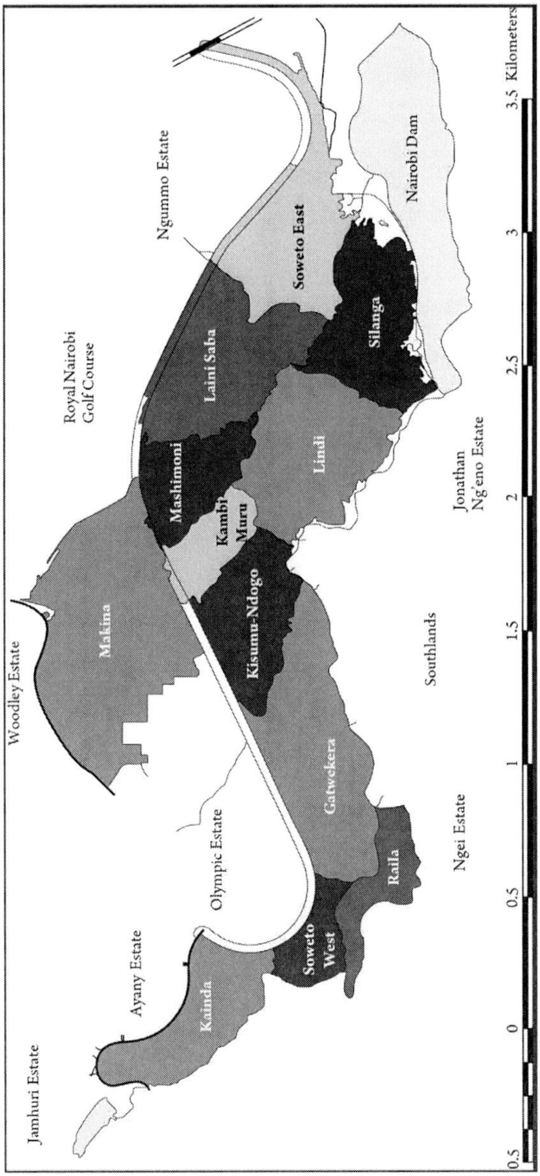

Map of Kibera
Where There is No Government: Enforcing Property Rights in Common Law Africa by Sandra F. Joreman

Christ the King Catholic Church

Although the primary focus of this research is limited to a four-year period in the 2000s, a brief review of how the parish evolved is helpful to contextualize the OHR's interventions. The parish started in 1974 as a small sub-parish of St. Michael's, a middle-class parish located near the southeastern boundary of Kibera. The priests assigned to administer St. Michael's were Guadalupe missionaries from Mexico. In 1987 the first missionary in Kenya to live fully immersed in a slum moved to Kibera. Because Kibera was public land, the government agreed to give the Archdiocese a plot in the village of Line Saba so the Guadalupe priests could build a small, semi-permanent church, priest's house and office.

The founding parish priest administered the parish until 1995; at that time, Catholics numbered around 1,000. Catholics participated in the church primarily in two ways; the first was by the attending mass at the main parish compound on Sunday mornings. About 10% of the parishioners were also members of one of eight small Christian communities (SCCs), groups of 15 to 35 Catholics, organized by their specific locale that met on a weekly basis. At a typical meeting, members might recite the rosary, sing hymns, and read and discuss passages from the Bible. Some of the groups also organized funerals, visited sick members, raised funds for mutual aid and organized support for parish liturgies and fund raisers. Each SCC had an elected leadership that included a chairman, secretary and treasurer who were responsible for the overall management of the SCC.

Although many observers frequently draw parallels between the SCCs and the base Christian communities from Latin America, there are important distinctions. In Latin America, the base communities were grass-roots organizations that emerged in the 1960s in the context of liberation theology. They provided church members opportunities to worship together, discuss common concerns and take action toward concrete goals, often in the form of grass-roots politics. Although the SCCs were influenced by the Latin America model, it is important not to overstate the parallels. The SCCs in East Africa evolved in a different context and for different purposes.

In 1976 the Kenyan bishops along with bishops from the other AMECEA (Association of Member Episcopal Conferences in Eastern Africa) countries adopted the formation of SCCs to improve the organizational base of the church by shifting from a centralized, clerical model into a more localized one that enhanced the role of the laity. Prior to 1976, the church followed a traditional model imported by European missionaries; the parish priest resided in a central compound and was the focal point of the parish's administration and sacramental ministry. Catholics typically traveled considerable distances from their village to the parish center to fulfill Sunday obligations and then returned home. The creation of SCCs was a significant break from this pattern. The aim was to form small, local communities where lay Catholics could meet regularly to pray, read the Bible, help one another with daily problems and eventually form new ministries that would respond to the social reality of the community. Whether or not the SCC model has been effectively established in Kenya is still open to debate.[106] However, even the most enthusiastic supporters of the SCC initiative admit that the SCCs have not become a vehicle of social transformation in the manner observed in Latin America and elsewhere.[107]

In 1995 the founding parish priest returned to Mexico and was replaced by another Guadalupe missionary who administered the parish until 2001. During that time, the parish priest divided the parish into several, smaller units called sub-parishes to help administer pastoral activities. The sub-parishes were located in Soweto, Lindi and Shilanga; each rented a small structure to use as a meeting place and chapel. The parish priest also invited a number of missionary congregations and donors to set up programs in the mid-1990s. Unlike other parishes in the Archdiocese of Nairobi, the Kibera parish was fully immersed inside the slum and did not have a middle-class sector to supplement the financial operations of the church. The Guadalupe priests also did not have the level of financial resources that many European congregations enjoyed so they invited other missionaries to assist them. For example, a group of missionary brothers were invited to start a drop-in center for street children that later became an informal primary school. An international Catholic donor set up a health clinic in the parish to provide low-cost medicine and basic medical examinations. A brother provided support for a parish-based youth group. A congregation of missionary priests built a vocational training center to train young men in carpentry, masonry and plumbing. A group of missionary sisters started a home-based health care

[106] See Laurenti Magesa, "The Church in Eastern Africa, Retrospect and Introspect," in *How Local is the Local Church? Small Christian Communities and Church in Eastern Africa*, ed. Agatha Radoli (Eldoret, Kenya: AMECEA Gaba Publications, 1993), 6 and AMECEA, *Small Christian Communities 20 years later*, Amecea Documentation Service, (Nairobi, June/July 1997).

[107] See Joseph Healey, and Jeanne Hinton, ed., *Small Christian Communities Today: Capturing the New Moment* (Maryknoll, NY: Orbis Books, 2006), 97.

program for AIDS patients. Another group of sisters started a tailoring program for young girls in the parish.

Efforts to invite other missionary congregations to assist the parish had mixed results. Although the services provided were greatly needed, the approach was fragmented and rife with conflict. Apart from the primary school, which was eventually handed over to the parish, none of these programs was under the control of the parish priest or the parishioners. Each missionary congregation designed, administered and financed its own project; the parish's only official role was to provide physical space for their offices and programs. As a result, there was little accountability or effort to coordinate activities. Instead, each missionary carved out his or her niche and operated independently. Some of the projects were not sustainable because they were dependent on the personal commitment of the individual missionary and his/her access to necessary funds. As a result, in a number of circumstances the projects ended as soon as the missionary left.

In 1998 the Archdiocese officially recognized Christ the King as an independent parish and secured a title deed for the main parish compound. By 2001, it was estimated that there were 3,000 active Catholics in the parish; the number of SCCs had grown to 16, but the overall percentage that joined a SCC remained around 10%. Parishioners also participated in a number of parish-based groups started by the missionaries such as the women's group, youth group, liturgy committee, choirs and pro-life group. There was also a parish-based justice and peace commission (JPC) that consisted of two representatives from each SCC and two elected leaders. The JPC was affiliated with the Archdiocese's Catholic Justice and Peace Commission (CJPC) started by Archbishop Ndingi in 1998 to support pastoral action designed to promote justice. In addition to representing the parish at the diocesan-level meetings, the JPC facilitated the KEC's annual Lenten Campaign that highlighted a specific socio-political issue during every week of Lent as well as civic education and other justice-related activities.

There was an elected leadership called the parish pastoral council (PPC), which was composed of two representatives from each SCC and parish group. The PPC occasionally met the parish priest to discuss parish-wide issues such as church construction, fund-raising efforts and other administrative matters. Most of the leaders in the PPC came from the lower strata in terms of education, experience and commitment because many of the educated parishioners were employed outside Kibera and largely unavailable for parish activities. As a result, leadership in the PPC was of a low quality. There was also a pastoral team comprised of the parish priest, an assistant priest, the catechist, a Guadalupe lay missioner and two parishioners who worked with the youth and women that met on weekly basis to discuss activities planned for the coming week.

In 2001 a Guadalupe missionary priest who had worked for nearly a decade in the rural Amazon was appointed as the new parish priest. During his first year, he restructured the parish to reflect the model he worked with in Brazil, a style heavily influenced by Latin American liberation theology. His immediate priority was to involve parishioners in the larger Kibera social, political and economic reality. To accomplish this goal, the parish priest created several new ministries starting with the women's ministry designed to organize women to meet, reflect and act on the issues facing them. In addition, he started the self-reliance department to respond to the economic and employment needs of Kiberans by promoting job creation, vocational training and capacity building in the areas of business management, job searching and income generation.

The parish priest also started a new ministry known as Human Rights and Popular Movements and assigned the social worker for the primary school, a trained community organizer, to manage it. The creation of a specific human rights ministry was a break from other parishes in the Archdiocese, all of which relied on parish-based JPCs to pursue human rights issues. The new parish priest started the ministry because he was frustrated over the leaders of the JPC and their failure to promote social justice issues in Kibera. Shortly after the parish JPC was formed in early 1999, two parishioners whose primary motivation was to access parish resources, not to promote justice and peace issues, took control of the JPC. According to the parish priest:

> I met the JPC in January 2000 and found out they were doing only the Lenten Campaign and they could not even do that. I waited for them to do something for one year and then I decided to do something different because it was clear that the JPC could not improve.[108]

However, following the creation of the new human rights ministry, the leaders of the JPC accused the social worker of usurping their authority and blocked all planned activities for more than one year. Following the violent rent clashes in December 2001, the parish priest asked the author of this book to coordinate and administer the office that had been renamed the Office of Human Rights. He also recruited new missionaries, including three religious sisters and three priests, to better staff the ministries and attract additional financial support. The pastoral team was expanded to

[108] Interview with CTK parish priest during 2001-2005, August 29, 2008.

include the priests as well as the coordinators of each ministry. A new layer of leadership at the sub-parish level with similar positions as the SCCs was also instituted. These leaders were asked to organize the activities for the cluster of four to five SCCs in each sub-parish.

In addition to restructuring the parish, the parish priest undertook the process of the pastoral circle, a planning methodology popular among Catholic parishes and groups that emphasizes participatory processes. Generally, there are five steps to the pastoral circle that are closely related–immersion, social analysis, theological reflection, pastoral planning and evaluation.[109] The aim of the pastoral circle exercise was to examine the root causes of the problems facing the parish community so a more systematic and holistic parish plan could be developed.[110] After hiring a Kenyan sister to design and implement a planning process, the parish priest assigned the members of the pastoral team different tasks to assist in the labor-intensive process. For two years, the members of the SCCs and parish groups (about 300 parishioners) met regularly to discuss, pray and reflect on the: (1) living conditions of Kibera, (2) African traditions and values, (3) socio-economic and political issues and (4) parish structures. The process culminated in a parish-wide plan as well as individual plans for each ministry and sub-parish for 2003-2008.[111]

---

[109] See Joe Holland, and Peter Henriot, *Social Analysis: Linking Faith and Justice* (Maryknoll, NY: Orbis Books, 1983).

[110] For details on the process, see Christine Bodewes, "Can the Pastoral Circle Transform a Parish?" in *The Pastoral Circle Revisited: a Critical Quest for Truth and Transformation*, ed. Frans Wijsen, Peter Henriot, Rodrigo Mejia (Maryknoll, NY: Orbis Books, 2005).

[111] The findings from the parish social analysis were summarized and published by the author in *Parish Transformation in Urban Slums: Voices of Kibera, Kenya* (Nairobi: Paulines Publications Africa, 2005).

CHAPTER THREE

THE CIVIC EDUCATION PROGRAM

Civil society advocates maintain that civic education is among the central functions performed by civil society organizations committed to the democratization process because it has the potential to increase the political capacity of citizens at the grass-roots level. In their view, individuals who participate in civic education not only learn about democratic values, norms and principles; they also cultivate skills in active participation, communication, organization and decision making. This foundation should lead them to take a greater role in promoting the community's common interests including holding the government to account for its abuse of power and corruption.

In March 2002, for the first time in Kenya's history, the CKRC formally invited civil society organizations to teach civic education as part of the country's on-going constitutional review process. Taking advantage of the newly created political space, the OHR coordinator and a team of Kenyan lawyers designed and implemented a civic education program for parishioners. Although the civic education program started as a four-month course on democracy, elections and constitutionalism for selected parish representatives, it turned into a four-year program situated in the SCCs that covered a broad scope of human rights topics as well as legal, social, political and cultural issues important in Kibera.

In this chapter, I analyze the OHR's civic education program to determine the extent to which civic education helped parishioners contribute to democracy building in the parish and the broader Kibera community. [1] I argue here that although civic education did play a role, it was not the role imagined by civil society advocates. During the initial course, the number of parishioners who were interested in learning about

---

[1] Earlier versions of this chapter were published as "The Catholic Church and Civic Education in the Slums of Nairobi," *in Jesus and Ubuntu: Exploring the Social Impact of Christianity in Africa*, ed. Mwenda Ntarangwi (Trenton, NJ: Africa World Press, 2011), 147-76 and "Civil Society and the Consolidation of Democracy in Kenya: An Analysis of a Catholic Parish's Efforts in Kibera Slum," *The Journal of Modern African Studies* 48, no. 4 (2010): 547-72.

their human and legal rights was relatively small. The majority were consumed with meeting survival needs while others were not interested due to apathy, fear and avoidance of matters related to the political arena. It is further argued that the second phase of civic education helped inculcate democratic values and behavior among a small percentage of parishioners (around 15%) in a number of ways including improving parish leadership, participation, respect for the rule of law, conflict resolution skills, accountability, and tolerance and respect for different views. However, the vast majority of the participants who were educated about their rights did not use their new knowledge and skills to promote the community's interests in the civil and political arena. Most parishioners were inhibited from holding local government officials to account for their corruption and abuse of power due to fears of retaliation, restrictive church protocols and a lack of capacity and resources.

Civil Society's Historical Role Providing Civic Education

Although the CKRC's invitation to civil society organizations to teach civic education within a legal framework was unprecedented, certain sectors within civil society, including the Catholic Church, had been providing democracy education for three decades. In order to contextualize the OHR's civic education program, I provide a brief review of the Catholic Church's historical role in promoting civic education. I also explain the political changes in the country that led to the CKRC's invitation and the response of the Kenyan Catholic Church and the parish.

In the early 1970s, expatriate Catholic missionaries pioneered an innovative development education program known as DELTA (Development Education Leadership Teams in Action).[2] Rooted in Catholic biblical teachings and the theory and practice of Brazilian educationalist Paul Freire, the classes taught the psycho-social method of community education, communication skills and leadership training. Over three million Catholics were trained in DELTA before the Catholic bishops bowed to political pressure from President Moi to end the program in 1982, following an attempted coup to overthrow the government.[3] Even though the bishops' disavowal of DELTA marked the end of the Catholic Church's effort to promote a grass-roots social movement in Kenya, the

---

[2] Anne Hope, and Sally Timmel, "A Kenyan Experience for Faith-Based Transformative Action," *Development* 46, no. 4 (2003): 96.

[3] Jerry Crowley, *Go to the People: An African Experience in Education for Development* (Eldoret, Kenya: Gaba Publications, 1985), 14.

church continued to provide Catholics with voter education prior to the 1992 and 1997 elections. The national CJPC and the NCCK published and distributed pamphlets and books for voters and organized mass seminars that popularized the principles of democracy within the context of church teachings.[4] Through its highly organized structure that connected the dioceses to the parishes to the SCCs, the Catholic Church had a ready-made network for disseminating information to the grass roots.

A growing number of NGOs also provided civic education classes.[5] Leading up to the 1997 election, the number of providers grew from 30 to 130 as Western donors channeled unprecedented levels of funds to the NGOs. Civic educators, however, did not have a free hand to teach. The state labeled civic education as anti-government and the PA regularly harassed and intimidated civic educators. Some even destroyed their teaching materials and denied them permission to hold workshops. As a result, civic educators were often forced to disguise their efforts and, in many parts of the country, the only safe havens for classes were inside churches.

The overall impact of civil society's efforts prior to the 1992 and 1997 elections was quite limited for a number of reasons. Not only were civic educators blocked by the Moi government, there was also a lack of coordination and poor planning by the providers. Most damaging to the initiative was that many providers did not make a clear distinction between civic education and political advocacy. It was not uncommon for opposition politicians and, even NGOs, to use civic education forums to promote political candidates.[6] In addition to political co-option, the unchecked flood of donor money turned civic education into a commercial enterprise. According to Maria Nzomo, the number of "briefcase" NGOs, organizations started overnight by individuals interested mainly in accessing donor funds, outnumbered the experts who had a genuine commitment to democracy education.[7]

---

[4] Sabar-Friedman, "Church, State," 48.

[5] Marcel Rutten, Ali Al Mazrui, and François Grignon, *Out for the Count: the 1997 General Elections and Prospects for Democracy in Kenya* (Kampala: Fountain, 2001), 68.

[6] Karuti Kanyinga, and Carl Wesselink, "Transition to Democracy-The Role of Civic Education in Kenya," Phatlaslatsa Newsletter (December 2002), 3.

[7] Maria Nzomo, "Civil Society in the Kenyan Political Transition: 1992: 2002," in *The Politics of Transition in Kenya: From Kanu to Narc*, ed. Walter Oyugi, Peter Wanyande, and C. Odhiambo-Mbai (Nairobi: Heinrich Boll Foundation, 2003), 197.

The modalities of providing civic education were also criticized. Civic education was characterized as a short-term "hit and run" initiative that occurred only in the months before an election. In general, the curriculum was limited and abstract focusing on political functions to the exclusion of governance, development and second-generation rights that dealt with social, economic and cultural issues. It also failed to take into consideration the particular dynamics and needs of the local community. Providers frequently were not qualified and used teaching materials in English, which the majority did not adequately comprehend.[8] A strong NGO-bias for the urban, middle-class also resulted in unequal access to civic education; a 2007 nation-wide study of civic education showed that only about 30% of Kenyans had ever attended a civic education forum.[9]

Notwithstanding government opposition and mounting criticism of civic education, pro-democracy NGOs continued to promote civic education in the post-1997 election period as part of their constitutional reform agenda. In 1999, to develop a more coordinated, non-partisan approach, a consortium of 10 Western embassies funded 74 NGOs to provide civic education under the aegis of the National Civic Education Program (NCEP). Although the program was heavily criticized as a project of foreigners, Steven Finkel's 2003 study showed that the program changed the democratic orientations and behavior of the participants, especially those who attended more than one or two classes.[10] Steven Orvis's 2004 study of several civic education providers also suggested improvements had been made. According to his research, Orvis found that civic education programs were still "quite small, with limited national impact," and had "not provoked a revolution in political knowledge or attitudes," but they had begun to make a positive difference in people's awareness and knowledge about their legal and political rights and debates about constitutional reform.[11]

---

[8] Catherine Ndungo, "Language, Gender, Political Participation and Democracy in Kenya," (Paper presented to Language Project Conference, University of Maryland, November 2004), 158-59.

[9] *Political Patronage, Access to Entitlements and Poverty in Kenya, Final Report of Findings of a National Survey* (Nairobi: KEC-CJPC and Dan Church Aid, 2007), 49.

[10] Steven Finkel, "The Impact of the Kenyan National Civic Education Program on Democratic Attitudes, Knowledge, Values and Behavior," (Report prepared for U.S. Agency for International Development, Nairobi, AEP-I-00-0001800-00, December 30, 2003), 91.

[11] Orvis, "Kenyan Civil Society," 265.

The CKRC's invitation to civil society to provide civic education was prompted by two watershed events in Kenya's political history. First, a 10-year struggle by pro-democracy groups to reform the constitution reached an important turning point in March 2002 when the CKRC was empowered by parliament to hold public hearings to listen to views of ordinary Kenyans and convert them into a new constitution. This was the first time in Kenya's history that citizens were given an opportunity to participate in deliberations that would determine the country's governance structures. At the same time, the CKRC was authorized to facilitate civic education to raise awareness on constitutional issues in order to enable widespread participation. Lacking adequate resources of its own, the CKRC invited civil society organizations to supplement its efforts.

Second, in another unprecedented move, the CKRC invited civil society organizations to provide civic education to the general public in order to raise awareness on constitutional issues and prepare citizens for the December 2002 general election. Since President Moi was constitutionally prohibited from seeking another term, many Kenyans viewed the December 2002 election as an opportunity to make a fundamental break with the KANU government whose decades of plunder, greed and corruption had caused widespread poverty and deprivation. Optimism was heightened further because the opposition parties had finally united to support one candidate. When President Moi, determined to continue his patrimonial regime by proxy, endorsed Uhuru Kenyatta, the young and politically inexperienced son of his predecessor, a number of key Moi supporters including Raila Odinga defected from KANU and joined the National Alliance Party of Kenya, a coalition of the three main opposition parties and 12 small, ethno-regional parties that had come together in January 2002. The new coalition, renamed the National Alliance Rainbow Coalition (NARC), endorsed Mwai Kibaki as its presidential candidate.[12]

The Catholic Church's response to the CKRC's invitation to teach civic education was markedly different from its prior initiatives. Instead of preparing civic education materials that incorporated the church's teachings or organizing seminars for Catholics at the grass-roots parish level, the CJPC opted to teach the secular civic education curriculum created by the NCEP program. The workshops were limited in number and designed for the upper echelons of the laity at the diocesan level. Moreover, in contrast to the 1990s when the Catholic bishops were at the

[12] For details on the 2002 election, see Makau Mutua, *Kenya's Quest for Democracy, Taming Leviathan* (Boulder, CO: L. Reinner Publishers, 2008).

center of the country's movement for political reform, in 2002 they did not speak publicly as a group about the election or constitutional review process. The bishops also did not issue any pastoral letters advising Catholics how to approach these issues.

In the Archdiocese of Nairobi, organized civic education was almost non-existent. Archbishop Ndingi, the one-time heroic advocate of democratic reform, had seemingly abandoned his personal crusade and the activities of the diocesan JPC. Starting in 2000, the Archbishop had gradually begun to shift the Archdiocese's priorities to economic development.[13] Faced with growing costs and expenses attendant to managing over 90 parishes, the Archdiocese relied more and more on donor-financed development projects to supplement its administrative costs. Except for the vocations office, all the Archdiocese's independent programs such as the JPC, education, health, women, agriculture and micro-finance were put under the control of the diocesan development office.[14] Because the coordinator of the development office was interested primarily in projects that could generate funds, the JPC initiative was given scant attention and resources. In 2001 the layman who coordinated the JPC was dismissed and most local justice and peace activities terminated.

Despite the institutional church's reluctance to get involved in the constitutional review process, demands for guidance by parishioners started in the early months of 2002. During numerous meetings with the OHR and the parish JPC, the chairman repeatedly requested civic education to prepare parishioners for the upcoming election and to teach parishioners about their legal rights. The JPC representatives also admitted that they did not have the capacity to teach civic education and they asked the OHR to take the lead. While these discussions were taking place in the parish, a number of missionaries from the Kutoka network suggested that the parishes should develop a civic education program that addressed the particular socio-political issues facing Catholics in the slums.[15] The missionaries felt the parishes were well suited for the task because they possessed moral credibility, the loyalty of large constituencies and were generally viewed to be non-partisan. The convener of the Kutoka asked a small committee to develop a curriculum that could be used by all the parishes. However, after one meeting the committee concluded that a joint

---

[13] Archdiocese of Nairobi, *Strategic Plan 2003-2008* (Nairobi: Archdiocese of Nairobi), 2002, xi-xiii.

[14] Interview with former director of the Nairobi Archdiocese JPC, September 22, 2008.

[15] Kutoka Minutes, April 11, 2002.

civic education program was not realistic because the parishes had vastly different demographics, needs and ideas about civic education. In addition, the network lacked sufficient capacity, including human resources and financial support, to undertake such a large project.

When the plan for a common program was canceled, the OHR coordinator decided to facilitate civic education in the parish and presented her plan to the pastoral team in March 2002. The parish priest supported the project if the coordinator raised the necessary funds. The other ministry coordinators also gave verbal support for the idea, but viewed it as the personal project of the OHR coordinator, not a parish-wide initiative. The pastoral team's response was typical of the way the coordinators interacted; the different ministries generally operated independently with little joint support from one another. The coordinator solicited donations from her missionary organization and family and friends in the United States to cover the anticipated costs for the teaching materials.

The OHR's Development of a Civic Education Program

The first step taken by the OHR coordinator in developing the parish civic education program was to recruit a team of qualified volunteer lawyers to design and teach the classes. The OHR coordinator asked five Kenyan lawyers, who had previously worked with her at the KCS, to develop the curriculum, teach the classes and provide free legal advice and representation for parishioners who might act on their rights. Four of the lawyers were working in private practice and one was working for a national NGO that specialized in civic education and paralegal training. All five agreed to volunteer in the parish program. The coordinator also invited a missionary priest who was the director of a Jesuit-based program working on social policy and advocacy to help the lawyers incorporate the church's teachings into the civic education curriculum.

The OHR next assessed the knowledge and understanding of parishioners about democracy and human rights as well as the political environment in Kibera. In addition to distributing a questionnaire to the SCCs, the coordinator and community organizer in the OHR spent months visiting parishioners in their homes, SCCs and other parish groups to talk about the particular social-political issues affecting them. The assessment revealed several key findings. As an example, the SCCs in the parish varied a great deal depending on their history, region and leaders. Some of the older SCCs located in Soweto and Line Saba had received training and formation classes and had active leaders that met on a regular basis, but mostly to pray and read the Bible. In contrast, many of the SCCs in Shilanga and Lindi met infrequently; some operated more like savings groups, gathering for the primary purpose of contributing and loaning money. A few had stopped meeting altogether. Apart from a few SCCs in Soweto that periodically visited the sick, the vast majority were not engaged in activities outside their SCC including justice and peace issues.

The OHR assessment also revealed that most parishioners had little knowledge about the basic structures of the government or the laws of Kenya. More than half the parishioners had not finished secondary school or participated in any adult education programs. Unlike other slum areas, Kibera had largely been ignored during the civic education boom of the 1990s. Most NGO providers viewed Kibera as a dangerous and politicized place and were afraid to teach civic education in the community. Although some parishioners regularly listened to the radio and, to a lesser degree, read the newspaper, many, especially the women, had not been exposed to social and civic issues through the mainstream media. The parish JPC, lacking training, financial resources and the desire, had done little to fill the gap. The result was that most parishioners were susceptible to the political propaganda being promulgated by local ethnic-based politicians.

Other factors contributed to low levels of knowledge and participation. The political environment was volatile and unstable. Violence was a recurrent feature of the electoral process in Kenya, but the potential for violence was particularly high in Kibera because it comprised the majority of Raila's electoral base, making it a hotly contested political constituency. Raila was also notorious for dispatching NDP youth wingers to generate political support for him, typically with the use of the force. The threat of violence was at a historical high in advance of the 2002 election as the community feared that politicians would exploit ethnic hostilities still simmering from the 2001 rent clashes to garner votes.

There was also on-going government harassment of civic education providers. At the time the CKRC started public discussions about the proposed constitution, it was widely believed that it would have the ability to stop the government from obstructing civic education. That was not the case. Viewing civic education as an initiative to incite the masses in favor of NARC, the government tried to undermine it using harassment and intimidation tactics reminiscent of the 1992 and 1997 elections. In July 2001, President Moi publicly demanded that the churches and NGOs stop conducting civic education and declared "only politicians would be allowed to carry out civic education programs as selfish 'foreigners' were manipulating the church and non-governmental organizations through their programs."[16] Even though a number of Catholic bishops quickly rebuffed Moi's threats, the government's intimidation tactics had a chilling effect in Kibera. Some parishioners, particularly women, said they were afraid to attend civic education classes in fear of violent reprisals by the chiefs, which could range from verbal harassment to a physical beating to being thrown in a cell at the DO's camp.

During election periods, Kibera, like most slums, was viewed as a "vote bank." Although vote buying transcended class structures with over 60% of Kenyans admitting to selling their voter card to politicians. In Kibera, the selling of voter cards was rampant due to acute economic needs.[17] Starting in mid-2001, NDP youth wingers started their campaign to buy voter cards. Every Sunday afternoon after drinking alcohol, the youth, carrying sticks and making threats, moved door-to-door to buy voter cards. Although parishioners were not willing to admit that they sold their card, the OHR coordinator believed that most parishioners did so in exchange for a cooking pot, cloth or money. A card was worth anywhere from 15 to 100 Ksh, depending on how much time remained in the campaign. In admitting to the practice, a number of parishioners explained that there was no moral judgment attached to the practice, it was just someone's "good luck" if they could profit from the politicians.

The final step in the OHR's planning process was developing a suitable pedagogy. The lawyer who was in charge of her NGO's country-wide civic education program took the lead in developing the modalities for the program. In her experience, classes were more effective when taught in smaller groups over a sustained period of time because they allowed for greater participation and analysis. Even though it was clear that many of the SCCs were weak, the election was less than six months away, which meant there was not adequate time to create new groups. Based on their prior experience at KCS, the lawyers knew that group formation in the slums was a timely and labor-intensive process because the community's overriding preoccupation with survival needs, ethnic divisions and the repressive tactics of the chiefs. Such a process would be even more difficult and time-consuming in Kibera because the community had been sharply polarized along ethnic and political lines during the 2001 clashes.

The lawyers decided the best way to reach a large number of people quickly was to train trainers from the existing parish groups who would then transmit the classes to their group members. The groups were the 16

[16] "Churches, NGOs in Kenya Told to Stop Voter Education," *Daily Nation*, Nairobi, July 24, 2001.

[17] *Political Patronage*, 62.

SCCs as well as 10 parish groups.[18] The coordinator added a secondary target group, parishioners who were not members of the SCCs and were commonly known as the Sunday Christians because their only connection to the parish was attending weekly mass. The Sunday Christians would be taught the main points of the core curriculum during 10 to 15 minute inputs after Sunday mass or through dramas enacted during the mass. Between March and May 2001, the OHR coordinator met each group to explain the project and recruit two representatives for training. Because of their historical exclusion from the political arena, each group was asked to send at least one woman.

Civic Education prior to the 2002 Election

The lawyers, working in teams of two, facilitated classes on eight Saturdays from September through November 2002. Despite the unstable political environment, attendance was higher than expected; on average, 80 to 90 parishioners participated in the classes. Between 30 and 40 participants were the appointed representatives from the SCCs and parish groups while the other participants were youth members. At least one representative from 22 of the 26 groups attended regularly and only three parishioners did not turn up because of threats made by the NDP youth wingers and the chiefs.

The classes had a strong Catholic bias; each session started with prayers and a scripture reading that related to the topic followed by a short theological reflection led by one of the participants. At the start of the course, one of the lawyers dedicated one day's input to explaining the Kenyan bishops' historical support for multi-party democracy, constitutional reform and civic education as well as the Christian perspective on the key points in the curriculum. The lawyers taught classes on nation building, constitution making, democracy and good governance. At the end of the course, as fears about potential election violence escalated, the coordinator invited a local NGO to teach the group about peace building and active non-violence. During every session, the lawyers went beyond the abstract concepts and directly confronted the difficult issues facing Kibera residents such as political violence, tribalism and the corrupt practices of the chiefs and police. The lawyers also facilitated

[18] The 10 parish groups were two choirs, the youth group, women's group, job seekers in the parish-based employment group called Help Employment Need in Kibera, primary school teachers, pastoral team, catechists, the JPC and the parish health workers.

discussions on democracy and good leadership not just in the government, but also in their families, SCCs, the parish and the Catholic Church.

Due to low literacy rates, the lawyers did not teach in a typical classroom lecture style; instead, they used a participatory methodology that incorporated dramas, role plays, small group discussions, pictures, flip charts and songs. All classes were taught in Kiswahili to ensure maximum comprehension. In addition, the lawyers prepared written summaries of each subject in English and Kiswahili, which were distributed to help the trainers teach the subject matter in their groups. The lawyers taught on Saturdays to accommodate the schedule of most parishioners who worked as day laborers during the week. Class periods were deliberately kept to a half-day in order to allow parishioners adequate time to open their shops and manage household responsibilities.

During the participants' evaluation of the course, discussions about the classes as well as the new government were hopeful and positive, a reflection of the national euphoria that swept through Kenya following Mwai Kibaki's landslide victory. Virtually every participant voiced positive feedback on the lessons, particularly the class that addressed the election process. One participant expressed the sentiments of many when she said:

> We thought voting was for strong people who were looking for jobs or people who wanted to work for the government. We had stopped voting because as slum people we thought it was a waste of our time, but then we learned why we needed to vote and make the politicians deliver what they have promised.[19]

For many, the highlight was being given a sample ballot and walked through the process of how to vote. Women in the group felt especially empowered. According to one participant, "I learned that it is my right to participate in elections as a woman and I can't be denied the right to vote. I have to participate and I need to know the person I vote for is the right person and will help me."[20] A number of participants also commented about the impact of lawyers teaching the classes. The following comment is illustrative: "It was the first time for lawyers to come to us. There was a feeling that lawyers were rich people and could not come into Kibera especially when it was raining, but the lawyers were there all the time."[21]

---

[19] OHR Evaluation, February 1, 2004.

[20] Interview with Saturday group member D, September 29, 2008.

[21] Interview with OHR team member A, September 22, 2008.

Despite the positive assessments and affirmation for the course, there were also limitations in the classes. Several participants said they wanted to learn more about activism and concrete actions they could take; they felt it was not enough to just learn their rights. Some also noted that incorporating the teachings of the Catholic Church were very important to them especially as they related to tribalism and religious differences, but the lawyers did not have enough background on the church's social teachings. Further, the evaluation of the four-month course showed that the overall impact of the program was very limited, namely, because most parishioners who had been targeted for classes did not receive them. Only six of the 16 SCCs were able to teach the lessons in their SCCs. Of those six, three felt that they adequately communicated the lessons to their members. Although five trainers requested and received assistance from the OHR team, eight of the 16 SCCs did not receive the lessons. For those that received the inputs, the quality of the classes varied considerably; some trainers were given only 10 or 15 minutes while others were allowed a full hour to teach the class.

The parish-based groups also varied in the degree to which the membership participated. Overall, the impact was very low. Only one of the ten groups succeeded in adequately teaching the full curriculum, a group of 40 young men and women who met every week with the self-reliance coordinator. This group was highly motivated to attend the classes because they were vying for factory jobs being allocated after the classes. Despite the sincere commitment of most trainers, there were a number of obstacles that prevented them from teaching their members. The OHR coordinator and the lawyers were aware of some of the obstacles, but they did not adequately understand or anticipate the complex dynamics at play.

Lack of Time

The number one challenge for the trainers was the lack of time. The limited availability of parishioners was linked to their economic reality and their daily struggle to meet survival needs. During the evaluation, trainers repeated a common mantra that SCC members were "too busy looking for their daily bread" to spend time studying the constitution. A number of the young men who attended the Saturday classes had higher levels of education and skills to teach, but they could not attend their SCC meetings on a regular basis because they worked in the factories with unpredictable schedules. Men were not the only ones limited by time. Many of the women expressed similar sentiments especially those coming from the Shilanga region, most of who were single mothers under daily pressure to earn enough to feed their children. Faced with the choice to close their roadside stands where they sold household food products or attend their SCC meetings, it was not realistic to expect these women to choose civic education over the well-being of their families.

Another common time constraint for parishioners was the constant need to return to their rural homes to assist relatives. Since many parishioners were the sole wage earners in their extended families, cultural norms dictated they assist family members struggling with financial matters especially illness and funerals. As a result, a number of participants were consistently unavailable for the Saturday classes. The growing number of HIV and AIDS cases was also a factor. In two SCCs, there were parish leaders in the final stages of the disease that required the other SCC members to care for the dying members' families rendering all other activities impossible. In addition, at least three of the trainers were known to be suffering from AIDS and were frequently unable to attend classes because of reoccurring illness. Women were faced with additional demands because of their household responsibilities. There were also a number of trainers that admitted they were just too tired and overwhelmed at the end of the day to teach a class in their evening SCC meeting.

Authoritarian Leaders

The nature of leadership in the parish was also an inhibiting factor for several SCCs and groups. Leadership in many of the SCCs mirrored the top-down, paternalistic patterns characteristic of the Moi government. According to one parishioner:

> We have elected leaders in our SCCs, but some are just like KANU because we are not free to speak out during our meetings; only a few people have a voice in the SCCs. There is no democracy in our SCCs. Being a leader in the SCC is just like being a MP; they don't want to hear about our problems. They are supposed to serve the church, but for many, leadership is just a title.[22]

Since the SCC leaders had been given limited training, many were capable of doing little more than reading the Bible or leading the group in prayer. Some ran their groups like a personal fiefdom, holding office year after year with little to no opposition, discussion or participation. The civic education program introduced a novel approach to the SCCs. In the past, only the priest and catechists visited the SCCs for the purpose of

---

[22] Interview with Saturday group member C, September 30, 2008.

celebrating mass or imparting religious teaching. When the OHR asked ordinary SCC members to teach their fellow members, it was a direct threat to this cadre of leaders. In several SCCs, the elected chairpersons viewed the trainers' attempts to teach about democracy and good governance as a way to undermine their power and they refused to give the trainers an opportunity to teach.

There were also a number of group leaders who overtly blocked the trainers from teaching. Even though the chairman of the JPC had repeatedly asked for civic education and participated in planning the curriculum, he and his small circle of followers stopped attending after the first class because the lawyers did not single him out to lead the group discussions. Accustomed to monopolizing most parish meetings, the JPC chairman boycotted the classes and started a verbal campaign against the OHR asserting that it had wrongfully overtaken the designated role of the JPC. As a result, trainers from two SCCs in the Lindi sub-parish where he lived and held influence also stopped attending the lessons.

It was not just parishioners who obstructed the classes; a member of the pastoral team also opposed civic education. Just prior to the start of the civic education classes, the new faith formation coordinator, an expatriate missionary sister, started a training program for parishioners who had agreed to work as part-time catechists in the SCCs. The trainers for the catechists attended the first two classes but were told that civic education was not appropriate for religion teachers.[23] She characterized civic education as "NGO work" that was secular and political in orientation and should not be taught in SCCs because they were the exclusive purview of prayer and faith formation. She also asserted that only religious sisters or priests, not a lay missioner or lawyers, were qualified to teach Catholic social teaching. Warned that if they attended civic education they could not be catechists, the two catechists stopped attending the course because they did not want to relinquish their monthly catechist allowance.[24]

Financial Motivations

Numerous trainers reported that some of their SCC members did not attend the classes because the OHR refused to pay allowances. According to one trainer, "People in my SCC didn't show up for the classes because they want to be paid. They think I'm crazy because I am doing this for

[23] Interview with OHR team member C, October 3, 2008.

[24] Interview with parish lead catechist, October 2, 2008.

free."[25] Faced with a chronic impoverishment, many parishioners were not willing to participate in activities unless they provided a tangible benefit, either in the form of money or a skill that could be parlayed directly into a job. In the experience of most parishioners, civic education provided neither and its possible long-term benefit of promoting greater democracy and accountability in the government was not perceived as a value.

Expectations for payment were not unreasonable given that the payment of allowances was a wide-spread practice among NGOs that taught civic education. According to one volunteer lawyer:

> As NGOs we had to pay slum dwellers to attend our classes or we would not have had any programs to implement for our donors. We were outsiders with no point of access to the community so we gained entry by paying sitting allowances. We enticed people to attend by putting them up in nice hotels, paid their transportation and gave them posh meals. For most of the participants, it was nothing more than a money-making venture.[26]

NGOs were not alone in using money as an incentive for participation; this practice also had a history in the parish. For example, the 24 SCC members who assisted the parish health clinic by visiting AIDS patients and distributing medicine to bed-ridden patients boycotted the civic education classes because of money. During the first class, over 20 people attended, but once they realized allowances would not be paid, only eight returned for the second class and three for the final class. According to their trainer, "The health workers wanted to be paid by the OHR to attend the classes because many of them ran small businesses. They felt that since they had to close down their businesses to attend the meetings, they should be paid so they didn't go home empty-handed."[27] Their expectations of payment were based on their experience with the congregation of missionary sisters who started the program. In order to attract "volunteers" for their program, the sisters had financed a number of income-generating projects for the health workers. Although this practice provided much needed assistance, it also eroded the health workers' spirit of volunteerism. Aware that the OHR was coordinated by an expatriate missionary, the health workers automatically assumed they would be paid money in exchange for their attendance.

---

[25] OHR Evaluation, February 15, 2004.
[26] Interview with volunteer lawyer A, September 21, 2008.
[27] Interview with Saturday group member C, September 24, 2008.

Even though the OHR coordinator and the lawyers anticipated that parishioners would expect financial allowances, they deliberately decided not to pay them. The OHR not only lacked the financial resources people, the program was also designed to be a long-term project that would require a high degree of volunteerism. The lawyers wanted to involve parishioners willing to learn and share their learning, not those motivated merely by financial gain.

Apathy

During the evaluation, the trainers also pointed out that many parishioners simply were not interested in civic education and many frequently referred to it as "a waste of time." Much of the community's ambivalence and apathy was directly related to Kibera's political reality. Decades of neglect by an authoritarian government that survived on ethnic patronage and violence had caused most Kiberans to turn away from the state. There was a sense among most parishioners that the government and politicians existed only to serve the interests of rich and they had no ability to influence the process. One parishioner noted, "We only see politicians during the elections when they need votes. We don't know where their offices are or even how to reach them."[28] Others pointed out that teaching civic education was a futile exercise because, regardless of what people learned, the police still asked for bribes and parishioners still paid them.

The greatest indifference to civic education was demonstrated by the Sunday Christians. The OHR coordinator asked the Sunday Christians who attended mass in the main parish compound (approximately 800 adults) to stay after mass for a short input on the election, but fewer than five people remained. In response to this situation, the OHR coordinator asked the parish priest to allow the youth to enact dramas after the homily about the election violence and vote buying. The dramas were well received and parishioners were able to easily grasp their meaning. These occasions, however, were limited to two because the youth, having spent considerable time to write, rehearse and perform the dramas for the Saturday classes, wanted free time on Sundays to purse their regular activities.

The OHR's strategy for the priests to preach about election-related topics also never took hold. Although the parish priest frequently preached generally about tribalism and election violence, he did not have time to attend the course and therefore was not able to use the pulpit to

[28] Interview with Saturday group member D, September 29, 2008.

disseminate detailed information. The plan for trainers to give short inputs on the curriculum during mass in the sub-parishes also did not work. There were few trainers who were both willing to and capable of teaching a large group on Sunday morning and, apart from the parish priest, there was no clerical support for this plan. With only one full-time priest, the parish relied on visiting missionary priests to say Sunday mass in the sub-parishes, most were newly ordained and afraid to get involved in civic education because of its political overtones.

Fear of Politics

Trainers from almost every SCC reported that some of their members resisted the classes because they objected to the parish talking about the government and the election, topics that most parishioners felt were strictly off limits for the church. Many felt that the SCC meetings were the exclusive preserve of religious matters such as prayer and Bible reading, not issues of a secular, social or political nature; some complained that the classes were interfering with saying the rosary and prayers.

Like many Kenyans, some parishioners had a negative view about civic education because they associated it with corrupt politicians and vote buying. A few trainers reported that their SCCs objected to being taught civic education because they thought civic education promoted certain political candidates and such a practice should not be brought into the church. Some parishioners held this view because in the past the JPC leaders had used civic education to promote the political agendas of their ethnic leaders. A few parishioners thought that because Mwai Kibaki was Catholic, the parish was conducting civic education to support his candidacy. In one SCC, two members left their SCC in protest because they thought civic education was a gimmick to register people for the NARC party. The repressive tactics of the chiefs and youth wingers also were a factor. Some parishioners were afraid to meet and discuss issues that could be interpreted as political and might therefore invite retribution from the PA.

Dysfunctional Groups

The inherent dysfunction of numerous groups also deterred the trainers. Nearly one-third of the SCC trainers reported that they could not teach because their SCCs did not meet on a regular basis. There were two parish groups–the women and youth–that stopped meeting altogether. With respect to the women's group, there were four women who attended the classes and were among the most active members in the discussions. Their group of about 50 women, however, disbanded shortly after the course started. Historically, the women's group had been supported by a congregation of missionary sisters who provided financial support to start income-generating projects such as baking, tailoring and handicrafts. When the parish priest asked the women's group to be more inclusive and address social issues such as the women's groups he had worked with in Brazil and expand membership to non-Catholics, the women parishioners stopped attending and the group quickly disbanded.

The youth group experienced a similar outcome. The number of youth who participated in the Saturday classes was unexpectedly high with 20 to 40 young people regularly attending classes and preparing and performing dramas on the course topics. The youth's interaction with the rest of the group was noteworthy since it was the first time the youth had consistently participated in a parish activity with adults. The efforts of their trainers to teach the classes to the broader youth group, however, failed. As with the women's group, the parish priest asked the youth group to open its membership to non-Catholics. Unwilling to share their limited resources with outsiders, the youth stopped meeting all together.

Cultural Biases

Cultural practices restricted the ability of some female trainers to teach. In a number of SCCs, women faced a particular challenge in teaching the classes, especially the women trainers who were characterized as "single mothers." Approximately 75% of the women in the parish fit into this category of unmarried women with children, a situation related to the lifestyle common in Kibera. Because the majority of men in the settlement had left their wives and children upcountry in their rural homes where expenses are substantially lower, it was common practice for these men to take a "city wife" to prepare their meals and wash their clothes in exchange for paying rent or school fees. There was a surplus of single women in Kibera willing to play this role due to economic necessity. Many women had fled bad marriages or were widows who had been disinherited. Others had left to escape the poverty and deprivations of rural life; some were simply lured by the promise of a better life in the city. With little education and even less employment opportunities, they had few alternatives.

Although 75% of the women in the parish were single mothers, they were often treated as second-class citizens and referred to as people of "bad character" because they were believed to be "always searching for another woman's husband." Discriminatory attitudes were reinforced by church rules and practices. Because single mothers were not legally married, they were precluded from receiving communion at mass, and as a result, prevented from holding office or taking responsibilities in many of the SCCs. The eight single mothers who were trained in civic education all struggled with varying degrees of success for the chance to teach in their SCCs.

In addition to gender obstacles, in at least one SCC the trainer was blocked because of age bias. The trainer, a woman aged 28, was prevented from teaching by her fellow SCC members on the grounds that she was too young. From the perspective of the elders, it was an insult for a young woman to hold herself out as knowing more than they did. As a result of the cultural taboo, she was not given time during the SCC meetings to teach the curriculum even though she had dutifully attended every meeting.

Limited Capacities

The individual capacity of the trainers was another factor that impacted their ability to teach in the SCCs. A number of female trainers from Shilanga who had low literacy skills struggled to convey the information. Illiteracy, however, was not necessarily a negative. For example, two SCCs in Soweto reported that their trainers, all of whom were illiterate women, managed to convey the courses using their verbal skills, hand-outs and pictures. A more significant factor than education was the trainer's personal ability to facilitate a meeting. Contrary to the lawyers' expectations, the lessons on how to teach the information to their members were not adequate; virtually no one had prior experience in facilitating a class. As a result, the majority of the trainers did not know how to teach a group of largely uneducated people in a participatory manner.

The 2003 Program

The next phase of the civic education program started in the aftermath of the 2002 election. Despite an outpouring of national jubilation and high hopes that the new NARC government would usher in a period of political reform including a people-based constitution, only 35 people regularly attended the Saturday classes in 2003. The OHR coordinator recognized that most people were interested in civic education only at election times and expected the number of participants to drop and it did, by more than half. The reason for the decline, however, was not limited to the close of the election period. The OHR coordinator learned that the majority of the original participants had initially volunteered for the program out of financial motives; they believed that their participation in civic education would lead to their selection as election monitors. In the past, the JPC leaders had handed out the coveted jobs of election monitoring that paid 3,000 Ksh to parishioners who attended their workshops. Once they realized that civic education did not provide a job opportunity, many of the participants, especially the men, stopped participating.

The reduction of the group fitted with the coordinator's original plan to single out the most interested and committed parishioners. The 35 parishioners who stayed active in the Saturday group represented all but three of the SCCs and half the parish-based groups; the group was mixed with respect to ethnicity, age and gender with an almost equal ratio of men and women.

During the evaluation of the pre-election phase and planning for 2013, the Saturday group members voiced an interest in learning more about the CKRC's proposed constitution and their legal rights.[29] Three of the lawyers took turns facilitating 15 Saturday sessions on topics chosen by a small committee.[30] During the first six classes, one of the lawyers explained the current constitution, the subsequent amendments, the proposed changes in the CKRC draft and the impact of the changes at a national and local level. Special reference was given to contentious issues related to land, the PA and the devolution of power. Two other lawyers each taught a pair of classes on the rights of the accused, worker's rights and inheritance law and a community organizer from Pamoja Trust facilitated two classes on slum upgrading. The Saturday group also prepared a year-end mass and feast that featured food and customs from their different ethnic communities in order to celebrate their new knowledge as well as their ethnic diversity.

---

[29] The product of extensive public consultation, the CKRC draft of the constitution tried to create more accountability and balance the powers of the government especially within the executive branch. Although it was supposed to be debated and amended during a National Constitutional Conference before being sent to parliament for ratification, President Moi dissolved parliament in October 2002 to prevent the Conference from occurring prior to the election. Despite the fact that the status of the CKRC draft was unclear, the Saturday group felt that given the centrality of the reform issue in the country's political life, it was important to understand it so Kibera residents would be prepared to engage in the national debate should the process be revived.

[30] In 2003 the OHR paid the lawyers a small fee to cover transportation costs.

During the mid-year evaluation, members of the Saturday group expressed a unified sentiment that learning their legal and human rights had improved their lives, but they also said that more people in the parish should be learning them, especially parishioners in the SCCs. One participant expressed the views of many, "We have come here as students and we leave as teachers, but there are many who are missing out. We have a responsibility to them too, don't we?"[31] This feeling reflected the group's awareness that the civic education lessons had helped them and could have a similar impact on others. In recognition of their limitations as teachers in the SCCs, the group members asked the OHR coordinator to hire a full-time civic education teacher for the SCCs. When the parish priest agreed to expand the office, the coordinator raised funds from her missionary organization to fund civic education for the Saturday group and SCCs; she did not include the parish groups and Sunday Christians because of their lack of interest.

After the funds were available, the Saturday group proposed that the OHR coordinator recruit a part-time team from their own membership, not another community organizer to replace the one who had left the parish in March 2003 to work for a NGO. It was agreed that a parish-based team would be accepted more readily in the SCCs than an outsider. The group identified a number of criteria that the members should satisfy to be considered for a position in the OHR; a degree or certificate from secondary school was not a qualification because the group did not want to exclude women. Following a formal interview process, in May 2003 the OHR coordinator hired four parishioners from the Saturday group (the OHR Team), to work 20 hours a week. The OHR Team consisted of three men and one woman. Two of the men were in their late 20s and one was a member of the youth group, aged 22; all three had finished secondary school. The woman was also in her late 20s and had completed primary school. Prior to teaching classes in the SCCs, the OHR Team attended two months of training sessions taught by the lawyers on the legal substance of the curriculum as well as classes taught by a community organizer on how to use participatory methodologies effectively in the SCCs. The OHR Team also attended a three-day course taught by a professor from Tangaza College (a Catholic College operated by several missionary organizations) on Catholic social teaching that specifically addressed human rights and social justice issues.

Starting in June 2003, the OHR Team met each SCC to assess their level of comprehension and confirm the members' interest in proceeding

---

[31] OHR Memorandum, April 26, 2003.

with the classes. Of the 16 SCCs, 15 asked to participate; the only one that declined was the SCC controlled by the JPC chairman. Based on the feedback of the SCC members, the OHR developed a new methodology that better suited the needs of the SCCs. Working in pairs, the OHR Team taught four topics: what is democracy, how does democracy work, the principles of good governance and nation building. To facilitate greater participation and comprehension, the OHR Team taught the classes through small group discussions and role playing. The OHR Team first used several sessions to build consensus around the meaning and application of concepts such as equality, justice, the common good and the rule of law in their families and within their ethnic communities. They then facilitated discussions on these topics as they related to parishioners' SCCs, the parish, the Catholic Church and eventually Kibera and the country at a national level.

A year-end evaluation as well as personal conversations between the OHR coordinator and the SCC members showed the OHR Team resolved a number of problems that had faced the trainers. As official representatives of the parish OHR who had been trained in participatory methodologies, the Team had more credibility and skill than the trainers to teach the classes. The OHR Team also fully explained the purpose and goal of civic education and created a calendar of classes. The response of the SCCs was unexpectedly positive evidenced by the amount of time the SCCs were willing to give to civic education. In contrast to the trainers who had struggled for 10 or 15 minutes, most SCCs allocated anywhere from 45 minutes to two hours for each class. One Team member explained, "The SCC members expected to be taught about politics and the government, but we started with their families and the parish before we talked about the government and people were very open to that approach."[32] Half the SCCs were so enthusiastic about civic education that they asked for the classes to be taught on a weekly basis. A few SCCs that had stopped meeting reactivated to participate in the classes. Although the participatory methodology slowed the pace of the classes, it was more effective. One Team member observed: "The level of participation was high in the SCCs. People spoke freely regardless of their age or tribe because everyone wanted to share their experiences in their families and what they saw happening in society."[33]

---

[32] Interview with OHR team member A, September 22, 2008.
[33] OHR Memorandum, February 2, 2004.

The 2004 Program

Based on year-end evaluations of the 2003 classes by the Saturday group and the SCCs, the OHR coordinator expressed her desire to continue the program and the parish priest agreed. The coordinator applied for funding from several Catholic donors based in Europe that funded human rights projects in Kenya. Denied by the donors, the coordinator continued to raise funds from her missionary organization and personal contacts in her home country to secure funds to employ the OHR Team on a full-time basis in 2004.

At the request of the Saturday group, two of the lawyers took turns teaching a total of 10 sessions that covered the following topics: rights of children, marriage and divorce, advocacy and lobbying and landlord/tenant rights. In addition, a university student studying African culture and Christianity at Tangaza College taught sessions on poverty and African culture. The group also met for a planning/evaluation session and a year-end mass and party celebrating cultural diversity.

At the start of 2004, the core members of the Saturday group dropped from 35 to 20 with some classes attended by as few as 10 people. The cause of the decline reflected the reality of the Kibera environment. Five of the most active men in the group found jobs in other parts of Nairobi and moved to other slums. Two women suffered chronic illnesses and two others returned to their rural homes to care for sick relatives. A very active woman from the youth group started a hair salon and could not afford to close her shop on Saturday mornings. There were also a handful of middle-aged women who wanted to spend their Saturday mornings in their shops or houses taking care of their families and they felt they could learn the classes in their SCCs.

In an effort to attract more participants, the OHR invited all interested parishioners to attend as well as a number of neighboring churches and youth groups, but only a handful of people responded. The parishioners were either not interested in or available for the classes. The representatives from the churches and youth groups attended only once and did not return after they realized there were no allowances. The low attendance levels presented a dilemma to the OHR. Even though the Saturday group was small, the core members were very interested and they were the only parish group that consistently monitored human rights abuses as well as provided important information to the OHR. By this time, the JPC had ceased to exist because the chairman had found a job in another slum area and returned to Kibera infrequently. According to one lawyer:

> We all knew that if we wanted to see change in Kibera, we needed to start somewhere. It would take time to grow the number of active participants, but we felt it was better to start with a small group than to keep quiet and do nothing at all.[34]

The lawyers resolved the issue by committing to teach classes if a minimum of 15 participants attended.

The OHR Team also continued to teach classes in the SCCs; the topics were good governance, nation building, forced evictions, rights of an arrested person, children's rights and inheritance. In 2004 the number of SCCs increased from 16 to 21. The growth was attributed to revived interest by the parish priest who started saying nightly masses in the SCCs and assigned at least two catechists to each SCC. Attendance in the civic education classes remained high with an average of 10 to 20 people in each SCC attending the classes. There were, however, some classes that were attended by more people because the particular topic related directly to practical problems in their daily lives. For example, the topic in greatest demand was inheritance. The OHR Team taught it 71 times; approximately four times in each SCC. Interest in this topic was due to the high prevalence of AIDS-related deaths. According to most traditional practices, women are precluded from inheriting their deceased husband's property. Although these practices conflict with Kenya's Succession Act that grants females equal inheritance rights; this Act is not widely known and rarely followed. Upon learning the law, many women wanted to learn how to prevent their in-laws from taking their children and property when their husband died. In addition to learning about the law, the OHR Team spent several sessions discussing cultural practices related to death and inheritance. In later evaluations, SCC members identified these lessons as the most interesting component of the program because it gave them an opportunity to explain ethnic differences in a context that was not threatening.

Not all SCCs were interested in the classes. The JPC chairman's SCC continued to boycott the classes and there were three others that stopped participating. Leaders in two SCCs had been partially trained in DELTA and felt that they already knew their rights. The other SCC had ceased to meet. In addition, most SCCs reduced their meeting times from three to four times a month to once or twice a month. The reduced classes were due to a conflict between the OHR and the parish's faith formation department. As the civic education classes became more popular, a power struggle ensued between the catechists and the OHR Team. The catechists

[34] Interview with volunteer lawyer D, September 21, 2008.

felt the OHR Team was a threat to their status and influence because many SCC members preferred civic education classes over religious formation. The conflict also reflected a competition within the pastoral team for financial resources. Even though the OHR received no funding from the parish or the Guadalupe priests, the faith formation coordinator was angry that the OHR budget was larger and accused the parish of sidelining her department. She, along with a number of catechists, urged SCC members not to attend civic education classes on the grounds that only the catechists could teach about the Bible and Catholic social teaching. Eventually, the OHR Team took the lead in resolving the dispute. After meeting the catechists, it was agreed that each SCC should put in writing whether they wanted civic education and, if they did, they should choose one or two days a month that did not interfere with the catechists' schedule. Every SCC voted to continue with civic education classes.

The 2005 Program

Based on a positive year-end evaluation, it was agreed that the OHR coordinator should continue with the program in 2005. At that time, the OHR coordinator succeeded in securing donor funding from a Catholic donor in Ireland, Trocaire, to hire a full-time Kenyan lawyer to assist with the growing workload including managing the civic education program and assisting parishioners with legal advice. Trocaire made a commitment to fund the civic education program for three years starting in January 2006. In the meantime, the coordinator raised funds from her personal contacts to support the OHR salaries and activities.

Although attendance in the Saturday group remained relatively stable in 2005 with around 15 to 20 participants, the number of classes was fewer. The lawyer agreed to the group's request that they be given a chance to meet once a month to debate and discuss issues that related to second-generation human rights. Between April and July 2005, the new OHR lawyer taught four sessions on international debt, tribalism, political and economic rights and two sessions on planning and evaluations. The Tangaza student facilitated additional sessions on culture and witchcraft. The group also met for its traditional year-end mass and cultural celebration.

At the start of 2005, the OHR coordinator and the new lawyer visited each SCC (which had grown to 28) to assess the impact of the OHR Team's teaching and the level of interest in the project. Feedback during the individual SCC assessments was positive and of the 28 SCCs, all but two new SCCs, whose structures were not yet in place, asked for classes.

When several SCCs that had previously resisted civic education discovered that the other SCCs were learning about inheritance and property rights, the women in these groups insisted that the OHR Team teach civic education in their SCCs. From January to August 2005, the OHR Team taught classes on inheritance, marriage, divorce and slum upgrading.

In September, the lawyers in the OHR suspended all scheduled civic education classes so the office could prepare parishioners for the upcoming constitutional referendum.[35] In April 2003, President Kibaki had reconvened the national constitutional conference so delegates from around the country could debate, amend and adopt the CKRC's proposed new constitution. The deliberations quickly became acrimonious when President Kibaki reneged on his campaign promise to reduce the executive powers of the presidency. The delegates who purported to represent the government walked out of the conference, but the remaining delegates continued with their deliberations and in March 2004 submitted a final version of their draft (the Bomas draft), which reduced executive powers. A year of political wrangling ensued and sharply divided Kenyans along ethno-regional lines. In August 2005, the Kibaki regime unexpectedly published a draft constitution (commonly known as the Wako draft) hastily put together by the president's inner circle and announced that Kenyans would be required to vote for or against its ratification in a national referendum to be held on November 21, 2005. The Wako draft weakened the role of the new post for a prime minister and conspicuously eliminated provisions from the Bomas draft that reduced executive power.

The referendum campaign symbolized the power struggle between President Kibaki and Raila Odinga and by extension the ethnic communities that they represented. Amidst the political grandstanding on both sides, politicians failed to explain the complex document to the public and instead used the rallies (many became violent) to politic and jockey for power in anticipation of the 2007 election. Civil society sectors that had been so vocal in their demands for constitutional review also failed to assist the citizenry understand the review process and the document that they were voting for or against. A number of NGOs, which typically provided civic education, started their programs too late, well

---

[35] For details, see Cottrell, and Ghai, "Constitution Making," and Alicia Bannon, "Designing a Constitution-Drafting Process: Lessons from Kenya," *Yale Law Journal* 116 (2007): 1824-72.

after politicians had poisoned the referendum campaign with ethnic partisanship.[36]

Religious leaders from most of the mainline Christian churches including the Catholic bishops invoked a position of neutrality arguing that they did not want to polarize their politically diverse memberships. Their official position was that Kenyans should "vote with their conscience," a stance that evoked widespread criticism for "sitting on the fence" when the country seemingly required them most.[37] Moreover, the real position of the Catholic Church was ambiguous because several bishops made partisan statements for and against the Wako draft, which only added to the level of confusion.

Because the Catholic bishops had invoked a position of neutrality and the Archdiocese distributed no official teaching materials, the parish was left to pursue civic education without any guidance from the local church. The two lawyers in the OHR created an 80-page booklet, which explained the changes made by the different versions of the constitution and distributed it to SCCs, groups and individual parishioners as well as the parishes in the Kutoka network and different Catholic groups outside Kibera.

In evaluating the classes taught in 2005, the greatest amount of interest, attendance and participation was in the classes taught to prepare parishioners for the constitutional referendum. In total, members of the OHR taught the class 125 times between September and November. All 28 SCCs participated and the number of people attending the classes in the SCCs rose to an average of 35 or more. For the first time, leaders in all sub-parishes asked the OHR to facilitate classes after mass. Attendance at these classes was also high with an average of 50 to 60 people attending on a weekly basis.

Second to the constitution, SCC members indicated the topics related to their day-to-day problems were the most popular and highly attended. For example, the OHR Team was asked to teach the classes about marriage 51 times. The laws in Kenya on marriage are complex because they recognize three different kinds of marriages–church, civil and traditional ceremonies. The vast majority of parishioners were in "come we stay" relationships where a man and woman stay together without a formal church or civil ceremony. The women were keen to learn whether

---

[36] Committee of Eminent Persons on the Constitution Review Process, and B.A. Kiplagat, *Report of the Committee of Eminent Persons on the Constitution Review Process* (Nairobi: Government of Kenya, 2006), 57-58.

[37] Andrew Teyie, "Catholic Bishops Won't Tell Kenyans how to Vote," *East African Standard*, Nairobi, August 30, 2005.

they were legally married and if they had custody of their children or any rights to marital property. Most parishioners were unaware that traditional marriage laws require a couple to take certain customary steps beyond merely staying together to legalize a marriage. The lessons on the rights of the accused were similarly in high demand; the OHR Team taught classes on this topic 50 times. In an environment where corrupt police and chiefs regularly arrested people to generate bribes, parishioners wanted to learn their rights and how to respond to a false arrest.

The Impact of Civic Education

Measuring the impact of the civic education program is complicated. Not only is it difficult to assess rising levels of knowledge and empowerment, the impact is also not always obvious or immediately visible. In some cases, the impact may evolve gradually and become manifest long after the lessons end. Despite these limitations, the annual evaluations and on-going conversations between the participants and the OHR revealed a number of positive findings about the impact of the civic education lessons on the Saturday group and SCC members.

Increased Knowledge

Overall, there were approximately 500 parishioners who enhanced their knowledge and awareness about the rights and duties of democratic citizenship, good governance, constitutionalism and a wide array of legal and human rights. In addition, about 1,000 parishioners were educated on the country's constitution during the referendum campaign. The classes not only helped demystify the law and equip parishioners with information, both legal and non-legal, they also enhanced parishioners' ability to respond to socio-political and cultural issues that they considered important. Taught from a Christian perspective, the classes also helped parishioners begin to connect their faith to the responsibilities of democratic citizenship.

Despite the increased levels of knowledge and awareness for the participants, the scope of the civic education program remained small; 85% of the parishioners chose not to participate. Learning about democracy and human rights was not a priority for most parishioners because of their preoccupation with survival needs. Civic education had also been politicized in Kenya. In an environment heavily influenced by ethnic politics, many parishioners were afraid to be associated with civic education because of its political overtones. Others lacked interest in learning about the government and political processes due to feelings of apathy, frustration and cynicism caused by decades of government corruption and mismanagement.

Although the number of participants was small given the population in the parish and the Kibera community, the program led to an observable change in the participants' democratic behavior and practices in the SCCs and in the personal lives of the participants in a number of ways. The classes, however, did not empower parishioners to defend and promote the community's common interests or human rights. Before analyzing the reasons why the program did not cause parishioners to enter the civic and political arena, I first describe the ways in which it enhanced democratic behavior, values and practices.

Improved Leadership

The most visible impact of the civic education classes in the parish was manifested during the elections for leadership in the SCCs and PPC in July 2004 when approximately 75% of the leaders were voted out of office; an outcome the new parish leaders attributed to raised awareness and involvement brought about by civic education. In the words of two different Team members:

> After we taught the classes on good governance, people realized they needed to hold leaders in the parish accountable, not just the government. The SCC members had been so scared of their leaders who had controlled everything for so many years but after the civic education classes, our people understood the values of Christian leadership and they changed their SCCs.[38]

> Parishioners realized that one of the most important things they could do was choose leaders who would represent their views. The idea that leadership in the SCCs was only for the elite changed and lots of SCCs threw out old leaders who had education but no leadership qualities. People realized that it was more important for the leaders to be honest and fair than a graduate of secondary school.[39]

Many parishioners also credited civic education with changing the approach and mindset of the leaders. As an example, the senior catechist in the parish observed:

---

[38] Interview with OHR team member B, September 20, 2008.
[39] Interview with OHR team member C, October 3, 2008.

> After civic education, you could see that the leaders were different because they were much more open to real issues. In the past, they had spent their time discussing small, petty issues. After they learned about governance and democracy, leaders in the SCC and the PPC started addressing the bigger social issues like violence and tribalism. Before civic education, the SCC people couldn't discuss anything outside the Bible. The Catholics never talked about social and political issues and they did not feel they had a duty to do something about it, but that changed. Parishioners now talk openly about the government and even politicians in their SCCs.[40]

In addition to removing the clique of ineffective leaders, the SCCs also voted for a two-year cap on all leadership positions, a practice they learned during the classes on good governance.

Enhanced Participation

In addition to improved leadership, the civic education program also enhanced the level and depth of parishioners' participation in the SCCs and the Saturday group. Many of the leaders in the SCCs adopted the methodology used by the OHR Team and started giving everyone in the SCC the opportunity to speak as a matter of routine. One Team member explained, "When the SCC leaders started to change their approach, for the first time, so many people had the opportunity to talk and share out their feelings and ideas."[41] Heightened participation was most notable among groups that were traditionally excluded, the illiterate and single women. Several women noted that before the civic education classes started, they did not feel free to pray in public in front of men because they feared being ridiculed. One woman explained, "In the SCC I now can say what I feel and I even disagree with men because I learned about my rights in civic education. I am no longer afraid that I will be laughed at."[42]

Parishioners' ability to discuss and debate difficult issues improved in an even more visible manner in the Saturday group. According to one lawyer:

> The Saturday group started out with a lot of facilitation because they expected the lawyers or the church to have all the answers. Later there was much more listening by the lawyers and very little facilitation. The participants led the discussions and my role was to give the dialogue some direction and a bit of content. They questioned and challenged everything

---

[40] Interview with parish lead catechist, October 22, 2008

[41] Interview with OHR team member C, October 3, 2008.

[42] Interview with Saturday group member F, September 28, 2008.

> we taught which was very different from our past experience. We were able to tell them the law and they had the ability to question it and talk about what it meant in Kibera in their reality.[43]

Another lawyer observed a similar outcome:

> The parishioners showed a noticeable difference from other students I had taught. In Kibera, because we had the luxury of time, the participants started to have self-awareness and they would ask questions that challenged me as a lawyer. They realized that many of their friends and neighbors were not aware of the problems in their families and SCCs, but they could see them and they knew what to do to help others respond to those problems.[44]

In both the SCCs and the Saturday group, civic education also enhanced the ability of parishioners to discuss sensitive issues related to tribalism, marriage and divorce and property rights for women, taboo topics that most parishioners had refused to discuss during the social analysis. Interest in these topics was so high that the women in the sub-parishes of Lindi and Soweto organized special meetings with the OHR lawyer to discuss them in greater depth. In addition, parishioners grew in self-confidence and became less afraid to criticize the government or the parish. For example, in 2003 during the classes on good governance, members of the OHR Team reported that the class was difficult to teach "because people were not ready to criticize the government or ask questions." There were many people in the SCCs who felt the structure of the church was not following the structures of good governance, but were afraid to criticize the parish priest and leaders because they did not want to jeopardize their relationships especially if they were being given assistance with school fees or access to income-generating projects. The SCC attended by most of the parish workers refused to even discuss these topics out of fear that what they said might be repeated and they would lose their jobs for criticizing the parish. The situation was much different in 2005. After two years of openly discussing difficult topics, although a few SCC members still expressed reservations, most felt free to expose shortcomings in the parish including actions taken by the parish priest and other pastoral team members.

---

[43] Interview with volunteer lawyer C, September 24, 2008.
[44] Interview with volunteer lawyer A, September 21, 2008.

Respect for the Rule of Law

Another visible change in attitude was the participants' increase in the respect for the rule of law evidenced by the number of cases that they referred to the OHR lawyers for assistance. In 2003 parishioners active in civic education referred around five cases per month to the OHR for assistance. By 2005 the average number of cases rose to 45 each month. The increase in referrals was in large part due to the enhanced awareness of rights in the SCCs and the active role played by the Saturday group in referring Kibera residents for legal advice. Most cases related to landlord/tenant and domestic disputes, conflicts that had previously been resolved by paying a bribe to the local chief. In addition, there were numerous cases involving child abuse, rape and incest, illegal abortions and corruption on the part of the chiefs and councilors.

At the same time as the number of cases rose, the number of parishioners trained in civic education who visited the OHR for advice on personal legal problems gradually dropped. These parishioners started analyzing problems on their own and taking the initial steps to solve them; they came to the OHR only when they needed specific advice from a lawyer, not the basic information on the law. Parishioners' ability to resolve their own disputes was most visible in the area of landlord/tenant conflicts. The lawyer in the OHR responsible for assisting parishioners with legal matters for the years 2006-2008 explained the dynamic:

> Civic education lessons on the rental issue worked because both structure owners and tenants in the parish learned they each had a role to play and they started owning up to that role. The ones who came to the OHR already knew their rights. They only came because they wanted help drafting pleadings because they knew they could file a case in the tribunal and didn't have to pay the chief a bribe.[45]

In 2003, 20% of the cases related to landlord/tenant disputes. With the passage of each year, the percentage dropped. In 2004 these cases accounted for 15% of the cases and by 2007, rental issues numbered only 5% of the caseload.

Better Conflict Resolution Skills

Civic education also equipped participants with better conflict resolution skills. While it is not possible to measure with precision how

---

[45] Interview with OHR lawyer A, September 21, 2008.

many SCC members took personal actions to assist someone because many did not report their interventions to the OHR, it was observed that many parishioners who received civic education helped family and friends resolve personal conflicts and problems, especially those involving domestic matters, landlord/tenant disputes and demands for bribes by chiefs. As an example, one participant narrated:

> My SCC had a lot of widows from AIDS and there was a woman whose in-laws tried to take her land. They burned her house and were ready to chase her away. We told her what we had learned about inheritance laws in civic education so she went home and reported the actions of her in-laws to the chief and he stopped the in-laws from taking her plot.[46]

Another parishioner, an elderly woman who was illiterate, was able to help numerous Kibera residents. As an example, she explained: "When one of my neighbors told me her rent was going up, I told her about her rights as a tenant so she refused to pay the rent. She explained the law to her structure owner and he stopped trying to raise the rent."[47]

Enhanced conflict resolution skills were also observed at the parish level. As an example, in May 2002, the SCCs members from the Lindi sub-parish decided to repair holes in the walls and roof of their chapel. When the local assistant chief demanded that the parishioner pay a bribe before starting the renovation, they complied despite protests by the parish priest. Three years later, the same leaders were asked to pay a bribe to the NDP youth wingers in connection with the parish's purchase of 10 structures near their chapel to build toilets and a kitchen for the nursery school. The youth wingers threatened to burn down the chapel if the leaders did not pay the tenants who had been living in the structures. The leaders from the Lindi SCCs refused to pay a bribe or be swayed by the local community's call to use physical force in removing the tenants. Instead, relying on what they had learned during civic education, they organized the SCCs from the sub-parish and officially reported the matter to the local authorities. Following weeks of peaceful prayer meetings and negotiations, the tenants eventually moved.

The members of the OHR Team also improved their ability to assist parishioners in resolving conflicts. According to one Team member:

> Within the SCCs, people saw us as the people in the parish who could assist them with problems like domestic violence and child abuse. Everything was referred to us because we were seen as neutral. We were

---

[46] Interview with Saturday group member D, September 29, 2008.
[47] Interview with Saturday group member F, September 28, 2008.

> also called to solve internal problems in SCCs when people were competing over leadership roles during the parish elections and leaders were fighting with the catechists.[48]

In addition to helping parishioners in the SCCs, members of the OHR Team also routinely accompanied parishioners to court, the police station and the offices of lawyers and NGOs.

Internal Democratic Practices

The Saturday group also became more democratic in its internal practices. Unlike the early classes that were dominated by the educated men, by 2005 members of the group spoke much more freely and no one was excluded from the discussions. Moreover, the group on its own volition formed small committees to plan the curriculum and follow specific issues such as the Soweto upgrade. All decision making was by consensus, not dictated by a small clique. Accountability was also important. This was best exemplified in the group's insistence on following non-discriminatory employment procedures. The typical pattern in the parish was to hire people based on ethnic identity or levels of education. The Saturday group took an unprecedented step when it required parishioners to participate in a merit-based interview process with the parish priest. Members of the OHR Team were the first people hired in the parish's history that followed such a process and it set a precedent that was subsequently followed for all parish employees. The group also insisted on regular evaluations of the program and the OHR including its personnel, a practice that was eventually replicated in all parish ministries.

Heightened Tolerance, Civility and Respect

The program enhanced parishioners' tolerance and respect for other views. As a mixed ethnic group, the members of the Saturday group were keenly aware of the challenges of tribalism. But as the group discussed issues of tribe and ethnicity, the conversations became more open and respectful as the participants gained a deeper understanding of historical factors and their own role in perpetuating tribalism. Although few in number, their ability to meet as an ethnically mixed group and discuss deeply engrained prejudices and conflicts represented the potential of parishioners to address the multi-faceted issues related to ethnicity in the parish and Kibera. The group's diverse ethnicity was the center piece of

[48] Interview with OHR team member B, September 20, 2008.

their annual liturgy and feast to celebrate the successes and losses of the year. In 2005, in order to reconcile the ethnic fissures that arose during the referendum campaign, the group invited the parish leaders, catechists, teachers in the school and the pastoral team to join together for a mass and meal to honor all ethnic traditions equally.

Reluctance to Pursue Advocacy

Notwithstanding the positive impacts of civic education, contrary to the expectations of civil society advocates, four years of civic education did not empower parishioners to proactively confront the local government about the myriad human rights abuses in Kibera particularly those related to the illegal chang'aa trade, slum upgrading in Soweto and the threat of forced evictions that are discussed in greater detail in the subsequent chapters. Although some individuals in the OHR Team and Saturday group took small steps, the majority remained either uninvolved or dependent on the OHR to lead them. In evaluating the reasons why parishioners remained passive the OHR Team identified three key factors: fear of retaliation, restrictive church protocols and limited capacity and resources.

First and foremost, parishioners were keenly aware of the dangerous and hostile political environment in Kibera; the chiefs and youth wingers would not tolerate any activity that addressed human rights issues or challenged the status quo. One Team member explained, "Parishioners knew their rights were being violated but they couldn't publicly mobilize against the DO or chief by writing letters or holding meetings because they were afraid they would be 'spotted' and then targeted later for retaliation."[49] The level of intimidation was high. The chiefs monitored the content of the classes and some members had already been questioned by the Line Saba chief about what they were learning and what they were doing especially during the classes on landlord/tenant rights and the PA.[50] Parishioners knew that if they confronted the chiefs they risked having their property destroyed and/or being flogged and thrown into a cell.

In addition to their fear of the PA, parishioners were afraid of the NDP youth wingers who worked for Raila. One Team member explained:

> As Catholics we were able to discuss sensitive political issues like corruption and bad governance by the PA, but we were not ready to take any action. If someone had tried to organize a meeting or protest an

---

[49] Ibid.

[50] Interview with OHR team member C, October 3, 2008.

> injustice, the NDP youth wingers and politicians would have known about it; they have agents everywhere and they know everything. If someone is from their tribe, the youth will send people to warn that person off. But anyone who did not listen to them would be attacked at night or targeted for harassment later and even killed. The politicians in Kibera allowed people to take actions only if it was in line with their political agenda. It was okay to meet to do clean ups or talk about water, but anything else wasn't allowed. So we knew our rights but we couldn't fight for them because the youth wingers were malicious and there was nothing we could do about it so we just didn't get involved.[51]

In 2004, more than 40 bodies were found dismembered along the railway line; all people who had been involved in a political issue.

Given the parishioners' fears and the real threat of danger, neither the Saturday group nor the SCCs wanted to become a strategic group within the parish that played a front-line role mobilizing for the parish's or community's interests. When parishioners shared their fears and concerns, the lawyers agreed that the threats were genuine and did not push members of the Saturday group or the SCCs in a direction that could risk their lives. In light of the political environment, parishioners preferred to take a less threatening role of attending meetings and gathering information that could be used by the lawyers to facilitate greater dialogue with the DO, chiefs, NDP youth wingers and councilors who had immediate influence over their lives. Unlike the residents of Kibera, the lawyers had greater immunity; they did not live in the community and their families and homes could not be threatened. They also knew how to use the legal system to protect their rights.

The parishioners' desire to avoid lobbying activities also related to restrictive rules and practices in the parish and local Catholic Church that prevented parishioners from discussing human rights issues in their SCCs and organizing other parishioners to respond to the issues. According to one Team member:

> A SCC member who raised any issue in his SCC that could be considered political like speaking out against corruption or the government would have been rebuked in front of everyone. Our Christians thought political problems needed to be solved by politicians and the church was there only for spiritual matters. If a SCC member raised a political issue it would have been seen as dividing people in the SCC because each person had his own

[51] Ibid.

political agenda. So we focused on issues like weddings or the illness of a member.[52]

In addition, the unspoken protocol in the parish dictated that a parishioner could not ask his or her fellow SCC members or the parish priest to take action on a socio-political issue unless the issue followed the chain of command. A Team member explained:

> An individual Catholic was not able to call a meeting after getting information on something that happened in Kibera. If he or she wanted to address an issue in the community, they had to first tell the leader of their SCC and ask him to address it and then the SCC chairman had to pass it up to the sub-parish leaders who had to ask the PPC and finally it was the PPC who could pass the issue to the parish priest.[53]

A parishioner who breached this practice and tried to take information directly to the community or the priest without first passing through the designated gatekeepers would have experienced retribution in his SCC; the leaders "would publicly condemn any person who tried to go around the leadership."[54] Group members were also afraid to single themselves out as knowing more than the others in their SCC. One active Saturday group explained:

> If you acted like you had new information for the SCC, people would start saying you were pretending to know more and wanted to be seen ahead of everyone else. No one wanted to be seen that way because you would have been abandoned by your friends and left on your own alone.[55]

In an environment where people rely heavily on friends and neighbors as a safety net, parishioners in the Saturday group, for the most part, chose to remain silent. "We could only ask the OHR for information, but we couldn't take action by ourselves."[56]

Parishioners' ability to take initiative on problems in the community was also inhibited by hierarchical practices endemic in the Catholic Church. Following a traditional Roman model, most parishioners, similar to Catholics throughout Kenya, paid a high level of deference to the bishops and felt they could not take a stand on a particular social or political issue unless Archbishop Ndingi first made a pronouncement on

[52] Interview with OHR Team member A, September 22, 2008.
[53] Interview with OHR Team member B, September 20, 2008.
[54] Ibid.
[55] Interview with OHR team member A, September 22, 2008.
[56] Interview with Saturday group member C, September 24, 2008.

the church's official position. The limitations of the church's hierarchy were also felt at the parish level; there was a strong culture of dependence on the parish priest to take the lead in all issues affecting the parish. One parishioner explained, "We waited for the priest to do something first for us because we believed that was the proper protocol. Any issue about justice and peace had to start up there with bishops and priests and then move down to us."[57] Although the parish priest spoke about the need for the parish to pursue human rights issues, his public statements were limited to generalized messages. As a consequence, many members of the SCCs felt that they could not act because the parish priest was not fully behind them.

Finally, the Saturday group and SCCs lacked the requisite capacity and resources necessary to lobby the government. According to Robert Fatton, for a voluntary organization to participate effectively in advocacy, the members of the group require relatively high levels of education, access to financial resources and free time; all attributes of the middle class.[58] Parishioners had none of these attributes. Most had low levels of education and even less knowledge of complex policy matters related to land, housing and corruption. They also did not possess adequate resources to undertake advocacy; they had no electricity, computers, printers, telephones and office supplies. People who participated in civic education were wholly dependent on the OHR coordinator to fundraise for basic materials such as pens and paper. They also had no formal leadership, organizational structure or access to decision makers. Parishioners in the SCCs and Saturday group also did not share the same goals and aspirations. Although four years of meeting together, praying and supporting one another on a personal level had created a new level of trust and friendship, parishioners were still divided along ethnic lines. Their willingness to expose the underlying tensions around the issue of ethnicity and share their customs and traditions did not translate into a broader sense of solidarity or a shared sense of Kiberan identity that trumped ethnic identities. As a result, even if they had overcome other inherent obstacles, parishioners were not in a position to mobilize a united front on the key issues that had political or ethnic overtones.

---

[57] Ibid.

[58] Robert Fatton, *Predatory Rule, State and Civil Society in Africa* (Boulder, CO: L. Reinner, 1992), 5.

Conclusion

The civil society advocates' hope that civic education can transform ordinary citizens into political actors is not realistic in an environment like Kibera where people struggle with poverty, ignorance, violence and corruption on a daily basis. Although the findings in this chapter show that the impact of learning about democracy and human rights had an important impact in the SCCs and the parishioners who participated, they represent fewer than 15% of the parishioners, a small percentage of the parish and a minuscule number in Kibera. Contrary to the advocates' assumption that citizens in fledgling democracies are ready and willing to learn about democracy, the majority of parishioners preferred to use their time securing a daily wage or maintaining the status quo.

The advocates' belief that citizens trained in civic education will use their enhanced knowledge and skills to influence the local political arena is also overstated in Kibera. After four years of consistent participation in civic education classes, apart from a handful of parishioners, the majority of people in the Saturday group and SCCs did not take initiative to confront the state about a variety of injustices regularly meted out by the government functionaries. The key reason for avoiding the political sphere was related to fears of violent retaliation by corrupt government officials, politicians and youth wingers. Parish structures and practices in addition to limited resources and capacities also did not foster a supportive environment for active participation in social justice issues.

Given the repressive political environment in Kibera, the most important role of civic education was to break the culture of silence in their families, the SCCs and the broader parish. The main concern of the parishioners was spreading their new knowledge and responding to the personal legal problems of their families, neighbors and SCCs. As a result of decades of government-enforced silence and ignorance, holding the state to account was not as important as securing a place for open and honest dialogue where they felt their input was valued. Members of the Saturday group wanted to create a sense of community within the parish and discuss things together beyond issues related to their basic survival. Even though they lived almost on top of each other, they were not a community. They were too divided and too busy trying to cope to create a proper community. Dialogue and debate on social and political issues was a luxury, especially for the women. Through their Saturday discussions, the participants were able to see that they had common interests and they started to try to reconcile their differences and find a different way to respond. They wanted to find equal footing with other Kenyans in terms of their knowledge and understanding of the government, politics and the legal system. Although their dialogue did not empower them to immediate action, it was an important step in reclaiming their dignity and identity as Kenyans citizens.

CHAPTER FOUR

THE CAMPAIGN AGAINST CHANG'AA

In the previous chapter, I set out the OHR's efforts to promote democracy and human rights generally through a civic education program taught to parishioners in the SCCs and Saturday group. In this chapter I examine parishioners' efforts to confront corrupt local officials in the trade of illegal spirits known as chang'aa. [1] I analyze the parishioners' actions during three distinct phases: (1) prior to the parish social analysis; (2) during the OHR's campaign against chang'aa and (3) as the Soweto sub-parish's priority issue. The primary aim of this chapter is to challenge the assumption of civil society advocates that ordinary citizens have the requisite desire, ability and resources to expose corruption and the abuse of power by low-level government functionaries in a place like Kibera.

It is argued here that fear of violent retaliation by local government officials, politicians and police who profited from the illicit chang'aa trade made it impossible for parishioners to expose their role in the proliferation of the illegal brew. As a result, parishioners relied on the intervention of the OHR coordinator, a missionary lawyer, who had greater immunity from local threats of retaliation as well as access to donor funds to address the chang'aa problem. This chapter illustrates how efforts by the OHR coordinator to mobilize a parish-wide campaign against chang'aa failed not only to elicit the support of parishioners and other local civil society actors, but also to penetrate the deeply entrenched layers of political patronage and corruption that protected the illegal trade. It also examines how a combination of fear, lack of interest, limited capacity and poor parish planning prevented parishioners in the sub-parish of Soweto from contributing to the chang'aa campaign, even after they chose it as their priority issue.

---

[1] An earlier version of this chapter was published as "Chang'aa Drinking in a Kibera Slum: The Harmful Effects of Contemporary Changes in the Production and Consumption of Traditional Spirits," *African Journal of Drug and Alcohol Studies* 9, no. 1 (2010): 49-56.

The Issue of Chang'aa prior to the Social Analysis

In November 2002, during the social analysis phase of the pastoral circle, members of the pastoral team met parishioners in each sub-parish to discuss 15 social, economic and political problems that had been previously raised by parishioners. The issues were abortion, HIV and AIDS, alcohol and drugs, crime, the elderly, environment, housing, illiteracy, land, politics, prostitution, tribalism, unemployment, women and idle youth. Anywhere from 25 to 40 parishioners attended these meetings, the majority of whom were active members of the SCCs; typically, only a handful of Sunday Christians participated. The discussions were led by the Kenyan sister in charge of the social analysis who asked the participants to describe how each problem manifested itself in their families and neighborhoods, its impact on the community and how parishioners could respond to the problem. In every sub-parish, particularly Soweto, the issue of illegal alcohol commonly called chang'aa was identified as the leading example of the local government's abuse of power and provoked the most emotive discussions during the two-year social analysis.

Chang'aa is an alcoholic spirit distilled from fermented maize or sorghum sold locally by small-scale operators in the informal sector. Served in old tins, plastic tubs or reused bottles, it is the most popular alcoholic drink in Kibera and other slum areas. A glass of chang'aa cost five times less than a bottle of beer and it is potent, with an alcoholic content similar to distilled whiskey.[2] Chang'aa is also readily available throughout Kibera. In 2003, there were 441 chang'aa sellers within the parish boundaries, the vast majority were women who sold chang'aa out of their houses.[3]

The production and consumption of locally made spirits started in Kibera during the early 1900s when Nubian soldiers first inhabited the area.[4] By the 1920s, using traditional distillation techniques, Nubian women had commercialized the production of Nubian gin into a profitable

---

[2] On average, chang'aa has an alcohol content of 36% versus a bottled beer that has 4.2%. Mugane Kamande, "Microbiological, Physical and Chemical Analysis of Local Alcoholic Brews in Korogocho (Nairobi)," (Report prepared for St. John's Catholic Church, Nairobi, 2000), 56.

[3] In May 2003 the coordinators of the health and pro-life departments made a survey of all health clinics and dispensaries, abortion clinics, bars and video kiosks in the parish.

[4] For a history of alcohol use in Kenya, see Justin Willis, *Potent Brews, a Social History of Alcohol in East Africa 1850-1999* (Nairobi: The British Institute in Eastern Africa, 2002).

business with the nearby army barracks and growing town providing a sizable market. Throughout the 1940s and 1950s, Kibera was infamous for its illicit liquor dens and prostitution.[5] In the late 1960s and early 1970s, new migrants to Kibera copied the Nubian distillation techniques and produced their own spirits that they called chang'aa.

Despite its ubiquitous presence, chang'aa is illegal. President Moi, a strict teetotaler, viewed the drinking of chang'aa as an affront to modernity and orderly development. In his view, men who spent all day drinking in chang'aa dens were unable to school their children, and some could not even feed or clothe their families. In 1980 he criminalized the manufacture, sale and consumption of chang'aa and gave police wide powers to enforce the ban. Notwithstanding occasional crackdowns and stern public pronouncements, the chang'aa business was too lucrative to be banned effectively by the law; it generated profits five times larger than the legal trade in bottled beers, wines and spirits combined.[6] Moi's prohibition merely drove the illegal chang'aa business underground where brewing was done in hidden, domestic environments. Facilitated by multiple tiers of corruption and local political patronage, councilors, chiefs and the police used their control of markets to create space for clients to produce and sell chang'aa in exchange for a percentage of the proceeds.

By the late 1980s, Kibera's expanding population meant there was no longer room near the rivers for chang'aa manufacturers to operate their stills without detection. Most Nubian distillers closed their gin businesses and started investing in house rentals.[7] Kibera quickly became the exclusive market of distillers operating in the slum area of Mathare Valley located on the eastern side of Nairobi and in the rural areas of western Kenya. To facilitate the transportation of their spirits to Kibera, manufacturers created an elaborate smuggling ring, paying police bribes at road blocks in exchange for safe passage.

In the mid-1990s, drinking norms in Kenya changed as more and more people experienced acute economic hardship. Many drinkers, especially the poor, began drinking chang'aa less as a social drink and more as a coping mechanism; premium chang'aa was considered to be the kind that caused the drinker to black out with as few drinks as possible. Motivated by a desire to boost earnings, manufacturers increased the potency of chang'aa by adding substances such as formaldehyde, sisal juice,

---

[5] Parsons, "Kibra is Our Blood," 95.

[6] Justin Willis, "Kenya's Illegal Alcohol Industry," *BBC News*, November 24, 2000.

[7] See Johan de Smedt, "Kill me Quick: a History of Nubian Gin in Kibera," *International Journal of African Historical Studies* 42, no. 2 (2009): 201-20.

fertilizers, alkaline battery content and even airline fuel, substances that also contained poisons like lead, copper, mercury, DDT and cobalt.[8] Local names given to the enhanced chang'aa reflected its increased strength: Kill Me Quick, El Nino, Tornado, Tarzan, Medusa and Jet.

Instead of trying to curb the unscrupulous manufacture of adulterated chang'aa, the police exploited the booming black market. Corruption in the chang'aa trade was no longer limited to extorting protection fees paid in exchange for turning a blind eye. Many members of the Kenya police joined the lucrative trade and began acting as the main transporters of the illegal brew, using their police vehicles to smuggle jerry cans of chang'aa into slum areas during the early morning hours.

Drinking chang'aa turned lethal in 1999 when manufacturers started adding ethanol, an industrial-strength substance intended for the production of legal spirits as well as vehicle fuel. On a number of different occasions, chang'aa manufacturers, unable to tell the difference between ethanol and methanol, a wood alcohol used in varnishes and anti-freeze, mistakenly added methanol to their chang'aa batches causing the death and blindness of hundreds of Kenyans and serious injury to thousands more.[9] The rash of chang'aa-related deaths provoked a national outcry as the illegal brew was blamed for a broad range of Kenya's social ills including an increase in illness, death, road accidents, domestic violence and infertility.[10] Chang'aa was also characterized as a drag on the economy with alcohol-related inefficiencies and absenteeism causing businesses millions of shillings in losses. Some church leaders also condemned it, including Archbishop Ndingi, who appealed to Catholics to "help the government curb the sale and drinking of the brews" and report anyone engaged in the illegal vice to the PA.[11]

In addition to these pronouncements, women's group from across Kenya took to the streets to demonstrate against chang'aa, arguing that it had made their husbands impotent and caused them to ignore family responsibilities. For example, more than 300 women living in Kangemi, a low-income settlement on the outskirts of Nairobi, with support from a local NGO working on women's issues, marched to the PC's office.[12] When the PC failed to respond, the women forcibly closed several

---

[8] Kamande, "Microbiological, Physical," 22.
[9] Dennis Onyango, "Deadly New Content in Illicit Brew," *Daily Nation*, Nairobi, July 21, 2002.
[10] Ibid.
[11] "Protests Mount over Brew Deaths," *Daily Nation*, Nairobi, November 20, 2000.
[12] Peter Kimani, "Women Up in Arms against Brew," *Daily Nation*, Nairobi, January 22, 1999.

chang'aa dens.[13] Although the national media generated by the women's actions caused a small dip in the production of chang'aa, the women's protestations did not reduce the demand for chang'aa or the illegal protection provided to the sellers by corrupt chiefs and police.

At the same time, a small group of politicians called for the legalization of chang'aa arguing that the number of alcohol-related deaths would decline if the brew was regulated and inspected for minimal quality standards. Some Kenyans, including Anglican Bishop Otieno Wasonga, argued that chang'aa should be legalized so ordinary people including the poor could afford to drink.[14] Despite the emerging movement in favor of legalizing chang'aa, in 2000 President Moi characterized traditional liquors as "doomsday drinks" and emphatically refused to lift the ban, blaming the growing number of chang'aa-related deaths on the opposition and religious groups who had lobbied for the reduction of the chief's powers during the 1997 IPPG reforms.[15] Although Moi ordered officials to enhance their efforts to clamp down on the production of chang'aa, the state was too fractured to suppress the illicit trade.

The Impact of Chang'aa

During the social analysis, parishioners identified many of the same concerns about chang'aa that had been raised in the national debate. They also revealed a more nuanced analysis of the impact that chang'aa had on their day-to-day life. The comments that are in quotations in this section were made by parishioners during the social analysis meetings.

In the early 2000s, the five main chang'aa distributors in Kibera operated their depots in the village of Soweto because of its access to the main road, which facilitated the police in making their drop offs. The distributors bought large amounts of pure chang'aa from manufacturers and then sold it in 20-liter containers to household retailers. The distribution of chang'aa was one of the most lucrative businesses in Kibera, netting a distributor a monthly income of 25,000 to 50,000 Ksh, almost 20 times more than the average wage earner. Some distributors were also retailers. The household retailers usually diluted the chang'aa with boiled water and sugar or honey to double the batch size and sold it in small tin glasses for 5, 10 or 25 Ksh, earning anywhere from 1,000 to 10,000 Ksh per month.

---

[13] Kutoka Minutes, November 20, 2003, 4-5.

[14] "Poverty Link in Lethal Brew Deaths," *UN Integrated Regional Information Networks*, November 24, 2000.

[15] Onyango, "Deadly Brews," 14.

Although the drinking of illicit spirits had always been part of Kibera's social make-up, many parishioners, especially the women, voiced emotional concern about the number of youth drinking chang'aa and the fact that in recent years, the chang'aa sellers had violated an unspoken rule that prohibited the sale of chang'aa to young people. About half the parishioners shared personal stories of how they had "lost" their children to the illegal brew. Constituting over 60% of the population, the vast majority of Kibera's youth could not afford to pay school fees; only one in five aged 12 to 24 attended school.[16] Since the majority of young people were school leavers with little access to employment, unable to afford recreational facilities and possessing unlimited free time, they were particularly vulnerable to chang'aa. Chang'aa drinking, however, was not limited to the uneducated. One parishioner narrated:

> Young boys, even well-educated ones who have degrees but no jobs, were drinking chang'aa. They have used up their family's resources to go to school and they have nothing to give their parents in return. So now they are desperate and drink until they black out and many of these have become addicted to chang'aa.[17]

Parishioners were also angry about the fact that chang'aa was exposing their children to prostitution and greater risk of AIDS. About three-fourths of the chang'aa sellers incorporated prostitution into their businesses, paying young girls (from 13 to 20 years) a small commission to engage in commercial sex with chang'aa drinkers.

In addition to its negative impact on the youth, chang'aa was identified as the root cause of the community's main economic, health and social problems. The most serious consequence was that it increased the level of poverty in many families. During the parish social analysis, one parishioner reported that, "people are using money meant for food, rent and school fees for drinking. Children end up sleeping hungry because parents are too drunk to take care of the family's needs." Chang'aa drinking also was blamed for a host of employment-related problems. Numerous young men in the parish had "been sacked for drinking on the job" which had led to more unemployment and poverty. Some turned into full-time "idlers who could no longer contribute anything to their families." Chang'aa drinking also negatively affected people's health

---

[16] Frederick Mugisha, Jacqueline Arinaitwe-Mugisha, and Bilhah Hagembe, "Alcohol, Substance and Drug use among Urban Slum Adolescents in Nairobi, Kenya," *Cities* 20, no. 4 (2003), 232.

[17] Interview with OHR team member B, September 20, 2008.

causing untold illness and even death. It also was blamed for the spread of HIV and AIDS. "More and more people are drinking and roaming around at night and AIDS is spreading because of this. We are living in the dark and don't care about what happens in our lives." Chang'aa drinking was also identified as one of the leading causes of family breakups and divorce and several parishioners noted that domestic violence increased because men who came home drunk frequently beat their wives.

The most scathing comments were about parishioners who sold chang'aa, especially the ones who sold it to young people. These complaints were most vociferous in the sub-parish of Soweto where there were four women active in the SCCs who sold chang'aa; two were large distributors/retailers and two were household retailers. Three of these women belonged to the same SCC. Virtually everyone who participated in the social analysis discussions complained about these parishioners, asserting that it was hypocritical for them to attend mass and then sell illegal chang'aa. A few people voiced their frustration that the former parish priest had shown the sellers special favor because of their regular financial contributions to the parish. Several elderly parishioners were so upset that they asked that the priests refuse the sellers communion at mass.

There was a small but vocal cadre of parishioners who repeatedly complained that the Catholic Church in Kibera had a reputation as being a church of drunkards, which had caused it to lose credibility and even prompted some Catholics to join Pentecostal churches because of their prohibitions on alcohol. There was no empirical evidence to show that Catholics drank more than other Kiberans and it was impossible to know how many or what percentage drank chang'aa. No one was willing to admit to drinking illicit spirits because they were afraid of being reported to the authorities or ostracized by the priests and parishioners.

Parishioners' Response

In describing the impact of chang'aa, parishioners admitted that neither the parish nor any other group in Kibera had ever tried to address the problem. Even though parishioners were keenly aware of its negative impact, they felt they were powerless to do anything about it. Parishioners highlighted several reasons to explain their inaction. First, based on long-standing parish protocols, parishioners felt that they could not speak out on the alcohol issue because the parish priest did not support their view. In fact, many felt the former parish priest had encouraged drinking by serving alcohol at parish events and openly drinking with parishioners in their homes and in the priest's house. Second, even if the parish priest had shown an inclination to address the issue of alcohol, the parish structures and operational modes inhibited efforts to mobilize Catholics on socio-political issues. The vast majority were Sunday Christians whose only involvement in the parish was attending mass. The 10% who were organized into SCCs were not equipped to respond to a controversial social issue. Shallow in their base and functionality, they operated primarily as prayer groups and lacked meaningful leadership, not to mention experience or skills in addressing a complex issue such as chang'aa. Third, parishioners lacked financial resources. Without funds to pay for awareness raising, organizing and lobbying efforts, the community could not mobilize a response. Parishioners also had no ability to access donors directly; they lacked personal contacts and relationships with individuals in the donor community, as well as institutional support, bank accounts and requisite expertise to implement a project.

All these deterrents combined, however, did not equal the number one reason parishioners took no action; they were sincerely afraid to confront the influential people involved in the chang'aa business. The police and low-level government officials not only protected the illegal trade, but they also participated in and profited from it. During the social analysis, one parishioner explained:

> We all know that it is the government car driven by police officers that is bringing chang'aa into Soweto every morning between 3:00 and 4:00 a.m. If we try to report it, we will be harassed. The police will arrest us and put us in a cell just because we have complained about the chang'aa.

Another pointed out, "We are very few in this church today because many parishioners are afraid the police will find out we are talking about chang'aa and we will be targeted for harassment later." They were also afraid of retaliation by the chiefs who were involved in the illegal trade. "The chang'aa sellers have their own association where they collect money to give to the chief so he keeps quiet. Anyone selling chang'aa that doesn't pay will be arrested by the chief and put in a cell." Parishioners also feared that the area councilor, a known protector of local Luo distributors in the Soweto area, would send NDP youth wingers to harass or evict them if they complained about chang'aa. They were equally afraid of confronting the sellers who had close contacts with the corrupt officials in the PA and police whom they regularly bribed to facilitate their trade.

Aware of their vulnerability, many parishioners repeatedly asked the OHR coordinator to address the issue. They felt local government officials would not retaliate against an expatriate lawyer who could use the legal system to protect the community's interests. During the social analysis, parishioners suggested a number of possible ways the OHR should facilitate the parish in responding to chang'aa. The biggest concern for most parishioners was reversing its negative image as a church that encouraged drinking. Participants suggested that the parish priest make a public statement against chang'aa. They also asked the OHR to hold workshops for the SCCs to educate them on the dangers of alcohol and that the parish priest should preach about the harmful effects of chang'aa during Sunday homilies. Parishioners suggested that Catholics pray about the issue in their SCC meetings and ask their catechists to give lessons on what the Bible says about alcohol. Some advocated that the parish revive the Pioneers Abstinence Association that had previously existed in the parish.[18] Others suggested that the parish ask Alcoholics Anonymous (AA) to start a support group for parishioners.

Parishioners also wanted to deal directly with the sellers. A small but vocal group wanted to have the chang'aa sellers arrested, but the overwhelming majority wanted to find a way to help the women voluntarily close their chang'aa dens. One sub-parish leader asked, "Can the church find other work for the women that are selling chang'aa?" Others suggested that the chang'aa sellers be given priority in the parish micro-credit project so they could start new businesses. Others suggested that they could talk quietly to the sellers and try to convince them to stop selling chang'aa.

Finally, most parishioners felt that the OHR should try to pressure the local government officials to enforce the law prohibiting chang'aa, but they did not know how to accomplish this goal without provoking retribution. One parishioner suggested the parish follow a common NGO practice of signing a petition. Several others promoted the idea of a public march like the marches of the Kangemi women. Further discussions, however, revealed that Kibera was a very different kind of settlement. Although Kangemi shared many of the physical attributes of a slum, most structure owners owned their plots, which made them far less vulnerable to the threats of evictions by the chiefs. The Kangemi women also had benefited from years of leadership training from a local NGO that had helped create a network of churches and community groups. In contrast, the chiefs and NDP youth wingers in Kibera could evict the parishioners at any time; moreover the Kibera community was not organized into groups or trained on how to protect their rights.

---

[18] Started in 1898 in Ireland for Catholic teetotalers, members of the Pioneers take a voluntary pledge to abstain from alcohol for a certain period of time or even for life.

The OHR's Campaign against Chang'aa

In response to the repeated requests by parishioners, in April 2003 the OHR coordinator and the volunteer lawyers decided to launch a campaign against chang'aa. Parishioners in the OHR Team and Saturday group responded positively and agreed to assist in implementing the campaign. The response from the pastoral team was more reserved. The members who lived in Kibera and felt its impact on a personal level as well as the sister who facilitated the social analysis were very supportive of the campaign. Others, however, were less enthusiastic. In the view of the parish priest and several other missionaries, chang'aa drinking was too entrenched and the sellers would never willingly give up their lucrative businesses. Despite the parish priest's personal reservations, he told the OHR coordinator to pursue the campaign if she could secure funding. Several months later, an Irish missionary arranged for Trocaire, an Irish donor, to visit the parish with a film crew to shoot footage for Trocaire's Lenten fundraising campaign. During this visit, Trocaire's country director met a number of pastoral team members including the OHR to learn more about the parish and its activities. The OHR coordinator shared the idea of a campaign against chang'aa and asked for funding. The Trocaire director responded positively and agreed to fund the campaign for one year starting in October 2003.

Following Trocaire's funding commitment, the OHR coordinator along with two volunteer lawyers designed a campaign to accomplish the goals identified during the social analysis. Aware of the limitations of the SCCs and JPC, the coordinator planned that the primary activities in the campaign-awareness raising and lobbying would be done by the Saturday group and OHR Team with support from the coordinator and lawyers. In addition to empowering parishioners to address the issue, the OHR coordinator also wanted the campaign to build the organizational and lobbying capacity of the Saturday group and involve the other churches and religious groups in Kibera. With that in mind, the lawyers developed a three-phased campaign. The first and overriding goal was to sensitize parishioners, particularly the youth, about the physical dangers of chang'aa and its harmful consequences in an effort to reduce the level of chang'aa consumption. Second, the campaign sought to lobby local government officials to enforce the law that prohibited the sale and use of chang'aa and stop the police from distributing it in Kibera. Third, the campaign sought to help the women in the parish who sold chang'aa find another livelihood.

In developing the methodology, the lawyers did not follow the typical NGO model of staging a one-day event where special guests were invited to speak and t-shirts were handed out as an incentive for people to attend. They also did not want to mobilize community members to march to town in protest. According to their prior experience at the KCS, they knew a rally or march could attract several thousand people as well as the media, but the message would be forgotten quickly and would have little, if any, long-term impact on the parish's goal to educate Kibera youth about the dangers of chang'aa and eradicate it from the community. Instead, the lawyers decided to raise awareness about the dangers of chang'aa with a musical tape/compact disc (CD) that contained songs about the negative impact of chang'aa written and sung by Kibera youth. The CD would allow the message about chang'aa to be repeated for years to come and it would be communicated in the youth's own words using a popular medium. The members of the OHR held a talent show to select songs for the CD. They also invited well-known Kenyan musicians to add profile and credibility to the project. To launch the campaign against chang'aa, the songs were performed at a live musical concert in Kibera. Because accessing musical artists and producing a CD would require music industry experience, the OHR coordinator hired a part-time coordinator to manage the musical component of the campaign.

Parishioners' Role

Based on discussions during the social analysis, the OHR coordinator believed that parishioners were able and willing to address the issues related to chang'aa. However, once funding for the campaign was attained and the plans finalized, only a small group of parishioners in the Saturday group and Soweto sub-parish were willing to get involved; the vast majority of parishioners wanted nothing to do with the campaign. The reasons for their lack of interest varied. Even though there were chang'aa dealers in every section of the parish, the majority of parishioners viewed chang'aa as a Soweto problem. From their perspective, because the key depots were located in Soweto, addressing the problem should be the responsibility of parishioners living there. Some felt the chang'aa issue was too deeply rooted in Kibera's social economy and any effort to eradicate it was a waste of time. Others associated the chang'aa business with corrupt police and sellers, two groups they wanted to avoid. Others stayed quiet because they drank chang'aa and wanted to continue to have access to cheap liquor.

Parishioners from Soweto expressed similar reservations, but their primary concern was the potential for violent retaliation. Since they lived near the sellers and were known by them, they feared that if they were seen to condone the campaign publicly, both the sellers and the police would harm them. Contrary to expectations by the OHR coordinator, the presence of the lawyers did not dissipate that fear. The parishioners knew that they could be beaten, evicted in the middle of the night or thrown into a cell and there was little the lawyers could do to prevent that. Moreover, if their property was destroyed, the lawyers would not be able to replace it. In the balance of things, it was too risky for them to get involved. There were also some parishioners from the Soweto area who had been very vocal during the social analysis discussions who, once they knew the OHR had money for the campaign, felt it was the OHR's responsibility to implement the campaign. Parishioners were not accustomed to playing an active role in community activities; in their experience many projects run by the parish as well as the NGOs were implemented in a top-down manner with few opportunities to participate in decision making. They felt their role was limited to attending events or meetings to receive what was being given out, little more.

Despite the reluctance of most parishioners to get involved in the campaign, there was a small group of 30 that included a handful of youth, around 15 members of the Saturday group and a few SCC members from Soweto who regularly volunteered to work on the campaign. Notwithstanding this group's sincere commitment and willingness to get involved in a risky issue, they were too few and lacked the requisite skills and ability to play a significant role. In the vacuum of interest and capacity of the parishioners, the campaign was largely driven by the OHR and two volunteer lawyers. From the campaign's initial conceptualization and planning to its implementation, the OHR coordinator played the dominant role; she wrote the proposal, arranged for the international funding and developed the methodology. She and the lawyers also played the primary role in organizing the awareness raising and lobbying activities.

The coordinator's centralized approach limited the impact of the campaign on several levels. Unaware of the complicated political interests in the chang'aa industry, she initially believed that parishioners would be willing to lobby local government officials about chang'aa if they had support from the parish OHR, but that was not the case. Neither the parishioners nor the OHR was immune to the threats made by the people running the chang'aa business. Furthermore, the issue of chang'aa turned out to be much more complex and dangerous than anticipated. The advocacy work required skilled negotiations and was not appropriate for the Saturday group members who had no prior experience in lobbying or conflict resolution strategies. In addition, the awareness-raising activities planned by the coordinator were not appropriate for building the capacity of the Saturday group. Because the donor required the funds to be spent within one year, the OHR coordinator was rushed during the initial planning and implementation of the campaign events; there was not adequate time to train the OHR Team and Saturday group on how to organize an event including designing the theme, message and advertising materials. Organizing the musical events proved to be complex and required sophisticated and professional skills that the parishioners did not have. Even if parishioners had the skills, they did not have the time. Consumed by attending to survival needs, most Saturday group members were not in a position to participate fully; they simply were not able to sacrifice their daily wage needed to feed their families so they could work on the chang'aa issue.

Notwithstanding the lack of widespread participation, efforts to raise awareness on chang'aa were successful. On November 15, 2003, more than 1,500 people attended the talent show, mostly young people from the parish. There were 48 musical acts that included youth, children, adult choirs and elderly women who sang original songs describing the impact of chang'aa on their lives. The judges, three of Kenyan's internationally recognized musicians, Eric Wainaina, Suzanna Owiyo and Roughtone, chose seven winners. Almost one month later, on December 14, the three musical artists who judged the talent show along with the well-known musical groups of Kayamba Africa and Bakalutu joined the talent show winners to put on the first live musical concert in Kibera. More than 5,000 people attended the event that was staged in the playing field in Line Saba.

For the talent show, the members of the Saturday group volunteered to do the non-skilled tasks such as publicizing the event and mobilizing people to attend by handing out flyers and posters and making announcements in their SCCs and sub-parishes. With support from the OHR Team, members of the Saturday group also helped set up and managed the registration process, crowd control and the stage on the day of the event. The skilled tasks that required access to communication systems and technology, however, were undertaken by the coordinator and lawyers who prepared the advertisements and organized the logistical details of the talent show.

The role of the Saturday group was much more involved for the concert than the talent show due to its size and venue. Apart from occasional political rallies, the concert was the largest event ever organized inside Kibera and required hundreds of volunteer hours.

Working with the OHR Team, the lawyers and the OHR coordinator made arrangements with the performers, secured contracts with service providers, arranged for publicity, invited special guests, notified the press and organized a heavy police presence as well as private security due to fears that the sound equipment could be stolen or damaged and that the sellers might use force to disrupt the event. Most Saturday group members, again, volunteered to publicize the event and mobilize people to attend by putting up posters and making announcements. They also helped set up the staging area, manage the crowd and clean up the event. Staging an event in Kibera presented unanticipated logistical challenges that the Saturday group assisted in resolving. For example, since the electricity source was inadequate for the speakers, a five-ton generator had to be transported to the venue that required the Saturday group to place hundreds of stones along the path so the water pipes beneath the road were not crushed.

The Saturday group's willingness to volunteer for the talent show and concert was in contrast to the youth's response. Prior to the talent show, with the belief that the youth who had been part of the parish youth group (a mix of about 45 boys and girls from the ages of 18-25) would enjoy meeting and interacting with the famous Kenyan musicians, the coordinator invited the youth to be volunteers. However, apart from five young men, the youth declined to participate because the OHR was not willing to pay allowances. Their response reflected one of the greatest challenges to soliciting volunteers for events in Kibera. Most residents, especially young people, had grown up in an environment where many activities designed by anyone not resident in Kibera (including NGOs, politicians, churches and missionaries) paid residents to participate in the form of allowances, jobs or food. Charitable donations of this kind had a very negative consequence. Most young people viewed activities planned by outsiders as an opportunity to negotiate for fees. Moreover, since the project and money came from the outside, residents felt little, if any, sense of ownership or personal responsibility for the activities, regardless of whether they were designed to improve Kibera.

Following the concert, the OHR coordinator worked with a local production studio to produce a CD that contained the winning songs in addition to a song donated by each of the professional artists. The recordings were in the process of being mixed when the production studio was robbed in October 2004. Because the production studio had no backup of the recorded songs or access to other recording equipment, the OHR coordinator wrote the project off as a complete loss. Six months later, the production company unexpectedly recovered some of the stolen equipment. After the OHR coordinator raised funds from family and friends to cover the expense of replacing the tapes and CDs that had been stolen, the project was restarted and finally completed in August 2005. After nearly a year of delays, the OHR launched the CD entitled "Rhythms of Life," at two different venues. The CD was first launched on August 6, 2005 at the production studio in order to accommodate journalists who were not willing to enter Kibera to cover the event. The event was widely covered by print, radio and television media. Following the launch, the OHR coordinator also distributed the chang'aa CD to the major radio stations, media houses, city officials, government ministers and diplomats as part of the campaign to raise awareness.

Just a week later, the parish was robbed by an armed gang in the middle of the night. During the raid, the new parish priest was forced to hide on the roof of his house as the parish guard was badly beaten. The gang ransacked the offices of the OHR and the priest's house stealing computers, printers and other valuables. Although the police called to investigate the incident said there were no suspects, local contacts revealed that the robbery had been orchestrated by a number of large chang'aa sellers from Soweto intent on intimidating the parish into dropping the chang'aa campaign. The robbery was a significant setback for the parish. Fearing future reprisals, most night-time activities including SCC masses and civic education classes were temporarily suspended. Without any computers, administrative work as well as numerous activities also came to a halt including the OHR's plan to launch the CD in Kibera. Lacking a financial reserve, the Guadalupe priests asked the OHR coordinator to raise funds to replace the stolen equipment. It was not until October 2005, after the OHR coordinator raised the necessary money from two donors as well as family and friends, that the OHR finally launched the CD during a parish-wide mass attended by over 1,000 parishioners.

Unlike the talent show and concert, the process of preparing and launching the tape/CD was done almost exclusively by the OHR and the lawyers. The tasks related to the production did not lend themselves to group participation because they primarily involved negotiations with the production studio and performers. Moreover, after the production studio was robbed, the project lost its momentum and interest among the Saturday group and the parish naturally waned.

Other Faith-Based Organizations

In anticipation of significant resistance by the police, PA and local politicians, members of the OHR wanted to broaden the range of support for the campaign beyond the parish and collaborate with other churches and religious groups both inside and outside Kibera. To that end, members of the OHR met a number of priests, pastors and an imam in Kibera as well as the missionaries in the Kutoka network to solicit their participation in the campaign. Although the priests and clerics in Kibera were all quick to agree that chang'aa was an enormous problem, none of them was willing to pursue the campaign because of limited interest, time, resources and fear of retaliation, leaving the OHR to pursue the issue in Kibera alone. A number of the Catholic missionaries in the network who had access to resources joined the campaign.

The OHR coordinator and Team first met the parish priests from the two neighboring Catholic parishes, Our Lady of Guadalupe and St. Michael's. Our Lady of Guadalupe was primarily a middle-class parish also administered by Guadalupe missionaries whose boundary included approximately 40% of Kibera. Even though they were sister parishes, there was little official collaboration between Christ the King and Our Lady of Guadalupe. The two parishes had very different modes of operation that reflected the personal interests and views of the individual parish priests. The parish priest at Our Lady of Guadalupe followed the conservative pastoral approach used by the majority of Mexican priests in his congregation; his primary focus was evangelization, sacraments and devotional prayer. When the OHR coordinator and Team members met him, he was supportive of the campaign but he was not willing to get involved personally because he was busy planning a parish-wide novena. He referred the OHR Team to a representative of the JPC in the parish. Although sincere in his intentions, he was a part-time volunteer with limited education and financial resources; the most he could do was put up posters announcing the events and personally encourage people to attend.

St. Michael's parish was a middle-class parish located along the southern boundary of Kibera that included approximately 10% of the slum. The parish did not have a working relationship with St. Michael's even though it had been started and administered by Guadalupe priests before they handed it over to the Archdiocese. When the OHR met the parish priest, he was sympathetic to the problems of chang'aa but he, too, was not willing to get involved in the campaign. Reflective of the general trend of most diocesan priests in Nairobi, he was not interested in getting involved in controversial socio-political issues. Since there was no JPC representative in the parish, he referred the OHR Team to a sister responsible for health issues who agreed to put up posters, but admitted there was little else she could do.

Since the parish did not belong to any ecumenical groups in Kibera or regularly collaborate with other churches or religious groups, the OHR coordinator relied on the personal relationships of Team members to contact two religious leaders. One Team member arranged for members of the OHR to meet his neighbor, the imam from the Lindi mosque. The local imam was an enthusiastic supporter of the campaign; he was personally opposed to alcohol because of his religious beliefs and he also felt chang'aa was responsible for the spread of AIDS. The coordinator and two Team members also met a well-regarded Pentecostal pastor whose church was in Line Saba and approximately 30 other Kibera pastors who were part of his fellowship group. Initially surprised that the Catholic Church was addressing the issue of alcohol given the widely-held perception that it was a church of drinkers, the Pentecostal pastors welcomed the chance to build a united campaign against chang'aa. Similar to the imam, their support was motivated not only by their religious opposition to alcohol, but also their shared belief that eradicating chang'aa was critical to reduce the growing number of AIDS-related deaths.

Both the sheikh and pastor joined the acting parish priest who was filling in while the parish priest was on home-leave to lead the prayers at the concert, during which time the imam declared that it was the first time in 40 years that he had been invited by the parish to participate in an event and that he enthusiastically supported the campaign. Despite the newly formed friendship with the OHR, neither the Pentecostal pastors nor the imam took any concrete actions to expose the role of corrupt low-level officials or police in the chang'aa trade. These religious leaders had limited education and resources. They were also afraid to confront the local power structures. The Pentecostal pastor feared that if he spoke against chang'aa, the sellers would burn down his church and primary school. The imam was also afraid; he spoke privately about chang'aa but was not willing to address the issue outside his home.

The OHR coordinator also invited the missionaries working in the Kutoka parishes to join the campaign. Chang'aa was a chronic problem in all slum areas and one that the parishes in Kangemi and Korogocho had tried to address in the past. Because of limited time and resources, only five of the 14 parishes agreed to organize awareness-raising events on the same day of the concert. Prior to launching the campaign, the conveners of the network arranged for a press conference to publicize the campaign. Two missionary priests asked Archbishop Ndingi and the deputy mayor of Nairobi to attend the press conference. Consistent with his prior outspoken criticism of the chang'aa trade, the Archbishop accused government agents mandated to enforce the law against chang'aa of promoting it, noting that it was common to see police and local administration officials using government vehicles to bring chang'aa into settlements such as Kangemi, Kibera and Korogocho.[19] The deputy mayor also condemned the illegal trade and highlighted the need to target the youth who are the most affected by chang'aa in the slums.

On the day of the campaign launch, the parishes that participated in the campaign designed events that reflected the particular circumstances as well as their resources and capacities to organize parishioners. For example, building on efforts by the Kangemi women, the parish priest in Kangemi organized an ecumenical march to create awareness about the risks of drinking chang'aa; over 5,000 people including members of the parish SCCs as well as the Kangemi women's group, two Anglican churches and the area mosque participated. The missionaries in Korogocho who had funds from a donor in Italy organized a marathon. The youth of the parish recruited 5,000 people to run a 12-kilometer race to raise awareness about the dangers of drugs and alcohol. This event was attended by Italy's ambassador to Kenya and the area MP. The Consolata parish hosted a seminar on substance abuse and a football tournament for the youth that was attended by Archbishop Ndingi and the country's vice-president, Moody Awori, who was a parishioner. In Mukuru kwa Njenga, several hundred parishioners walked through the community with signs to raise awareness and then watched a video on the issues of drugs and alcohol. The choirs in Dandora parish wrote and performed songs about chang'aa and talks were given about substance abuse after mass.

The impact of the Kutoka's efforts to raise awareness and pressure the government to enforce the chang'aa law, however, was minimal both in the short and long term. Although numerous members of the print and television media attended events held in Kibera, Kangemi and Korogocho, media coverage was almost non-existent. Saddam Hussein was arrested on the same day and that story dominated the papers for the week. The only coverage of the chang'aa campaign was limited to one small report that the marchers in Kangemi had been stoned by drunken youth who thought the women were coming to destroy the chang'aa dens. Moreover, despite the missionaries' ability to reach thousands of Catholics at the grass roots, the network did not have the requisite organizational structure, financial resources or persons with the time and skills to mobilize a coordinated advocacy campaign. Most of the missionaries in the network were overwhelmed by other pastoral obligations and did not have sufficient

---

[19] Albert Kasemblei, "Body Formed to Eradicate Illicit Liquors," *East African Standard*, Nairobi, December 9, 2003.

time to dedicate to the campaign. As an example, no one in the network ever met any high-level government officials or the Archbishop following the launch of the campaign. As a consequence, for most parishes the campaign was a one-day event that did not reduce significantly the use of chang'aa or the corrupt role played by low-level government officials in the illicit trade.

There were only two parishes, apart from the OHR, that pursued the issue of chang'aa after the day of the launch. The missionaries working in Korogocho, with the assistance of an Italian donor and several full-time lay volunteers, set up an AA group that had 150 members and started a counseling program and a half-way house for alcoholics and drug addicts. The missionaries also gave 10 chang'aa sellers 10,000 Ksh to start new businesses; but more than half eventually returned to the chang'aa business because it was more profitable. In Kangemi, the parish leaders placed the names of four Catholic sellers on a list of shame that was read publicly in mass; one of the sellers closed her den but the others continued in the trade. In addition, a congregation of American brothers working in Kangemi started an AA group and built a half-way house for alcoholics.

Lobbying Efforts by the OHR

Because of fears and limited skills, the responsibility for lobbying for the enforcement of the chang'aa law in Kibera fell exclusively to the OHR coordinator, who with support from the lawyers and the OHR Team, used the information gathered by parishioners to lobby officials in the PA. In addition to having a greater degree of immunity from local threats, the coordinator had the benefit of resources, time, legal expertise, contacts and office support that were necessary to engage in lobbying work.

Although the OHR coordinator had certain advantages as an expatriate, she also had limitations including the lack of personal access to high-level decision makers. The OHR coordinator therefore summarized the parish's findings on chang'aa in a memorandum and sent it to the PC, the mayor of Nairobi and the Kibera DO, describing the role of the police in transporting chang'aa into Kibera, its impact on the community and a request that the government enforce the law prohibiting the production and sale of chang'aa. The responses of the government officials were mixed. The mayor never replied. However, to the surprise of the OHR, the PC and the DO of Kibera responded with unexpected enthusiasm. The PC sent numerous letters to the parish priest and OHR coordinator expressing both his and the NARC government's support for the campaign. During various meetings with the OHR members, the DO also indicated that the government was in full support of eradicating chang'aa from Kibera and pledged his support as the government's senior representative in the community. He also indicated that, as a Muslim, he wanted to rid Kibera of illicit brews and he personally committed himself to the campaign.

In order to publicize the PA's support, the OHR coordinator invited the DO to be the special guest at the concert. The DO addressed the audience with a strongly-worded statement warning all chang'aa sellers that the Administrative Police had prioritized the eradication of chang'aa from Kibera and that anyone caught selling or drinking chang'aa would be arrested. The DO also read a speech by the PC who planned to attend the event, but cancelled at the last minute due to a family emergency. His remarks appealed to all the residents of Nairobi to volunteer information to the chiefs and the police about chang'aa use stating, "Where the Public is convinced that officers have been compromised, do not hesitate to write to me or see me in person in view of correcting such action of misguided Officers who are a liability to the NARC Government."[20] On the day after the concert, the PC attended a public meeting in Kibera where he announced his support for the parish's campaign and instructed all members of the PA to crack down on chang'aa sellers, distributors and transporters.

In response to the PC's and DO's public statements, the Administrative Police started immediately arresting chang'aa sellers. Within six months, nearly half of the 60 chang'aa dens in Soweto had been closed, either by the Administrative Police or voluntarily by the sellers. In addition, as a result of the heightened surveillance, people accustomed to drinking chang'aa reduced their consumption because they were afraid of being arrested in one of the frequent raids ordered by the DO. According to one OHR Team member:

> For the first time the sellers had their doors locked because they knew they were being monitored and what was happening on the ground was being reported to the police who might react. Customers went in and drank in two minutes and left. Before they would hang out and relax and drink. That situation totally changed after the concert.[21]

In addition to the increased police activity, the chief from Soweto/ Highrise, who was the brother-in-law of a Team member, increased his surveillance and arrests of chang'aa sellers in his region.

---

[20] Statement of PC, December 14, 2003.

[21] Interview with OHR team member B, September 20, 2008.

Despite the closure of numerous chang'aa dens, the gains made were short-lived and had only a limited impact in curbing the chang'aa trade. Since the PC and DO lacked jurisdiction over the regular police force, the police ignored the directive and the early morning drops of chang'aa continued unabated. It was only the Administrative Police, who could be dismissed directly by the DO that responded to the call for more rigorous patrolling of chang'aa dens. Despite the efforts of the Administrative Police, two chiefs and all seven assistant chiefs ignored the order to arrest the sellers and the DO could do nothing to compel his corrupt subordinates to follow his directive. The chiefs and assistant chiefs were political employees hired through the Office of the President; their job security was dependent on their personal loyalty to NARC officials, not on whether they performed their jobs.

The PC and DO, who had the full weight of authority of the central government as well as physical force at their disposal, were also powerless to counter the corrupt forces that had taken permanent root in Kibera where the most powerful players were the area MP and his agents, especially the councilors and NDP youth wingers. For example, when the OHR Team members met the assistant chief of Soweto/Highrise, an active parishioner, to solicit his support for the campaign, he said that he did not want to be associated with it regardless of what the parish or DO said; his primary loyalty was to the area councilor, a fellow Luo and political ally. Furthermore, when the chief of the Soweto/Highrise area tried to crack down on the chang'aa trade, he was blocked by the area councilor. After the chief and his two staff tried to stop a group of Ugandans from another slum area from delivering over 1,000 liters of chang'aa, all transported in police vehicles, they were attacked and beaten by NDP youth wingers sent by the area councilor.[22]

In addition to the PA's inability to enforce the laws because of political interference and corruption, the constant shuffling of the local administration brought about by political pressure also limited the impact of lobbying efforts undertaken by the OHR. The area DO, the campaign's strongest ally, was transferred abruptly from Kibera in September 2004 after publicly confronting the NDP youth wingers. This incident was related to a struggle over land. Following two years of negotiations, a large international donor had agreed to build an informal primary school on land located in Lindi after the DO agreed to allocate the plot of land to the school. The tenants who lived in the structures located on that plot were Luo youth protected by NDP youth wingers and they refused to leave

[22] OHR Memorandum, October 26, 2004.

until they were paid a bribe. When the DO ordered a number of Administrative Police to remove them forcibly, a group of NDP youth wingers set fire to the chief's camp in Lindi and attacked the Administrative Police, sparking a full-scale riot during which a young man was shot and killed.[23] The NDP youth wingers alleged that it was the DO who shot the youth and threatened to lynch him if he was not removed from Kibera. Although the DO was innocent of the charges and was a respected leader in the community, he was permanently reassigned within two weeks of the incident.

The DO was not the only government official removed from Kibera because he confronted the politically-protected youth wingers and councilor. The Soweto/Highrise chief was also transferred. Shortly after he and his assistants were beaten for trying to prevent the importation of chang'aa, the chief was falsely accused of malfeasance and placed on indefinite leave without pay at the councilor's connivance.

The OHR's lobbying efforts were also undermined by the fact that despite pronouncements from high-level officials, the PA was too fractured to enforce its policies at the grass-roots level. Even though the Kibaki government had denounced chang'aa, the DO's support for the campaign was not institutionalized. The office of the DO was driven more by individual personalities than government policies. After the DO was transferred, his successors did not share his personal commitment to enforcing the chang'aa law and they did not follow the PC's orders. After spending over a year of time and effort to lobby the DO, the OHR had to start again and to no avail. The new DO was on temporary assignment and did want to engage in controversial issues. The subsequent DO who arrived in 2005 was young and inexperienced. Intimidated by the threats of the councilor and his youth wingers, he told members of the OHR Team that he did not want to get involved in the campaign. Thus, although the PC continued to send letters to the parish in support of the campaign throughout 2005, without local officials to enforce the law, the chang'aa trade gradually reverted to the status quo.

Chang'aa as the Priority Issue of the Soweto Sub-Parish

In November 2003, following the completion of the social analysis, the parish priest commenced the parish-wide planning process. He asked each sub-parish to identify one particular socio-political or economic problem

---

[23] Patrick Mathangani, "Man Killed as Kibera Erupts in Violence," *East African Standard*, Nairobi, August 30, 2004.

that it would address for the next five years and create a plan of activities for that problem, commonly referred to as the priority issue. His approach to the planning process was novel on several levels. In the past, parish activities had been limited to traditional religious activities such as liturgies, sacraments, retreats and masses. Parishioners had never been asked to address a socio-political issue. In addition, historically, parish planning processes had been done exclusively by the PPC leaders and parish priest; ordinary parishioners had never been involved. Nor had parishioners ever been asked to organize as sub-parishes. Thus, not surprisingly, many parishioners struggled to integrate and implement the multiple changes during the planning process.

As the first step, the parish priest invited the lawyers who taught civic education to facilitate the sub-parishes to select a priority issue from the list of 15 social, economic and political issues discussed during the social analysis. In the Soweto sub-parish, approximately 70 parishioners attended the meeting; the vast majority (nearly 90%) were SCC members. Lacking experience in planning, many parishioners in Soweto did not fully understand the process, their role in it and what choosing a priority issue involved or meant for the future. As a result, many parishioners did not participate in the discussions. In the vacuum, a few outspoken catechists and Pioneer members dominated the discussions and urged the group to choose alcohol as the sub-parish priority. The sub-parish's choice was also influenced by the fact that a number of parishioners felt that the OHR had money available from the campaign that could be used to fund activities in their sub-parish. After the sub-parishes chose their priority issues, the parish priest assigned a parish ministry to each sub-parish to assist the parishioners in implementing their chosen issue. In light of the OHR's on-going chang'aa campaign, the OHR was asked to partner the Soweto sub-parish.[24]

The members of the OHR initially hoped the Soweto sub-parish's choice of chang'aa would create an opportunity to involve more parishioners in the chang'aa campaign, but their enthusiasm quickly waned as the planning process unfolded. Concerned that the social analysis had taken too much time and delayed the parish leadership elections, the parish priest wanted to expedite the planning process. He decided not to ask the civic education lawyers to assist the sub-parish in developing plans because he felt their participatory processes would be too time-consuming. Instead, he assigned a small group of pastoral team

[24] The sub-parish of Shilanga chose abortion; Lindi and Highrise chose unemployment and Line Saba chose HIV and AIDS.

members, all Kibera residents, to draft a final plan for the sub-parishes. Apart from a weekend workshop, the planning team did not have professional training or experience in planning processes. They were also under time pressures. As a result, instead of meeting members of the Soweto sub-parish and the OHR to seek their input and build consensus over the specific activities and actions they wanted to take, the planning committee met selected SCC members. The parishioners knew little about how to identify shared goals, design activities and allocate resources for those activities. The planning team, therefore, adopted the activities which were already part of the OHR's campaign and added one additional activity, forming a committee to pursue the campaign in the sub-parish and undertake a social analysis on chang'aa in Soweto. The Soweto sub-parish, like the others, was not allocated a budget for their activities and there were no discussions about how resources would be raised or allocated for the activities.

The Sub-Parish's Role

Despite the legitimate concerns about chang'aa articulated by Soweto parishioners during the social analysis, once the issue was identified as the sub-parish priority issue, their interest dropped considerably. During the first meeting called by the OHR to form a chang'aa committee and plan how the sub-parish should proceed; only 40 of the 200 parishioners in the sub-parish attended. Those who participated were mostly members of the SCCs who had regularly participated in the social analysis discussions and were already accustomed to talking about chang'aa. The majority, however, wanted to avoid the taboo topic and quickly left as soon as mass finished. Most parishioners who left felt the parish had overreached its role by taking on the issue of chang'aa. For them, it was beyond the scope of the church's duty, which was to focus on "spiritual faith and Christian life not get involved in people's personal lives."[25] Many were also afraid that there would be retribution against the church if parishioners spoke out against chang'aa while others did not want to take sides; they preferred to remain neutral and not get involved in a controversial issue. There were also some who felt the campaign was a futile endeavor. Parishioners might condemn chang'aa publicly, but in private they were willing consumers.

Even though only about 25% of the sub-parish stayed, the OHR Team proceeded with the meeting where the practical challenges to pursuing the campaign at the community level were quickly revealed. Although

[25] Interview with Saturday group member E, September 29, 2008.

parishioners were willing to discuss the litany of reasons why chang'aa needed to be eradicated, when it came to confronting local officials or the sellers about their role in the illicit trade, most were not willing to take action because they were afraid that they would be arrested. According to one member:

> The police have no interest in arresting those people selling chang'aa. They will arrest people who complain about chang'aa. We can be thrown in a cell and left there just because we have been heard complaining about it.[26]

The threat of incarceration was a legitimate concern; a number of parishioners detailed their prior experiences in jail to emphasize their position. Kiberans who were arrested routinely stayed in the cells for days without being charged; they were often denied food and beaten.

Parishioners were also divided on how to confront the sellers; many feared that the sellers would retaliate against anyone who opposed them. One parishioner explained:

> The sellers are rich and linked to senior police officers and the crooks in the community. A lot of criminals take chang'aa so they have a close relationship with the sellers. If we confront the sellers, our lives will be in danger.[27]

Others felt that it was too late to try to talk to the sellers because they had been permanently alienated from the parish from the day of the concert. Some also asserted that they had been in the same SCCs for years and their personal relationship with the sellers prevented them from confronting them. In the words of one long-term parishioner, "The sellers are our friends. We do not feel comfortable telling them to stop selling their brews or reporting them to the police."[28]

Despite their reservations and concerns, six people volunteered to be part of the chang'aa committee, but they said they would not confront the local government officials; any action of that sort would be left to the OHR. Instead, the committee agreed to take on three activities: (1) gather more information about the chang'aa trade, (2) work with the OHR to organize speakers on alcohol-related topics during Sunday mass and (3) convince the sellers to find other businesses.

---

[26] Interview with Saturday group member C, September 24, 2008.
[27] Interview with parish leader from Soweto, September 29, 2008.
[28] Interview with Saturday group member F, September 28, 2008.

First Chang'aa Committee

Even though the SCC members had indicated a verbal desire to go ahead with the campaign, following the election of the chang'aa committee, no one in the sub-parish including the chang'aa committee, the sub-parish leaders, SCCs leaders or the SCC members took any steps to address the chang'aa issue. After two months of inaction, the OHR called the committee to attend a series of meetings to plan how to move the campaign forward. During the meetings, it was clear that the committee lacked the requisite knowledge and skills to facilitate the sub-parish to undertake any of the agreed-upon activities. Of the six members, only one had finished secondary school. None of the committee members had experience or training in basic communication and organization skills including how to plan activities, facilitate a meeting, keep records, build consensus or cooperate to achieve common goals, let alone accomplish the list of activities related to chang'aa, a controversial and potentially dangerous topic.

In addition to lacking capacity, the committee members were too afraid to take any concrete actions. In discussing how the committee could do further analysis of the chang'aa situation in Soweto, the committee members repeatedly said they were too scared to identify parishioners who sold or drank chang'aa. One parishioner commented, "We are afraid to enter into houses of the sellers because we will be seen as spies or agents for the police force and the sellers will come after us."[29]

Even if the committee members had been able to overcome their capacity limitations and fear, they did not share the same vision for the campaign as their fellow parishioners and the OHR. Two of the committee members were Pioneers who wanted to use their influence as committee members to eradicate all alcohol from Soweto. Adopting the position regularly heard in Pentecostal churches that all alcohol was sinful; they insisted that all parishioners stop drinking not only chang'aa but also traditional and bottled beer. Not surprisingly, they had no following in the sub-parish. Three others used their positions to remove the four SCCs members who sold chang'aa. Unbeknownst to the OHR, those committee members, two of whom were influential catechists, started a verbal campaign attacking the sellers, publicly branding them as sinners. The sellers were told that they should leave their SCCs and sub-parish and not return until they stopped selling chang'aa; they were also told they could

[29] OHR Memorandum, May 16, 2004.

not receive communion or serve as godparents or matrimonial witnesses. One Team member explained:

> These people in the committee had been angry so long and now they had a way to express that anger with the sellers. They felt the sellers were spoiling the name of the church and it was an opportunity to finally get rid of them from their sub-parish and they did it in a malicious way.[30]

As a bitter invective was exchanged, members of the SCCs started taking sides in favor of or against the sellers. Jealous of the sellers' privilege and money, some parishioners used the campaign to settle old scores unrelated to chang'aa. The conflict quickly threatened to split the Soweto sub-parish irreparably.

The behavior of the chang'aa committee highlighted a significant omission in the parish's planning process. The plan did not define the roles and relationships between the committee, sub-parish leaders, SCC leaders, the SCC members, Sunday Christians, OHR and the parish priest. Consequently, it was unclear who had authority to direct the committee's position, the leaders of the Soweto sub-parish who were largely uninvolved with the issue, the chang'aa committee members who were self-selected and had no following, the SCC members who had yet to act on the issue, the OHR whose role was intended to be one of support, or the parish priest who was not involved in the sub-parishes' priority issues because he wanted them to operate independently. The ambiguity of the situation created a dilemma for the OHR who felt pressure from the parish priest to help the sub-parish pursue its priority issue, but did not want to over-step the committee's role or unduly influence the sub-parish members. As a result of the confusion, combined with the fact that the OHR did not agree with the committee's personal vendetta against the sellers, the members of the OHR discontinued meeting the chang'aa committee and the campaign stalled.

The sellers reacted immediately to the committee's admonitions. The four chang'aa sellers stopped attending mass and their SCC meetings and they threatened to leave the parish. Their threats attracted the immediate attention of the priests and pastoral team. One of the women, whom I shall call Pauline, was the second largest chang'aa distributor in Soweto. She was also part of a small group of parishioners who attended daily mass in the main church compound and had been a close friend of the former parish priest and large contributor to the parish. When a missionary priest who worked part-time in the parish went to see her about her absence at

[30] Interview with OHR team member B, September 20, 2008.

mass, she told him that she was furious with the OHR and accused it of trying to ruin her reputation. She also threatened to stop her financial support for the parish and said she was taking steps to join another church. At the same time, the other large distributor, who I refer to as Margaret, also threatened to leave the parish because she was "tired of being treated like a sinner" by the members of her SCC. The missionary priest called the members of the OHR for a meeting and expressed his concern that despite the harmful impact of chang'aa, the parish's priority was practicing forgiveness and could not be seen to force parishioners out of the church. He suggested the OHR facilitate a reconciliation process in the Soweto SCCs and help the sellers find practical alternatives to selling chang'aa.

Suddenly the key issue for the OHR was no longer how to facilitate the committee to pursue the campaign against chang'aa, but how to keep the sellers in the parish and possibly facilitate reconciliation within the SCCs. The missionary priest took the lead in facilitating a dialogue with the sellers and their SCCs, periodically holding prayer services and mass in their homes that included the OHR, pastoral team members and SCC representatives. One of the OHR Team members also volunteered to spend time talking to the sellers in an effort to resolve the conflict in their SCCs. As news of these meetings with the sellers spread in the sub-parish, other SCC members began to meet and talk to the sellers on their own volition with the aim of reconciling the rift. Their combined efforts during several months eventually succeeded and the four sellers were invited back to their SCCs, albeit with a certain degree of lingering resentment and hostility on the part of some.

The situation that unfolded with the sellers demonstrated another flaw in the campaign strategy. At the time the coordinator and the lawyers designed the campaign, they lacked sufficient knowledge and understanding of the invisible power relations in the parish and the extent to which the sellers would resist the campaign. The coordinator mistakenly believed that the sellers would voluntarily start alternate businesses once the parish spoke out against it. The reality was far different. Even though Pauline and Margaret were openly criticized by most of their fellow SCC members, they were powerful players in the parish because of their financial contributions. In a parish where the average parishioner contributed $15 in a year, Pauline's annual contribution of $600 made her one of the parish's single largest local contributors. No one in the pastoral team or OHR wanted to jeopardize the parish's access to much needed funds. Thus, even though the campaign succeeded on one level by exposing the sellers in the illegal business, the sellers' threat to leave the parish and stop their financial support forced the OHR to reduce the very pressure the campaign was designed to generate.

Following their return to their SCCs, the two sellers met members of the OHR about finding alternate businesses. Margaret said that she was willing to stop selling chang'aa if the parish helped her start another business. Pauline emphatically declared that she would not give up the business until her four adult children, who relied on her for their upkeep, were employed. Their demands, again, demonstrated the complex issues at play with respect to the sellers which were not adequately anticipated or planned for.

The coordinators of the OHR and the self-reliance department met Margaret several times to discuss the possibility of setting up an alternate business but Margaret was unenthusiastic about her options and not willing to meet women in other slum areas who started small income-generating businesses. She had purchased a room in Soweto and wanted direct financial support in setting up a small shop. Neither the OHR nor the parish had money to loan her. The Trocaire funds had been used for the musical events and there was still a shortfall for the CD production. When Margaret realized that neither the OHR nor the self-reliance department had available funds for her, she stopped coming to the OHR. The coordinators of the OHR and self-reliance department also did not have the capacity to find jobs for Pauline's children, none of whom had prior work experience. When Pauline learned that her children would not be hired by the parish, she also stopped visiting the OHR.

Second Chang'aa Committee

Despite the stalemate with the sellers in Soweto, the parish priest did not want to abandon the priority issue in Soweto. In September 2004 he along with the OHR members met the Soweto sub-parish to try to revive the campaign by electing a new committee that was committed to a more inclusive attitude toward the sellers. Only 30 people attended the meeting; turnout was low because many people in the sub-parish did not agree with the approach taken by the first committee. During the meeting, much of the discussion was centered on concerns that the sub-parish was not well-positioned to take on the issue of chang'aa. One parishioner explained, "As Catholics, no one will listen to us talk about alcohol. How can we say we are against when even our parish leaders and the priests drink? Everyone knows it is Catholics that are the ones selling it."[31] In addition to

[31] OHR Memorandum, September 24, 2004.

their feelings of hypocrisy, fear of arrest had increased in the intervening time. There was also a general apathy within the sub-parish. Given the dominant role played by the OHR during the initial awareness-raising phase of the campaign combined with the perception that the OHR had access to a large amount of money for the campaign, many parishioners felt the campaign belonged to the OHR, not the sub-parish. However, not everyone in the sub-parish felt the campaign was a waste of time. One long-term SCC leader related her past history as a chang'aa seller and encouraged the group to do anything it could to lower the level of chang'aa consumption in Soweto. Another prominent member of the sub-parish who owned several local restaurants stopped selling chang'aa in his establishments.

At this point, most Soweto parishioners realized that they did not have the power or capacity to confront the police or the sellers, but at the parish priest's urging, five people volunteered to be part of a new chang'aa committee. Although the motives of the second committee were more sincere, they lacked the commitment and capacity to implement the sub-parish's plan. The issue was not a priority; committee meetings were frequently cancelled because members were not available. Moreover, like the first committee, the parishioners were not equipped to take any concrete action; they had no training or background in group dynamics, facilitating discussions, building consensus or planning or implementing activities. They also had no budget or resources to implement activities.

For example, the plan for the committee to find qualified speakers on alcohol did not work. As it turned out, there were few people in Nairobi who had the expertise or experience to speak about alcohol and addiction. Even the OHR coordinator, who had personal contacts in this sector, was able to arrange only for two speakers to teach about addictions and alcohol-related issues during the Soweto mass. Although these talks were well received and led several alcoholic parishioners to seek medical advice and counseling, the OHR coordinator was unable to arrange for additional lessons because of those people who were qualified; many did not feel comfortable entering Kibera. Others simply did not want to volunteer their time at 7:30 a.m. on a Sunday morning. Efforts to establish an AA group also failed. The OHR invited representatives from AA to speak during a Soweto mass, but the two representatives said they did not work on Sunday mornings, when parishioners were available. They also viewed the invitation as a money-making opportunity and wanted to be paid professional rates, which the OHR could not afford.

In early 2005, there was a growing sense of frustration by the members of the OHR that the chang'aa campaign had run its course. While the new committee was making an effort, it was not able to offer feedback from the sub-parish or articulate a strategy to advance the campaign. The coordinator raised the question of whether the OHR should continue to pursue the campaign against chang'aa, given its limited resources especially in light of the on-going crisis related to forced evictions and slum upgrading that affected tens of thousands Kiberans, not to mention the seemingly insurmountable obstacles related to the campaign.

At that time, there was a new parish priest and he did not want to abandon the sub-parish priority issues until he had an opportunity to evaluate them. He therefore urged members of the OHR to help the Soweto committee undertake the social analysis that the first committee had failed to implement with the hope that it might revive the campaign. After the committee members said they would not participate in the survey because it was too dangerous, the coordinator asked two members of the OHR Team to do the analysis. They created a questionnaire and interviewed over 60 people in Soweto about chang'aa. However, by the time the data was collected, the OHR coordinator had put all advocacy issues on hold in order to prepare the parish for the constitutional referendum. When regular OHR activities were resumed, the campaign was not a priority for the new OHR coordinator, a Kenyan lawyer who took over in January 2006, and the data gathered in the social analysis remained unused.

Despite the new OHR coordinator's limited interest in the chang'aa campaign, the second chang'aa committee continued to meet periodically during 2006 to talk about chang'aa. One of the OHR Team members also continued to meet Margaret who unexpectedly closed her chang'aa businesses in late 2006. The campaign clearly had an impact on her decision. Margaret explained: "I am a good Christian and I wanted to be fully back in the church so I started a small grocery shop and my daughter started selling water. I don't make very much money but I am clean."[32] During Soweto's year-end evaluation of the campaign activities for the year 2006, parishioners in the Soweto sub-parish celebrated that Margaret had given up the chang'aa business but they faulted the OHR for focusing too much on the sellers and not enough on the drinkers. They also complained that "they had been excluded from the planning stage that was done without getting their views."

Frustrations expressed during the Soweto evaluation were not unique. A parish-wide evaluation of the priority issues undertaken in early 2006 revealed that none of the sub-parishes was able to adequately implement

---

[32] Interview with Margaret, September 30, 2008.

their activities primarily because the parish plan was put into place without corresponding strategies and structures to implement it. Each sub-parish was given a list of goals, but the plans and objectives were too general and vague, making the goals impossible to achieve. It was also not clear what the committees were set up to do, how they were to implement the activities assigned to them and who would organize or implement the activities. In addition, the committees were not given leadership or skills training. As a consequence, members of the committees, including the chang'aa committee, lacked the requisite skills to organize meetings, mobilize attendance and facilitate participatory discussions on difficult and complex issues that in many situations cultural and social taboos prevented from being discussed. The greatest omission, however, was the absence of a budget and the allocation of parish resources. As part of the parish's decentralized management style, fundraising was left to the individual initiatives of each department coordinator. As a result, the ministries with a reserve of funds were able to implement some activities while others were not. In the case of the Soweto sub-parish, funding was limited to the Trocaire money and whatever additional funds the coordinator could raise from friends and family.

Although leaders within the sub-parish expressed disappointment about the committee's inability to implement the steps outlined in the sub-parish plan, they also acknowledged that the committee had raised the level of dialogue about the issue not only within the committee, but also in private meetings in the sub-parish and SCCs, which had led more people to speak publicly about chang'aa. The fact that the Soweto parishioners started to discuss the topic was not inconsequential, given that it had been the source of conflict for years and was highly stigmatized; many parishioners had been afraid to even mention it even during the social analysis. The committee also helped parishioners in the sub-parish reduce the level of intolerance for the sellers. Parishioners were able to engage in a number of constructive discussions, express their views, listen to opposing sides and learn the truth about the situation. This was a marked improvement from previous one-sided discussions that were largely based on rumors and gossip and led to finger-pointing and hostility.

Following the 2006 evaluation, the new parish priest decided to continue with the sub-parish priority issues but said that no further activities should take place until the parishioners were given a chance to participate in the planning process. Before that plan could go into effect, the new parish priest was reassigned to Mexico. His replacement did not subscribe to the social analysis methodology and discontinued most of the activities associated with the parish plan, including the priority issues in the sub-parishes. The new priest's unilateral decision to terminate a five-year process highlights one of the parish's fundamental weaknesses; the high turn-over of parish priests made it difficult for the parish to thoroughly implement any plan or policy.

Conclusion

According to civil society advocates, civil society organizations are well placed to hold government officials to account for their corruption and abuse of power. This case study shows otherwise. Civil society in Kibera does not function in the way the advocates would have us believe. Nor is it realistic to think that it can operate in such a way. It was the parishioners who raised the problem of chang'aa and the local government's corrupt role in facilitating it. Parishioners blamed chang'aa for a wide variety of social ills and repeatedly articulated the reasons why chang'aa needed to be eliminated. The parishioners, however, were relatively powerless to do anything about it because they were not willing to confront either the PA or the sellers. Most parishioners considered the issue to be too dangerous and beyond the scope of the parish's interest.

It was only because of the intervention of an expatriate missionary that the parish got involved in the issue. But even the presence of the OHR coordinator with her international donor funds and team of lawyers could not impact the chang'aa trade in Kibera. Given an opportunity to get involved in the issue, most parishioners were either not interested or were too afraid to participate. Those few who were willing to participate lacked the necessary time and skills to contribute to the campaign beyond volunteering for basic tasks. The campaign ultimately turned into the project of the OHR which lacked the capacity to hold government functionaries to account for their corrupt actions because the people who manufactured, transported, distributed and sold chang'aa were protected by powerful officials.

The failed effort of the Soweto sub-parish to implement the chang'aa campaign is further evidence that ordinary people in Kibera lacked the requisite capacity and skills to hold local officials to account. Most parishioners in Soweto, again, did not care to get involved. The ones who did either were motivated by personal vendettas or were too afraid to do more than talk privately among themselves and to the sellers in the parish. Moreover, the parish lacked the ability to empower parishioners to address socio-political issues. Notwithstanding the good intentions to facilitate a sub-parish response, the parish lacked the capacity and resources to provide parishioners with the tools to respond to the issue. It was not feasible to think parishioners could address a complex problem such as chang'aa without skills training, financial resources, a realistic plan and a functioning organizational structure, none of which was present in the parish.

CHAPTER FIVE

SLUM UPGRADING

In January 2003 the Kenyan government and UN-Habitat announced their decision to implement a joint slum upgrading project in the village of Soweto in Kibera. From the start of the project, the area MP and the local city councilor tried to co-opt the project to benefit their ethnic community. The government and UN-Habitat added to the problem by failing to inform the affected community adequately about the details of the upgrade or including them in the project. In this chapter, I examine the OHR's response to the broad spectrum of corruption, malfeasance and abuse of power that emerged during three periods of the project: (1) immediately following the announced upgrade; (2) subsequent to the election of community representatives and (3) after the councilor's co-option of the project. I also include an analysis of the efforts made by other civil society actors, namely, other churches and housing NGOs working in Soweto.

I argue that the civil society advocates' expectations for civil society are far greater than its capacity. The residents of Soweto were not equipped to hold the government, UN-Habitat or the politicians to account for their failure to implement a fair and corrupt-free upgrade because they were divided along ethnic and political lines. In addition, the affected community lacked the basic resources, leadership, organized community groups and political access necessary to lobby the project implementers. The Soweto churches and housing NGOs also were not able to hold the government, UN-Habitat or the politicians to account. Neither group had the sufficient expertise, collaborative networks or political access to curb the corrupt interference by local politicians or persuade the government or UN-Habitat to improve the channels of communication or levels of participation in the project. The only actors who were able to influence the project were international diplomats, particularly the Vatican's Apostolic Nuncio to Kenya, who intervened periodically at the request of the parish priest and OHR coordinator.

The Government's Plan to Upgrade Soweto Village

In November 2000, just months after being appointed the new executive director of UN-Habitat, Mrs. Anna Tibaijuka offered to spearhead a slum upgrading program in Kenya as a gesture of good will to President Moi for hosting the headquarters of UN-Habitat in Nairobi. Officials at UN-Habitat created a committee that short-listed and ranked nine slum settlements for the upgrade; the top-ranked slum was Huruma, a small settlement of 6,500 where Pamoja Trust had already started an upgrading project.[1] The next ranked slum was the village of Soweto located in Kibera, home to approximately 60,000 people. Even though Soweto was ranked lower, President Moi insisted that the upgrade take place there. In Kibera, it was widely believed that the upgrade was a political reward for Raila Odinga, the area MP and recent defector to the KANU party, who had promised Moi political support from his large Luo voting bloc in the upcoming 2002 election.

Many Kiberans felt that Raila's interest in Soweto was twofold: money and politics. Located along the railway line in the northeastern corner of Kibera with access to several middle-class neighborhoods, Soweto was home to the largest and most lucrative commercial area of the slum. The owners of the small retail shops and markets were almost exclusively Kikuyu. The Luo community had historically been denied access to Kibera's commercial hub; in 2003, less than 6% of the Soweto population was Luo.[2] During the months prior to the 2002 election, numerous parishioners reported to the OHR that during Raila's meetings with his Luo supporters, he repeatedly promised that Kibera would one day belong to them including its businesses and marketplaces. The upgrade provided an ideal vehicle to start this process since it would require the removal of the current population while structures were demolished and new ones built, which would give Raila an opportunity to move his constituents into the area. The removal of the Kikuyu population would also consolidate Raila's power in Kibera because it would eliminate a large percentage of his political opposition; the Kikuyu in Soweto had historically opposed Raila's agenda and consistently put forward rival candidates during election periods.

---

[1] For details, see Jane Weru, "Community Federations and City Upgrading: the Work of Pamoja Trust and Muungano in Kenya," *Environment & Urbanization* 16, no. 1 (2004): 47-61.

[2] Marie-Ange Goux, "Consultancy on the Habitat Project: Sustainable Neighbourhood Program Kenya Pilot Project: Preliminary Studies," (Report, Nairobi, 2003), 6.

Despite UN-Habitat's good intentions to improve the village of Soweto, the officials charged with coordinating the upgrade project were not prepared for the political machinations of the Kenyan government. The project stalled for almost two years as Moi tried unsuccessfully to control the international funds and procurement process.[3] After Mwai Kibaki was elected president in 2002, UN-Habitat officials renewed their push for a slum upgrading project. Concerned that the ethnic polarization and instability caused by the 2001 clashes would hamper the project if it took place in Kibera, they encouraged President Kibaki to choose a different slum such as Huruma. The new president, however, was adamant that the project go forward in Kibera. After the election, Kibaki had appointed Raila as Minister of Roads, Public Works and Housing, the government ministry responsible for the upgrading project.

On January 15, 2003, Raila Odinga and Anna Tibaijuka signed a memorandum of understanding that created the Kenya Slum Upgrading Program (KENSUP) to implement the Soweto upgrade. Placed under the Department of Housing, KENSUP's organizational structure included the Joint Project Planning Team that had representatives from UN-Habitat, the NCC, the National Housing Corporation (NHC) and a local NGO, Shelter Forum, to help implement the project. The project also anticipated the creation of two additional groups to enhance participatory decision making: the Settlement Executive Committee (SEC) to represent the community and the Multi-Stakeholder Support Group to include key consultants from the community, government, NGOs, donors and development agencies and private organizations.

UN-Habitat's press release stated the project would "improve housing, infrastructure services and the overall livelihoods of people," but it did not offer any details about the upgrade or address the most critical issues to the residents such as land ownership, compensation for lost structures, possible displacement and higher rents.[4] Residents were also not clear about which parts of Kibera would be upgraded; most believed the rumors that it was the whole settlement, not just Soweto. Taking advantage of the confusion, local politicians spread false information about the upgrade to gain political favor with their voting constituencies. Within days of the announced upgrade, numerous parishioners reported to the OHR that Raila had held the first of many rallies in Kibera for his Luo constituency whom

---

[3] Kristina Flodman Becker, "Follow-up Mission on Program Management Collaborative Nairobi Slum-upgrading Program," (Report prepared for SIDA, Nairobi, 2002), 3.

[4] UN-Habitat, "Government of Kenya," UN-Habitat Press Release, Nairobi, January 16, 2003.

he promised would be given priority in the distribution of new houses in Soweto. According to one team member who lived in Lindi:

> Starting in January, every weekend Raila held rallies in the village of Gatwikira and said that if the tenants supported him, they would be the first ones to get a house in Soweto and he told them the houses would be free. Raila promised all the Luo, not just those in Soweto, that they would get a house.[5]

Even though the promise of a free house seemed incredible to many observers, most Luo tenants believed Raila. Poor, uneducated and lacking any official information to the contrary, many tenants were easily manipulated by the misinformation propagated by their political patron. In the words of one Team member, "The truth didn't matter because the tenants worshiped Raila like a god and believed everything he said."[6] From the tenants' perspective, Raila finally had the power to deliver on his promises; he was the cabinet minister in charge of the project and there was a high expectation that he would use his position to compensate his constituents for their votes and support in the 2002 election.

The elected councilor for the city council ward that included Soweto helped Raila spread his promise to the tenants at the grass-roots level. Before the upgrade was announced, the councilor was considered a low-level operative in Raila's political retinue because the area he administered had a very small Luo population. His status changed when Soweto was chosen for the upgrade; the councilor became the MP's primary man in Kibera to ensure the upgrade benefited his ethnic community. With his new status, he became one of Raila's top "lieutenants" and was given unfettered access to the NDP youth wingers.

The councilor embraced Raila's message not only because he was a Luo politician and owed his election to Raila's patronage, but also because he knew that a larger Luo population in Soweto would secure his political future as the area councilor. The councilor, however, went even further than Raila with his promises to the tenants. Accompanied by large groups of youth wingers, he moved around Kibera telling tenants that since the upgrade was designed to benefit tenants, they no longer had to pay house rent.[7] The councilor's statements spread alarm and fear throughout the community because it was comments of this precise nature that precipitated the deadly clashes in December 2001. The subsequent refusal

---

[5] Interview with OHR team member C, October 3, 2008.
[6] Ibid.
[7] Ibid.

of many tenants to pay rent further divided the structure owners and tenants and added to the growing agitation and conflict. Even though the councilor's statements were viewed by most as dangerous and provocative, he acted with immunity because he was an important client and friend of not only Raila, but also the Director of Housing.

Immediately upon learning about the planned upgrade, the structure owners who lived in Soweto objected to the upgrade on several levels, not the least of which was Raila's attempt to commandeer the project for the exclusive benefit of the tenants. They were also angry that the upgrade would require the demolition of their homes, businesses and rentals. Unlike the other villages in Kibera, Soweto had a high number of small-scale, residential structure owners; they numbered approximately 30% compared to 5% in most villages[8] and they had the most to lose in the upgrade. One parishioner explained: "My only source of income is from the few structures that I rent. The upgrade will cause me to lose my tenants and my income. My houses will belong to someone else after the upgrade and I will have no other means to survive."[9] Another explained, "Our customers are here in this area. We will lose everything when they shift us. Where will the business people go to sell their wares after we are moved?"[10] They were also afraid that they would be displaced by the upgrade because they could not afford higher rents on the new houses. Residents' anxieties were based on their first-hand experience with the neighboring Nyayo Highrise upgrade. During the mid-1990s, the NHC initiated a housing project intended to benefit Kibera residents, but because the new rents were not affordable, the score of four and five-story stone buildings built on land that had been part of Kibera were now occupied by middle-class groups.[11] Many parishioners in Soweto were afraid of a similar outcome with the KENSUP program; not only would they be denied a new house, the loss of their current homes and businesses would also leave them worse off than before the upgrade.

During January 2003, many parishioners visited the OHR to verbalize their concerns about how the government's handling of the upgrade had divided them and was threatening to further destabilize an already fragile community. The parishioners, however, were not equipped to mobilize a community-wide response to protest the way the project was being mishandled or pressure the government to rectify the situation. Even

---

[8] Goux, "Consultancy on the Habitat," 9.

[9] OHR Memorandum, June 6, 2004.

[10] Ibid.

[11] Rob Neuwirth, *Shadow Cities: A Billion Squatters, a New Urban World* (New York: Routledge, 2005), 248-49.

before the residents knew how the project would benefit them, most Kiberans had mobilized for or against it based on their identity as a structure owner or tenant, a division with strong ethnic and political overtones. Within the parish and beyond, there were no organized groups or indigenous leaders who transcended these ethnic divisions or were capable of organizing the community to promote their common interests, namely, improving the living conditions in Soweto for all residents who lived there.

Fears by the structure owners that the upgrade would lead to their permanent displacement escalated in February 2003 when Raila unexpectedly announced that the residents of Soweto would be taken to Athi River, a small industrial town located 35 kilometers outside Nairobi.[12] Land in Athi River had been purchased by the Finnish government and given to the Kenyan government as part of a debt swap program.[13] According to Raila's announcement, the current residents of Soweto would be moved to Athi River during the upgrade where they would live in a housing project built by the Finnish government and then returned to their new homes in Soweto when the project was completed.

Raila's announcement sent shockwaves of fear and anxiety among the structure owners and confirmed suspicions among many Kikuyu that the upgrade was a political maneuver to permanently remove them from Kibera. Athi River was a financially depressed town where job opportunities were scarce. Structure owners complained that if they were forced to move far away to a place with very few customers, it would be nearly impossible to raise sufficient funds to finance their move back to Kibera. Even if they were able to return, their houses and businesses would already be occupied by Luo tenants brought by Raila.

As the situation worsened, a number of structure owners formed groups to try to stop the upgrade. These groups, however, were not able to substantially influence the project because they were too disorganized. Most groups were formed according to their particular home regions or locations within Soweto and operated independently. Many of the leaders were self-selected; they not only lacked popular support, but also financial resources. They also had little ability to influence the decision-makers in the project because they did not have access to KENSUP officials who were under Raila's ministry and they could not meet officials at UN-Habitat without an official invitation.

---

[12] Jeff Otieno, "Project on Slums Set to Begin," *Daily Nation*, Nairobi, May 6, 2003.

[13] "Finland Gives 750,000 Euros for Kenyan Slum Upgrading," UN-Habitat news release, Nairobi, May 8, 2003.

Moreover and perhaps most importantly, the number of structure owners who joined these groups was small; the active members were less than several hundred people. Most structure owners were afraid of retaliation by the Luo politicians and their NDP youth wingers who were promoting the project. Raila was no longer just the area MP; he was now the powerful cabinet minister in charge of the project and had the full support of the government. Many felt it futile to confront his agenda. In addition, some believed President Kibaki, a Kikuyu, would protect their property rights and investments when it came time to address that issue. Others were resigned to the government's plan; they thought they had no right to object because they did not legally occupy the land.

Lacking the capacity to organize a Soweto-wide response or lobby the project implementers, some of structure owner groups resorted to self-help and litigation. For example, a number of long-term structure owners in Soweto took secret oaths similar to those taken during the Mau Mau Emergency, pledging to fight to their death before they gave up their land. A group of younger structure owners organized the Kibera Landlords Multi-Purpose Cooperative Society, collected 1,000 Ksh from each of its members and retained a lawyer to file a case challenging the move to Athi River; a strategy that structure owners in Korogocho had used to stop a planned upgrade in 2000.[14]

In the aftermath of Raila's announcement about Athi River, the simmering conflicts between the tenants and structure owners started to boil over. According to one community organizer:

> There was a high level of tension on the ground and the situation got hotter every day. The structure owners said they would die before they left Kibera and the tenants were trying to arm themselves. There were alliances formed between the Luo and Kisii against the Nubians and Kikuyu creating a high possibility for clashes.[15]

Holding meetings of any nature in Kibera became difficult because most gatherings were commandeered by NDP youth wingers convinced that the meetings were being called by structure owners to strategize how to stop the upgrade. In addition, low-level violence became commonplace as agents of structure owners tried to use force to collect rents being withheld

---

[14] In August 2000 several hundred structure owners attained a court order that permanently stopped the mapping and enumeration process being undertaken by Pamoja Trust as the first step in a community-based housing upgrade.

[15] OHR Memorandum, March 12, 2003.

by tenants. Many Kiberans felt even the smallest of provocations could ignite a full-scale conflict.

Reaction of the Faith-Based Organizations

In the wake of the growing instability, numerous pastors from Pentecostal and AIC churches as well as the Anglican parish regularly visited the OHR to express their concern that the upgrade threatened to provoke further ethnic clashes. Despite their individual concerns, the religious leaders did not make a united objection to the way the project was being handled by the government and politicians. They not only lacked a collaborative network, they also did not have sufficient resources and capacity to advocate on behalf of the community.

The Christian churches and Muslims, many of who were Nubians, had been divided for decades by conflict about the land and rent issues. Moreover, notwithstanding their large numbers, the Christian churches in Kibera rarely met as a unified group. Apart from the Pentecostal churches that occasionally met for prayer fellowships, the churches typically joined together only during times of immediate crisis such as a large fire. The churches' inability to build a united faction was related to several dynamics. Some pastors did not believe that Christians who were saved should mix with Christians who were not saved. Others felt that churches that did not read the Bible literally or allowed for prayer in the form of public testimony were not authentically Christian. In addition, there were significant differences in how the churches viewed their public role. Unlike the mainline Protestant and Catholic churches, which had a history of engaging in social justice and human rights issues at a national level, the Pentecostal and the AIC churches did not believe it was their role to speak out on political or social issues. Moreover, the vast differences between the churches in terms of financial resources and expertise made it difficult to enter into equal partnerships. This was particularly true for the Catholic Church that was much better resourced than the other churches; the parish possessed a title deed for its main compound, had built permanent structures, and had access to the power grid and a full-time expatriate missionary staff. The financial disparity caused some smaller churches to feel inferior, jealous and distrustful of the Catholic Church.

The only time the churches came together to discuss the upgrade during this period was in September 2003 when the Pentecostal pastors, concerned about escalating violence and the increasing number of skirmishes, called a meeting of 40 local pastors and members of the OHR to discuss the upgrade.[16] It was the first time this group of pastors had invited Catholics to join their forum. During that meeting, the pastors complained that they had no information about the upgrade and many feared that they would lose their churches. After explaining that the parish had no role in the upgrade, the pastors agreed to the OHR's proposal that they invite the community organizer employed by Pamoja Trust who managed the Huruma upgrade, to explain generally the slum upgrading process and what might occur. During the follow-up meeting, the pastors learned about past slum upgrading experiences in Nairobi and also that the city's Department of Physical Planning had been calling meetings with NGOs working in Kibera to discuss the government's plans for the community and no churches had been invited. Surprised at their exclusion, the pastors wrote a letter to the NCC requesting information about the government's plans for Kibera. The pastors also agreed that they needed to visit Huruma to learn more about the upgrading process.

Despite their initial enthusiasm to get more involved in the upgrade, the pastors did not have the capacity or resources to pursue the upgrade. They did not understand the complexity of the upgrade and they lacked personal relationships with or access to decision-makers within the government, UN-Habitat and the NGO sector as well as basic resources such as electricity, computers and printers necessary to document and transmit information. At the pastors' request, the OHR prepared the pastors' letter to the NCC, which was circulated for signatures and mailed. When the pastors did not receive a response, their interest waned and they never followed up on the issue. None of the pastors pursued the plan to visit Huruma or held another meeting to discuss the upgrade. Many of the pastors' churches were not located in Soweto and when it became clear that their churches were not threatened by the upgrade, they were no longer interested. In addition, most pastors did not have prior experience raising objections to the government and they did not want to start with the upgrade. A number of pastors had been given plots for their churches and schools through patronage with the PA and did not want to jeopardize these relationships by complaining about a government-sponsored project.

Response of the Housing NGOs

The churches were not alone in their inability to elicit further information about the government's planned upgrade; most housing NGOs active in Kibera were equally frustrated in their attempts. At the time the

[16] OHR Memorandum, September 19, 2004.

upgrade was announced, the community looked to the five NGOs working on land and housing issues-Maji na Ufanisi, ANPPCAN, Pamoja Trust, KCS and Shelter Forum-to provide independent and accurate information about the upgrade, but none were willing or able to share that information. Shelter Forum, the NGO appointed by KENSUP to represent civil society in the project, regularly attended upgrading meetings with KENSUP, but it did not share information with the other NGOs. According to one NGO worker, Shelter Forum was in a "sibling rivalry" with other NGOs and "wanted to get a chance to do something with the upgrade and at the same time not let others get that chance."[17] The other NGOs could not access information; individuals at Pamoja Trust and ANPPCAN tried to solicit a response from UN-Habitat, but lacked sufficient clout to gain access to Habitat officials.

Although the NGOs did not operate in a uniform manner, they shared certain commonalities in their approach to Kibera residents that had a negative impact on their ability to respond to the upgrade issue. Their greatest weakness was that they did not have a working relationship with the affected community. There were several key reasons to explain the disconnection between the NGOs and Sowetans. First, apart from Maji na Ufanisi and ANPPCAN, none of the housing NGOs had a consistent physical presence in Soweto or the other Kibera villages. There was a common perception among many NGOs that Kibera was a hostile and dangerous territory for civil society. According to a KCS lawyer:

> Because of Raila, Kibera was the most politicized slum in Nairobi so we played it safe and didn't go in there before the upgrade started. We knew that the community was fractionalized so it was easier for the NGOs to provide visible services like toilets and drains, but the NGOs were afraid to address the social and political issues.[18]

A community organizer from Pamoja Trust explained:

> Kibera became a very visible and high-profile slum after the upgrade. We went there, but we had little direct contact with the community. Our approach was very project-based. We didn't have enough time to understand the settlement so we spent our time trying to push our agenda of starting savings groups.[19]

---

[17] Interview with housing NGO community organizer D, October 2, 2008.
[18] Interview with human rights lawyer B, September 28, 2008.
[19] Interview with housing NGO community organizer B, September 29, 2008.

Second, some of the NGOs were viewed by the residents as having a strong ethnic and/or political bias that undermined their ability to build trust and respect. For example, Pamoja Trust was viewed by most residents as a Kikuyu NGO with a preference for promoting the interests of structure owners. ANPPCAN, in contrast, was seen as having a strong bias in favor of the tenants. In addition, several of the NGOs were viewed as closely allied with the NARC government and therefore unable to criticize the government publicly.

Third, many residents resented the NGOs because they used a top-down approach that excluded the residents from the decision-making process. According to one Team member:

> After the upgrade, the NGOs came into Kibera but they did not involve the community or even try to meet the people first and make friendships. Because they didn't have any contacts, they couldn't mobilize people to attend meetings unless they paid people. They didn't do any analysis or allow us to choose our leaders. We didn't know their agenda and we didn't trust them.[20]

A community organizer explained the dynamic from the NGO perspective:

> When we entered into Kibera, we did not have enough time to convince people that they needed to participate in the upgrade and that it was their affair. We had no choice, we had to use money to entice them to come to meetings and get organized.[21]

Finally, since most of the housing NGOs had shown little attention to Soweto prior to the upgrade, many residents naturally assumed the NGOs primary interest in the upgrade was to pursue business opportunities, not represent their interests.

In addition to their disconnection from the community, the housing NGOs had limited collaborative networks with the churches in Soweto. The low-level staff of several NGOs who were physically present in the community worked closely with the OHR, but a number of NGO directors did not want to engage the OHR after the missionaries left the Land Caucus. The NGOs also did not have relationships with the pastors in the Pentecostal and AIC churches because they typically viewed these churches as small, ethnically biased and uninformed about complicated housing issues.

---

[20] Interview with OHR team member B, September 20, 2008.

[21] Interview with housing NGO community organizer C, September 26, 2008.

Unaware of the complex ethnic and political dynamic, some of the NGOs actually added to the level of confusion and agitation. As an example, in February 2003, a KCS lawyer held a community meeting to discuss the government's recently proposed housing policy. Because he was naively unaware of the level of anger and fear surrounding the upgrade and the fact that there was a rumor that Raila was going to attend, he was not prepared for the angry mob of 400 structure owners, who turned up demanding that title deeds be given to them as part of the upgrade project. The lawyer quickly lost control of the meeting. In a similar incident, personnel from Shelter Forum organized a meeting of 200 youth to discuss the upgrade at a church located in Line Saba. In the middle of the meeting, a number of NDP youth wingers stormed the church wielding whips and beating people declaring it illegal because the area MP and councilor had not been invited. No one was injured during the incidents, but news of the disturbance spread quickly throughout Kibera as did warnings for residents to avoid any upgrade meetings.

Alarmed at the growing insecurity in the community, in mid-March the OHR invited the community organizers working at Maji na Ufanisi, KCS, ANPPCAN, Shelter Forum and Pamoja Trust to a meeting to discuss how to proceed on the upgrade issue without provoking further conflict. During that meeting, the community organizers were in agreement that the NGOs were adding to the level of agitation because they were not working together despite the fact that they all claimed to assist the same affected community. According to a senior community organizer:

> We did not know what each other had been doing and it caused chaos and a high level of tension on the ground. KCS called a meeting on housing and none of us knew about it or what was even going on in that meeting. This could have been very dangerous and we all knew it. Clashes could have started with only a little provocation.[22]

Instead of creating a partnership and organizing a global community organizing strategy, the NGOs worked individually and in isolation from one another, sometimes even in direct opposition. For example, Maji na Ufanisi was meeting its CBO members and Pamoja Trust was meeting its savings groups but there were no coordinated efforts to bring these groups together. Some NGOs, such as ANPPCAN, formed new groups of tenants, but without any clear purpose or mandate. By individually disseminating their own perception about the upgrade, the NGOs not only duplicated efforts, they also further confused the community about the project's scope

[22] Interview with housing NGO community organizer D, October 2, 2008.

and implications and, in process, lost significant credibility in the eyes of many residents.

Even though the community organizers working at the grass-roots level acknowledged the NGOs' shortcomings and expressed their concerns to their bosses, the directors of the NGOs did not change their approach. A number of NGO staff active in the NGO Coalition, who met regularly to strategize about the eviction threat, proposed presenting a joint-position paper to KENSUP on how to better communicate with the community and involve them in the upgrade, but it was never prepared.[23] The NGOs were reluctant to share information or collaborate because many, low on funds, were in competition for donor funds and government contracts related to the upgrade. The competitive nature of NGOs created an environment of secrecy and suspicion among the NGOs and the community groups with whom they worked.

Advocacy by the OHR

Even though it was clear that the area MP and local councilor were deliberately exploiting the upgrade in a way that threatened violence and conflict, most parishioners demonstrated little interest in or ability to hold the politicians, the government or UN-Habitat to account for how the project was implemented. The passivity of the parishioners was related to two factors. First, parishioners were no different from the other residents of Kibera; they were deeply divided along ethnic and political lines. The majority of parishioners were tenants who viewed the issue of upgrading as a problem exclusive to the Kikuyu structure owners in Soweto. Not only did the tenants have little sympathy for the structure owners whom they viewed as wealthy and exploitive, they also did not want to oppose the agenda of their political leader who was vociferous in his support of the project and had promised to reward the tenants with free houses.

Second, the parish lacked any mechanism for parishioners to advocate for or against the upgrade. For example, many of the Kikuyu parishioners who were directly affected by the upgrade frequently visited the OHR to voice their frustration over the level of political interference in the upgrade, but they were not interested in organizing as SCCs or as a sub-parish to address the issue. In their experience, the SCCs were meant for religious activities, not pursuing socio-political problems. When it came to confronting the government, they preferred to use other channels. For example, many Catholic structure owners joined the Kibera Landlords

[23] NGO Coalition Minutes, April 7 and May 18, 2004.

Multi-Purpose Cooperative Society. The only function the SCCs played was to pass information back and forth to the OHR and parish priest. The sub-parishes were no different. The elected leaders took the same approach as the SCCs and chose not to get involved in any socio-political issues beyond what was expressly planned for by the parish priest. Although the parish priest preached about the upgrade and periodically advised the OHR on how to proceed, he was busy with other parish activities and did not identify it as a priority for the parish leaders. Similarly, the PPC did not get involved in the upgrade. Plagued by poor leadership, the PPC leaders did not speak out or act on any significant issues. In addition, the leadership within the PPC was dominated by Luo who supported the position of the MP and councilor and did not want the parish to block their efforts.

Despite the inaction by the parishioners, the OHR felt the office could not remain silent on the upgrade issue because the potential for violence was very high. In the aftermath of the announced upgrade, the coordinator, along with most Kiberans, was afraid that the upgrade project would rekindle the still simmering conflict between the Nubian and Luo communities over the rent issue. There was a widespread belief that the upgrade project would force the government to resolve the issue of land ownership and many feared that such a decision would ignite a conflict that could easily escalate to uncontrollable levels. The coordinator's fear that the upgrade would provoke violence was further heightened by her experience of the Mathare 4A slum upgrade, a well-known project that had been plagued with violence and conflict for over a decade. Upon hearing of the Soweto upgrade, many Kiberans naturally assumed structure owners would forcibly oppose the project like they had in Mathare 4A.

Given the strong influence of the Mathare 4A upgrade on Kibera, a brief description of the project is helpful. In the early 1990s, a Catholic missionary priest from Germany organized an upgrading project to build new houses and infrastructure in Mathare 4A, one of Nairobi's oldest slums that housed approximately 22,000 people. In order to prevent the land from being converted into personal use, the government transferred it to the Catholic Archdiocese of Nairobi to hold in trust for the residents.[24] Donor funding was channeled through the Archdiocese to set up the Amani Housing Trust to administer the project. From its inception, the project was marred by community opposition and violence. Absentee structure owners argued that the land should have been sold to them and

---

[24] Kefa Otiso, "State, Voluntary and Private Sector Partnerships for Slum Upgrading and Basic Service Delivery in Nairobi, Kenya," *Cities* 20, no. 4 (2003): 226.

used their political connections to periodically derail the project. The resident structure owners opposed the project because it turned them into life-time tenants of the Catholic Church and deprived them of their rental incomes. The tenants consistently lobbied for rent reductions with some refusing to pay any rent on the grounds that donors should provide them with free housing. Moreover, the only avenue for community participation was an inactive consultative board that had two resident representatives. Denied an adequate forum to voice their concerns, residents frequently resorted to public protest and demonstrations, some of which were violent.[25]

Tensions among the different groups in Mathare 4A eventually erupted into violence in July 1998 when hundreds of resident structure owners refused to hand over their houses to the project on the grounds that the compensation paid by the Trust was too low. Frustrated with their refusal to participate, the Trust hired a group of youth to remove the doors and roofs of the structure owners' houses as a means to compel compliance. The structure owners responded with violent opposition. In the wake of spiraling bloodshed, several hundred structure owners asked the KCS lawyers to sue the Archdiocese to suspend the project.[26] When the court dismissed the case on procedural grounds, more than 50 women living in Mathare 4A started a highly publicized hunger strike at the Catholic Basilica to protest the Archdiocese's role in the project. Following the arrest of the elderly protesters, several missionary priests and KCS lawyers active on the Land Caucus intervened and convinced the Archbishop to meet community leaders to devise a non-violent way to proceed with the project. However, the damage done to the image of the Archdiocese was significant. The incident left many slum dwellers with a dim view of upgrading and engendered negative feelings toward the Catholic Church throughout the slums.

In addition to their anxiety about escalating violence and the specter of full-scale conflict, the OHR team felt that KENSUP's failure to inform and include the affected community in the slum upgrade was a violation of international human rights law.[27] How to respond to the situation, however, posed a dilemma. Unlike most churches and groups whose

---

[25] For example, angry residents burned down the priest's office and kindergarten and eventually chased the parish priest from his home in the parish.
[26] Joseph Murithi, and Stella Nzoi, "Mathare 4A: The True Story," *Mwananchi* 274 (April 1999):1-2.
[27] See Malcolm Langford, Leslie Quitzow, and Virginia Roaf, *Human Rights and Slum-Upgrading: General Introduction and Compilation of Case Studies* (Geneva: COHRE, 2005), 9.

memberships were typically made up of one or two ethnically-related communities, the Catholic Church had members from every ethnic group. If the OHR gave vocal support for the project, it would alienate Kikuyu parishioners, while the failure to support the project would be viewed as counter to the interests of the Luo tenants. In light of the conflicting interests, the OHR coordinator consulted the pastoral team.

Although the upgrade generated a great deal of discussion and concern within the pastoral team, it was not a priority issue in light of other more immediate concerns facing the parish. The members of the pastoral team, including the parish priest, were focused on the core functions of the parish particularly the on-going spiritual formation of Catholics. The parish priest was also overseeing the construction of several buildings including a secondary school, two sub-parish chapels and a community library. The other ministry coordinators were administering their regular programs and they were particularly busy because the number of AIDS-related deaths spiked in 2003. Retroviral drugs for HIV and AIDS were not yet available in Kibera and the number of parishioners who required hospice care, the sacrament of the sick and funerals rose dramatically.

Even though it was not a top priority, the members of the pastoral team felt the OHR should address the issue because of the potential for violence. The parish priest and OHR coordinator agreed that the key priorities for the OHR were: (1) educating parishioners on slum upgrading generally and (2) gathering information about the proposed project in order to better inform the community. The decision for the OHR to get involved in the upgrade was driven almost exclusively by two expatriate missionaries, not the parishioners. Given that the OHR coordinator was operating with little support from the pastoral team and limited personal capacity, her ability to influence the process was curtailed from the outset.

The OHR's plan to educate parishioners about the upgrade started with the Saturday group whose curriculum committee identified the upgrade as an issue they wanted to learn more about. Since the only experience the OHR coordinator and the civic education lawyers had with upgrading was the Mathare 4A case, the coordinator invited a community organizer from Pamoja Trust to facilitate several classes. In addition to learning about the technical components of an upgrade, members of the Saturday group debated controversial issues related to land ownership, rent and power relations between the structure owners and tenants. Although the Saturday group felt free to speak openly about the difficult issues, the group did not take any steps to unify the two groups or promote greater participation in the upgrade process at a grass-roots level. As previously discussed in chapter three, the group's inaction was due to their fear of retaliation by the politicians and youth wingers and restrictive church protocols. Upgrading was considered a sensitive political issue because of Raila's involvement and because it related to land and housing. SCC members therefore felt they were not free to discuss it in the SCCs.

The members of the OHR also informed parishioners about the upgrade through civic education classes in the SCCs, regular announcements at mass and word-of-mouth. The parish priest frequently preached about the upgrade in his Sunday homilies and asked the parish to pray for peace in the upgrade. The OHR Team targeted the Soweto sub-parish providing regular inputs during the weekly Sunday masses and the OHR also organized a number of dramas performed by the youth during mass that explained particular issues arising such as the tension between structure owners and tenants and the councilor's unlawful role in the upgrade.

The impact of the OHR's education efforts was mixed. On one hand, as a result of the awareness-raising exercises, general information about upgrading started to spread throughout the community. Although the Saturday classes were attended by 35 parishioners, their impact was felt beyond the classes. Several parishioners who participated in the discussions later became important players in formulating opinions in Soweto about the upgrade; key among them was a structure owner in Soweto who was elected as one of two official representatives for structure owners. In addition, a parishioner who was active in the Muungano and helped formulate that group's position also was in the Saturday group.

On the other hand, because the OHR members had access to very few details apart from what was published in the daily newspapers, they were not able to educate parishioners about the specifics of the project. Moreover, once the initial clamor about the upgrade passed, many parishioners lost interest. After the OHR Team taught the basic classes on upgrading, only SCCs in Soweto asked for continued inputs. The lack of interest and solidarity with Soweto demonstrated a common phenomenon in the parish. The sub-parishes were not unified; they often operated independently and in relative isolation, paying little attention to the issues and problems of another sub-parish particularly when the issue carried ethnic overtones such as the upgrade.

As parishioners in the Saturday group learned more about upgrading, they quickly realized the need to gather additional information about the proposed upgrade, not only to learn what the government intended to do in Soweto, but also to dispel the rumors and political propaganda that threatened to provoke further clashes. Gaining access to additional information about the upgrade proved to be difficult. In April 2003 members of the Saturday group, lacking their own resources, asked the OHR coordinator to contact the project implementers and request that they provide the parish with further information on their plans for the upgrade. Since neither the OHR coordinator nor the parish priest had personal contacts with the project implementers, the coordinator sent letters to the officials. Apart from a brief letter from the Director of Housing promising the full participation of all stakeholders, the OHR received no response. During the next several months, as tensions continued to rise, the OHR coordinator sent several follow-up letters to KENSUP and UN-Habitat officials to inform them of the growing level of confusion and conflict. Neither KENSUP nor UN-Habitat responded.

In May 2003, UN-Habitat invited local civil society actors to attend a series of meetings addressing urban shelter strategies for the poor organized in conjunction with the 19th Session of the Governing Council of UN-Habitat. Three members of the Saturday group volunteered to attend the week-long meeting in the hope that information about the upgrade would be disclosed. During the meetings, the parishioners introduced themselves to several Habitat officials who expressed their surprise to see slum dwellers attending and stressed their desire to work with the grass roots. The parishioners told the officials they did not have enough information about the upgrade and invited them to visit the parish to learn how the lack of information was negatively impacting the community.

In a follow-up civic education meeting, the three parishioners reported on what they had learned in the workshop, including Mrs. Tibaijuka's statement that the Soweto upgrade was going to be an example for all Africa because it would empower civil society including NGOs, CBOs and the community to participate fully in the project.[28] One of the parishioners also reported that the official directly responsible for Soweto was born in his rural village and was known to his family. At the group's urging, he contacted the Habitat official who agreed to meet the parishioners and OHR Team. Although he listened to the parishioners' explanation of how political statements favoring one ethnic group had raised the level of anxiety and potential for violence, the tenor of the meeting was awkward and defensive. The Habitat official insisted that the community was fully apprised of the project and any miscommunications were due to false reports published by the media.[29] He was also not willing to share any details or plans for the project and promised that more

[28] OHR Memorandum, May 10, 2003.
[29] OHR Memorandum, June 17, 2003.

information would be forthcoming. When no additional information was provided, members of the Saturday group asked the OHR coordinator to send follow-up letters and e-mails to Habitat officials in June, July and August 2003, but no one from UN-Habitat replied.

Although members of the Saturday group showed initiative by seeking out more information on the upgrade at its start, as time went on, that initiative dwindled. According to one Team member:

> People constantly came to ask for information and to push the OHR to get more information, but they were not doing the same for themselves because they did not think they would succeed since even the lawyer couldn't get an answer.[30]

When none of the KENSUP or Habitat officials responded to the OHR's request for information, the group stopped inquiring.

Following several months of failed attempts to gather more information, the OHR coordinator and the parish priest asked the Archdiocese for assistance in responding to the escalating tension. During the April 2003 Kutoka meeting, which was attended by Archbishop Ndingi, the parish priest informed the Archbishop about the growing level of agitation and explained how ethnic politics and false promises had divided and antagonized the community.[31] The Archbishop asked the parish to document its concerns and submit them to him in writing so he could follow up with the proper government officials. The Archbishop, however, did not respond to the memorandum prepared by the OHR.

Despite the Archbishop's personal avoidance of the issue, it appeared that the development office's peace-building project for Kibera might support the OHR's efforts to promote a peaceful and inclusive upgrade. At the same time as the upgrade was announced, the director of the Archdiocese's development office, informed the parish that the Archdiocese had entered into a project funded by a Catholic donor in the United States, Catholic Relief Services (CRS), to implement a peace-building project in the parish as well as the parish located in Kariobangi that included Korogocho slum. The two parishes had been chosen by the Archdiocese because of their prior history with violent clashes. The parish priest's and the coordinator's optimism that the peace-building project quickly waned as the details of the program unfolded.

To the surprise of the missionaries in both parishes, the project was designed by the donor and was based on the NGO project model that

[30] Interview with OHR Team member A, September 22, 2008.

[31] Kutoka Minutes, April 10, 2003.

called for three years of surveys and workshops. It also planned that the parish-based JPCs would be the primary implementers of the project. During several follow-up meetings with the development office, the missionaries voiced their objection to the plan. In their view, the parishes were markedly different from the NGOs. The parishes were committed to the long-term transformation of the people and their environment, not short-term, result-orientated projects promoted by NGOs and their donors. The missionaries wanted to promote a more holistic approach to peace-building that was rooted in the parishioners' spirituality as well as their daily life, not hold one-day workshops where select people were chosen to travel to outside venues and listen to theoretical inputs on peace. Activities of this sort had been tried in the past by NGOs and had done little to reduce violence.

The missionaries also objected to using the parish JPCs to implement the project. A missionary priest working in Korogocho explained:

> Justice and peace groups in the slums are seen as a way of climbing the social ladder and a way to get money from either the church or NGOs. We have seen this process kill the spirit of our people. The project approach has created a very negative culture in the slum–a culture of dependency and expectation. We prefer to work with our SCCs, not the JPC.[32]

Parish-based JPCs throughout all the slum parishes were in a similar state. The JPCs, however, did not start that way. According to the first archdiocesan coordinator for the JPC, enthusiasm for the parish-based JPCs was high when they were started in 1998 because they were the first locally-based church forums where parishioners could discuss social and political issues.[33] The quality of the program declined because the Archdiocese did not prioritize the JPC, which meant it raised very little money for the training and formation of the JPC leaders. When money was made available, it was channeled directly to the JPC leaders in the parish who were not obligated to account for the funds to the parishioners or parish priests. Moreover, many priests did not engage with the JPCs because they viewed them as watchdogs within the parish and did not want the parish or their own behavior scrutinized. Because many JPCs were left on their own with no supervision and with access to money, the JPCs often attracted opportunistic and corrupt parishioners who became

[32] Interview with missionary priest B, September 5, 2008.

[33] Interview with former director of the Nairobi Archdiocese JPC, September 22, 2008.

powerful sub-groups in the parish operating according to their own set of rules and personal agendas.

Notwithstanding numerous efforts by the missionaries to change the project proposal, the director of the development office, who was dependent on the donor funds to offset administrative costs of her office, insisted the project go forward without further delay. Unbeknownst to the development office, the CRS official responsible for the project personally contacted the parish priest to confirm that the parish was in agreement with the plan and learned about the disagreement with the development office. In an effort to resolve the dispute, CRS personnel removed the JPCs from the program but proceeded with the project model. Although the revisions did not consume a great deal of time, the process created an acrimonious relationship with the director of the development office because she felt the missionaries circumvented her authority when they spoke directly with the donor.

Following the rancorous planning process, the peace-building project never took off. After interviewing numerous applicants to coordinate the project, the Archdiocese hired an elderly parishioner who had experience as a DELTA trainer, but he was blocked from undertaking any of the planned peace activities. The leaders of the parish in the PPC, aware that the project was funded by a large international donor, viewed it as a money-making opportunity, particularly since it included plans to hire a handful of parishioners for small project work. Just weeks after the peace coordinator was hired, two Luo leaders in the PPC accused him of making anti-Luo statements in the SCCs and promising to hire only Kikuyu to be peace teachers in the parish. The PPC refused him permission to attend their meetings as well as the SCCs. Unable to work with parishioners, the project languished. Despite repeated requests from the parish priest to hire another coordinator, the development office retained the original parishioner for almost one year fearing that he would follow through on his threats to file a lawsuit against the Archdiocese if he was fired.

When the original coordinator's contract expired, his replacement fared no better. The young man lived outside Kibera and had no prior experience working with slum communities; he was quickly frustrated by his inability to integrate into the parish community and quit after three months. The third project coordinator, a former youth member, was able to organize a few meetings with the youth to discuss the issue of peace, but was blocked from implementing most of the planned activities. The PPC leaders mobilized against the project after the development office paid youth, not PPC members, to undertake a baseline survey on peace issues and the project was never revived.

Unable to generate support from parishioners, the Archdiocese or the housing NGOs to address the growing level of tension and conflict, the OHR coordinator and parish priest reached out to other missionaries in the Kutoka network for assistance. During the September 2003 Kutoka meeting, the parish priest reported that Archbishop Ndingi had not responded to the parish's request for assistance and shared his fear that the level of conflict had risen sharply following Raila's plan to move Sowetans to Athi River. He also expressed concern that the parish might be targeted for violence because of false rumors that the Catholic Church was trying to attain the title deed for Kibera as it had in Mathare 4A.

A number of missionaries who had been active in the Land Caucus during the Mathare 4A crisis were alarmed by the report. Aware that the situation could quickly spiral out of control, they agreed that the parish needed immediate assistance in finding a way to communicate directly with decision-makers on the project to apprise them of the situation. They sent letters requesting an urgent meeting to the director of UN-Habitat and the Minister of Roads, Public Works and Housing as well as the Vatican's Apostolic Nuncio to Kenya, Archbishop Giovanni Tonucci; an Italian with whom several missionaries had a close relationship. As the Apostolic Nuncio, Archbishop Tonucci was the link between the local Catholic Church in Kenya and the international church in Rome. He also acted as the Permanent Observer of the Holy See to UN-Habitat. The missionary parish priest from Kangemi who advised the Papal Nuncio in matters related to UN-Habitat also sent a personal letter providing a more detailed background about the upgrade.

UN-Habitat did not reply to the network's letter and Raila sent only a short note inviting the parishes to participate in all public meetings about the upgrade. The Papal Nuncio, however, responded immediately. In early October, the parish priest and OHR coordinator met Archbishop Tonucci to present a written summary that described how the upgrade was impacting the parish and to discuss what, if anything, the church could do to prevent further destabilization.[34] In response, the Nuncio said that the Archbishop was not likely to get involved in the matter because he had been publicly criticized and embarrassed about Mathare 4A. The Nuncio also said that even though the Archbishop was not inclined to get involved, he was and would arrange for a meeting with Mrs. Tibaijuka.

On October 18, 2003, the Nuncio made his first personal appearance at UN-Habitat. During that meeting, Mrs. Tibaijuka, a Catholic, listened to the parish priest and OHR coordinator explain their concerns about how

---

[34] OHR Memorandum, October 9, 2003.

the project was further dividing the community because KENSUP's failure to provide the basic details on the upgrade or involve the community had allowed politicians to take advantage of the information vacuum to promote ethnic political agendas. The community was not able to counter this process because there were no cohesive groups to represent the varying interests of the community. The parish priest and OHR coordinator also expressed concerns that UN-Habitat officials did not fully grasp the complex dynamics of Kibera that made organizing the community exceedingly difficult, if not impossible. They suggested that Habitat start the project in another slum such as Huruma or Deep Sea because they were smaller and less politicized than Kibera. Moreover, community organizers had worked in those communities for several years to form organized groups. They also explained their fear that the project's continued exclusion of the community could invite public protests and violence as it had in Mathare 4A. The Nuncio emphasized that the church would do all that it could to support the project, but the church's first priority was the dignity and rights of the poor.

It was clear that the Nuncio, the parish priest and the OHR coordinator viewed the upgrade from very different perspectives from those of UN-Habitat. Mrs. Tibaijuka and her staff reported that they were concerned primarily with securing donor funding and political support for the project. Although they acknowledged the political interference, they downplayed it as a temporary distraction. From their perspective, the parish was overreacting and alarmist; the Habitat staff believed the community understood and supported the project and would not take steps to block its implementation.

In addition to the Papal Nuncio, the OHR coordinator utilized her network of international contacts to circulate information about the parish's concerns to the political advisers of the diplomatic missions that were part of the European Union's (EU) committee on land and some of the key donors in the project. She also invited them to visit Kibera to observe the situation with the hope that they would pressure the government or UN-Habitat to respond to the growing instability in Kibera. In September 2003, 12 diplomatic officials including the Ambassador of Finland, who had personally promoted the relocation of slum dwellers to Athi River, visited the parish to get a first-hand account of the events transpiring. After meeting parishioners from the Saturday group for a background on the impact of the upgrade, the officials, accompanied by parishioners, walked through Kibera to meet residents.

Although the diplomatic officials were not able to provide the community with additional information, they left with a clearer view of the situation and some of the officials took direct action. For example, the Finnish Ambassador reported to the OHR that he had been misinformed by the government that Kibera residents wanted to move to Athi River. His personal discussions with Soweto residents left no doubt in his mind that the community did not want to shift to Athi River. The Ambassador asked the OHR to replicate the tour of Soweto for Finland's Foreign Minister when she visited Kenya. He wanted her to hear directly from the residents the reasons why they did not want to move to Athi River before she met NARC officials to discuss the debt swap and the Athi River project. Shortly after the Minister's visit to Kibera, the Finnish Ambassador notified the parish that his government no longer supported the move to Athi River. Raila eventually retracted his statement and announced that the government would build a decanting site for Soweto residents only five kilometers away near the women's prison in an area known as Langata.

In addition to advising members of the diplomatic corps about the reality of the situation, members of the OHR and Saturday group also met a number of international consultants working for some of the project's donors as well as several human rights lawyers interested in monitoring the high-profile upgrade. These visitors contacted the parish OHR as their point of entry for several reasons. First, there was a paucity of organized groups in Soweto that could articulate viewpoints not influenced solely by ethnic and political interests. The parish Saturday group was ethnically mixed and included tenants as well as structure owners who had learned the fundamental issues about upgrading and were able and willing to express their views, concerns and ideas on the project. Second, many of the NGOs were viewed by outsiders as gatekeepers to the community who had a strong financial incentive in steering them exclusively to their groups in the hope that donor money would follow. Third, members of the OHR Team attended most of the meetings called by the structure owners, tenants, councilor, area MP and the CBOs and documented those meetings, which meant the OHR possessed an accurate and up-to-date written record of the community's views on the project. Finally, as a large church administered by expatriate missionaries, the visitors felt that the information provided by the parish OHR was not tainted by an underlying financial motive or ethnic and political chauvinisms commonly found in the other churches, NGOs and CBOs.

The Creation of the Settlement Executive Committee

Following the announcement of the Soweto upgrade, KENSUP officials undertook no activities in Kibera related to the project for nearly a year and a half until May 2004 when they held the elections for the Settlement Executive Committee, the 16-member group that was intended to represent the views of the various community groups during the design and implementation of the upgrade. Unfortunately, a number of the SEC elections were flawed because of the PA's incompetence and localized political corruption. Inexperienced with mobilizing the community for participatory processes, the DO was unprepared for the task.

The first group to elect SEC representatives was the FBOs, which included 26 pastors of small Pentecostal and AIC churches and the parish. The church leaders elected a local bishop from one of the small Pentecostal churches, because he had recently attended a meeting on the World Bank's infrastructure project and therefore was perceived to know more about upgrading than the other pastors. The pastors also wanted to elect the parish priest because they felt an expatriate missionary could more easily access information from the government and UN-Habitat; offices that the pastors knew would be reluctant to meet slum dwellers. They also felt the Catholic Church had more resources and expertise including a full-time human rights ministry and lawyer on staff. When he declined because his pastoral obligations would prevent him from regularly attending the meetings, the pastors elected the OHR coordinator in his stead.

Although the FBO election was rushed, some of the other elections were marred by outright corruption and political interference. As an example, the area councilor commandeered the election of the tenant representatives to favor his ethnic community. In the presence of a large contingency of NDP youth wingers, he paraded five young Luo men in front of the crowd and instructed them to vote through a process of public queuing. Fearing retaliation, the residents agreed to the councilor's selection. The election of the two CBO representatives was also flawed; only a two-day's notice was given and on the day of the election many qualified organizations with predominantly Kikuyu memberships were not allowed to enter the meeting or were intimidated from attending by the councilor's assistants.

Limited Interest and Capacity of the FBOs

During the elections of the FBO representatives, KENSUP officials from the Department of Housing as well as the NCC and UN-Habitat repeatedly stated that the FBOs had a special role to play in educating and mobilizing Soweto residents to participate in the upgrade. Their special status emanated from their position as indigenous leaders as well as their ability to reach large numbers of residents and influence their actions. Notwithstanding the pastors' initial expectations that they would play an important role in the upgrade, in reality, the FBOs faced numerous challenges that impeded their ability to effectively organize themselves or represent the interests of their members.

Immediately after the FBO representatives were elected, the bishop and the OHR coordinator arranged several meetings to discuss how the churches could be involved in the upgrade. Since the parish was the only church with a meeting hall, all meetings took place in the parish compound. To the surprise of the coordinator and the bishop, of the 26 pastors, only 10 to 12 regularly attended the introductory meetings. There were several reasons to account for the low attendance. First, many of the pastors did not have time to dedicate to the upgrade issue because they were busy struggling with survival needs. Since their churches were small and lacked independent financial resources, many pastors were employed either full or part-time in the industrial area or within Kibera. When the pastors learned that they would not be paid for their attendance at meetings, more than half chose not to participate.

Second, the pastors in Soweto did not have prior experience meeting as a group. Contrary to the views of the KENSUP officials, the religious leaders in Soweto were more divided than unified. Like most groups in Kibera, the main area of division was along ethnic lines. The majority of Kikuyu and Kamba belonged to the Catholic Church and many Luo and Luhya were members of one of the Pentecostal or AIC churches. Since these churches typically grew around the individual pastor, many of their memberships had exclusive ethnic identities and were reluctant to interact with churches that did not share their ethnicity. In addition, the pastors were in competition for followers. It was common for members of the Pentecostal churches to move back and forth between churches depending on the personal attention and charisma of an individual pastor. Given the crowded marketplace for churches, some pastors did not want to expose their members to other pastors because they might find them more appealing.

Third, some pastors did not attend the meetings because of the two FBO representatives. The elected bishop, a Luhya who was closely aligned to the Luo politicians, was viewed by some as a tribalist who wanted to use the upgrade to promote only the interests of the Luo and Luhya. As a result, the Kamba pastors did not want to be associated with him and boycotted the meetings. Some pastors viewed the OHR coordinator as an outsider while others did not want to work with the Catholic Church; it had a long history of operating alone and most pastors did not view it as a good collaborator. In addition, some pastors still believed the rumors that the Catholic Church was secretly trying to secure a title deed for all Kibera as it had in Mathare 4A.

Fourth, many of the pastors were intimidated by the upgrade; for most, the project was an alien concept that they had never before encountered. Lacking knowledge and experience on the process of upgrading, many felt the project was too technical for their understanding and that only experts with specific knowledge could contribute to the upgrading discussions.

Finally, some of the pastors were cautious in their approach because they were afraid it would change the status quo and the power structures. According to one NGO worker, "The pastors were the only visible non-state actors in Soweto and they had a big stake in its outcome. Since it would naturally change the power dynamics and their position, they saw the upgrade as a direct threat to their status in Kibera."[35]

Despite the low turnout at the meetings, there were a core group of pastors who attended the FBO meetings and took their responsibility to promote a peaceful upgrade seriously. During the meetings, the pastors articulated their concerns that were the same as the OHR's: ethnic-based interference by politicians, the lack of information and the community's exclusion. In addition to their fears that they would lose their churches, they also had considerable concern about future land ownership, unaffordable rents, the design of the house and compensation for structures owners. Since there was very little information available to communicate to their members, the OHR coordinator encouraged the pastors to focus on transmitting information from the community to KENSUP, especially given the DO's request that they provide the churches' views on how the upgrade should be implemented. Between June and August 2003, the sub-parish of Soweto along with 11 pastors collected and documented the viewpoints of their members.

The OHR agreed to prepare the findings of the churches and send them to the DO, the head of KENSUP and the UN-Habitat representative to KENSUP. When none of these individuals replied to the FBOs, some pastors turned against the project and complained that KENSUP's and

[35] Interview with human right lawyer B, September 28, 2008.

Habitat's repeated mantra that the upgrade would promote active participation by the community was insincere propaganda promulgated to appease the donors and international community. In addition, the process of meeting and documenting viewpoints had been time-consuming. The fact that the project implementers did not recognize the pastors' efforts confirmed their view that taking time away from their busy schedules to promote the upgrade was a futile endeavor. From their perspective, the Soweto upgrade was just like all the previous ones; the government had no intention of involving the grass-roots leaders or the community. As a result, some of the pastors gradually stopped attending meetings and disengaged from the project leaving only seven pastors, the bishop and the OHR coordinator in the group.

The exercise of gathering viewpoints, however, produced a positive result for some pastors who reported that the process provided them with an opportunity to raise the issue of the upgrade and communicate even a small amount of information about the process to their followers. For some, it was the first time many of their followers openly discussed taboo topics such as the divisions between structure owners and tenants, political interference and ethnic favoritism. In addition, the pastors recognized that they were not alone in their concerns and fears. They were empowered by the process and felt the churches should get more involved in the upgrade.

An opportunity presented itself in May 2004 when KENSUP announced its plan to enumerate the houses in Soweto. Some of the pastors were concerned that the enumeration process would be corrupted by political interference and proposed that the pastors undertake an independent enumeration that could be used to cross-check KENSUP's findings.[36] They felt that because of their status and physical presence, the pastors could elicit more truthful responses about who really lived in Soweto than the KENSUP staff who were strangers and unaware of the Kibera's reality. The pastors also felt the enumeration would give them a tangible way to engage the community in the project.

Since Pamoja Trust had undertaken a prior enumeration in Kibera, the pastors asked the OHR coordinator to invite community organizers from the NGO to help them create an enumeration form and train them on how to implement the process. On several occasions, two community organizers from Pamoja Trust met the pastors to talk about the logistics of implementing an enumeration. The pastors agreed to mobilize five members from their churches to attend a training session. On the day of the training, approximately 70 people attended, but the Pamoja Trust staff

---

[36] OHR Memorandum, June 12, 2004.

person who had agreed to train the pastors did not show up. The group left disappointed and frustrated. As it turned out, Pamoja Trust had decided to vie for a government contract to do the enumeration for KENSUP and did not want to support a competing process undertaken by the pastors. As a consequence, a number of pastors felt they were wasting their time and stopped attending the FBO meetings. Only four pastors returned for a follow-up meeting, too few to undertake a rigorous enumeration process and the plan to undertake the exercise was put on hold indefinitely.

Limited Competency of the Housing NGOs

Although the government frequently credited the housing NGOs with having greater professional expertise and skills on slum upgrading than the other sectors in civil society, in reality there were not enough competent NGOs in Soweto to represent the interests of the Soweto community. At the official level, the NGO sector was supposed to be represented in the upgrade through three different groups, the Joint Project Planning Team, the Multi-Stakeholder Support Group and SEC. None of these representatives, however, was able to build a coalition of NGOs or lobby the project implementers to ensure the affected community had adequate information or the ability to participate in the project.

KENSUP officials hand-picked Shelter Forum as its representative on the Joint Project Planning Team because it had political ties to the NARC government, but the NGO was limited in its ability to address the upgrade. Shelter Forum was not an implementing organization, but rather a membership organization that monitored a national network of NGOs involved in promoting shelter for the poor. The primary focus of its staff was research and documentation of other organizations' efforts; it had little experience in the field working with slum communities or the issue of slum upgrading. The Forum's personnel also had no grass-roots experience in Soweto or relationships with the Soweto community. As a result, Shelter Forum was not able to raise the community's concerns to KENSUP or organize the housing NGOs in Soweto. The Multi-Stakeholder Support Group similarly failed to give a voice to the NGOs because, just months into the project, KENSUP disbanded the group after a number of NGOs complained about the lack of community involvement.

The NGO designated to sit on the SEC was Maji na Ufanisi, not because of its expertise, but because it was the only NGO that had staff working on a regular basis in Soweto. Of the five housing NGOs active in Soweto, only one had practical experience in slum upgrading, Pamoja Trust, but KENSUP did not allow it to vie for inclusion on SEC because it had entered Kibera after the announced upgrade and had limited contact with the community. Although the community organizers who worked for Maji na Ufanisi were well-known, Maji na Ufanisi was not able to competently represent the NGO sector in the upgrade. The director of Maji assigned a community organizer to attend the SEC meetings, but his attendance was sporadic and tapered off completely in mid-September 2004 because of a management crisis in the organization. Following a lawsuit for alleged mismanagement of the organization's finances, most of the staff were fired and the office was temporarily closed. The position for the NGO representative on the SEC became vacant and was not replaced.

Despite the lack of official representation, Pamoja Trust and ANPPCAN tried to mobilize their savings groups and CBOs to participate in the upgrade during this stage, but their efforts were largely unsuccessful. Even though the SEC was intended to be a voluntary advisory group, in the mind of the councilor, the SEC not only had exclusive control over all upgrading activities, it was also a money-making opportunity. The councilor repeatedly insisted that he and other SEC members should be compensated for any and all activities related to the upgrade. As a result, the councilor refused to let anyone outside the SEC get involved in the upgrade, even on a voluntary basis. For example, during the months of June and July 2004, the NCC invited the NGOs to undertake a test run of the enumeration; 10 of the 60 volunteers were members of the Saturday group and the rest were members of Muungano savings groups. The day after the test run, the area councilor had two leaders of the Muungano arrested and detained on charges that they were "interfering" in the upgrade. He also threatened to arrest anyone who entered Soweto or tried to participate in any upgrading activities that were not authorized by the SEC. Even though the Muungano leaders were released the next day, the councilor's threats combined with his power to have people arbitrarily arrested crippled efforts to encourage active participation by the community. The house counting exercise was discontinued and many of the residents, fearful that they would be targeted by the youth wingers, declined to participate in any further upgrading activities.

Apathy of Parishioners

By June 2004, the vast majority of parishioners in Soweto had ceased to play a role in the upgrade apart from the OHR Team members who continued to attend sporadic meetings called by the NGOs or UN-Habitat and gave updates to the Saturday group and SCCs. The reasons for the community's lack of interest varied. Most were simply too afraid to get involved because of the councilor's threats and intimidation. They knew that if they voiced an opinion in contravention of the upgrade, they would likely be beaten by youth wingers. Others felt that any role they might have in the upgrade ended when the SEC was elected. In their experience, once the government designated community representatives, regardless of whether or not they were legitimate or competent, residents no longer had any standing to speak out on the issue. Also, interest in the upgrade ebbed as other issues of greater concern took center stage such as the government's plan to undertake forced evictions, an issue that will be discussed in greater detail in the next chapter.

There were also many parishioners who had lost interest in the issue. Since the government had taken no substantive steps to implement the upgrade a year after its announcement, many people thought the project had been abandoned. Their conclusion was in keeping with two prior upgrades in Kibera that had both fizzled out. In 1997 the city council partnered with an on-going World Bank project to install water mains. After three years of laying 80% of an extensive network of spaghetti pipes at the cost of $500,000, the project was abandoned due to disputes about project delays and cost over-runs; residents later pulled up the pipes and sold them for scrap.[37] Two years later the World Bank agreed to support a comprehensive project that would install water, roads and refuse collection.[38] In 2002 the NCC finally hired a consultant who submitted a master plan. However, due to the government's failure to address issue of land ownership in Kibera; two of the key donors including the World Bank pulled out of the project. Five years and more than a million dollars later, the project was shelved with little to show for their efforts. In the view of many Soweto parishioners, it did not make sense to spend valuable time that could be used earning money attending meetings on an upgrade that was not likely to happen.

The Councilor Co-Opts the Upgrade

Although the councilor had interfered with the upgrade from its inception, his efforts to commandeer the process for his own financial and political gain escalated in September 2004. During the SEC's first training

---

[37] Neuwirth, *Shadow Cities*, 245.

[38] Ministry of Local Government Urban Development Department, and Nairobi City Council Water and Sewage Department, "Kibera Urban Environmental Sanitation Project: Consultancy Services for Identification, Preparation and Implementation," (Report prepared for Government of Kenya, Nairobi, 2002), a-e.

session the councilor's two assistants called a secret meeting of select SEC members to tell them that they should elect the bishop, a political ally of the councilor, as chairman of the SEC and warned that any opposition would be met with a swift reprisal. According to one SEC member, "The SEC was a political committee where tribal issues were at the forefront. The councilor wanted the chairman to be a Luo or Luhya to protect the interests of the tenants."[39] The SEC members present at the meeting offered no challenge to the councilor's wishes. According to the parishioner who represented the structure owners, they were not only afraid of possible retaliation; the councilor had also promised them a free house in the upgrade in exchange for their votes.[40]

The next day when the NGO representative from Maji na Ufanisi and the OHR coordinator learned that the councilor had intimidated SEC members to elect the bishop, they declined to participate in the election. They also objected to the councilor's demands that KENSUP pay the SEC members 25,000 Ksh every month for attending meetings. They felt the payments would compromise the objectivity of the SEC as well as stifle the spirit of volunteerism necessary for the slum upgrade. Both the councilor and the bishop responded with fury to the opposition. The councilor publicly confronted the OHR coordinator and physically threatened her not to speak about Kibera in a public forum. Other SEC members who were not Luo or Luhya received similar threats. Although the KENSUP and UN-Habitat officials were present in the meetings and aware of the threats, they were unable to counter the councilor's corrupt behavior because he was protected by powerful political patrons.

The councilor's threats against the OHR coordinator created a difficult situation in the parish. It was clear that the councilor had hijacked the only mechanism for the community to voice its views about the upgrade, but the OHR coordinator and parish priest knew that any steps taken against the councilor would be perceived as anti-Luo and could provoke conflict within the parish. The PPC leadership was heavily dominated by Luo and the priests did not want to antagonize them out of fear that they would block other parish initiatives in retaliation. In addition, the threats of the councilor were a serious matter and the parish was vulnerable. The councilor had a large retinue of NDP youth wingers at his disposal who could easily destroy parish property and threaten and/or harm members of the parish in retribution for positions taken by the OHR coordinator. In light of these risks, the parish priest advised the OHR coordinator to

---

[39] Interview with SEC member, September 30, 2008.

[40] Interview with Saturday group member F, September 28, 2008.

continue to attend SEC meetings because it was important to monitor the situation and gather much needed information, but to take a low profile.

The councilor's unchecked intimidation also had an impact on the ability of the SEC to function. One of the representatives for the structure owners and one of the CBO representatives stopped attending the meetings. Although the OHR coordinator and the NGO representative continued to attend the SEC meetings, they could not influence the agenda or discussions because every aspect of the meetings was controlled by the councilor and the bishop. Instead of providing a venue for community representation, the SEC turned into the personal platform of the councilor who used every meeting to demand allowances and threaten to block any upgrade activities until his demands were met. The councilor's corruption was not limited to the SEC meetings. In late 2004, parishioners reported to the OHR that the councilor was demanding that Soweto residents pay him if they wanted their names included in the upgrade registry; tenants were told to pay 1,000 Ksh and structure owners 2,000 Ksh.

In October 2004, as the councilor's intimidation increased, the OHR coordinator summarized the details of the councilor's interference and its impact on the Soweto community in a memorandum and sent it to the Papal Nuncio with a request for his assistance. Before the Nuncio could act on the issue, he was reassigned to a new posting in Europe, but he agreed to brief his successor, Archbishop Alain Paul Lebeaupin, on the situation in Soweto.

Civil Society's Response

The parish was not alone in its inability to counter the corruption of the local politicians. Although the Soweto pastors were aware of the councilor's blatant corruption, they did not object publicly because of fears of retaliation. During several meetings of the pastors, the bishop, speaking on behalf of the councilor, warned the pastors to boycott all meetings called by anyone who raised questions about the SEC's legitimacy and capacity including any meetings arranged by the OHR coordinator. The bishop informed the pastors that if they criticized or questioned the authority of the councilor or SEC, they would be arrested. The bishop's statement had the intended result of scaring off most of the pastors. By the end of 2004, no pastors were willing to attend the meetings called by the OHR coordinator. According to one Team member, "The pastors were afraid that the councilor would retaliate against them by sending youth wingers to burn their churches down. Some were even afraid of getting hurt or killed by those youth."[41] In reflecting on the bishop's corrupt role in the SEC, one pastor commented:

> As pastors we had a big responsibility because we were the eyes of the community, but we failed to build unity in our community. Some of our pastors entered into the politics of this upgrade because money was moving in Kibera and it caused us to miss an opportunity to help our people.[42]

The housing NGOs also were not equipped to stop the corrupt actions of the councilor or the bishop. In early 2005, Pamoja Trust was the only NGO still working on the upgrade issue in the community; many felt the delays were permanent while others had moved on to other issues such as forced evictions addressed in the next chapter. However, the councilor made several public accusations that Pamoja Trust was improperly trying to hijack the upgrade from the SEC and warned its staff that if they entered Soweto, they would be "burned." Thereafter, the Pamoja Trust staff temporarily suspended their activities in Soweto. The councilor and the bishop also started a campaign to silence the Muungano leaders after they learned about their plan to file a lawsuit to declare the SEC invalid because of the corrupt election process. The bishop spread rumors that the Muungano was opposed to the upgrade and an enemy of the tenants that should be blocked. Shortly thereafter, the councilor, brandishing a gun, ordered the arrest of the local leader of the Muungano. The Muungano leader was released the next day, but not before NDP youth wingers assaulted his wife and ransacked his home.

The NGOs also did not have the ability to influence the UN-Habitat or the government to stop the councilor's corruption. Although a number of individual NGO workers had developed some contacts within UN-Habitat, their efforts to convince Habitat to respond to the councilor's corruption and interference in the project were unsuccessful. According to one Habitat official, Mrs. Tibaijuka was under intense international pressure to make sure the Soweto upgrade succeeded.[43] The Soweto upgrade was not Habitat's only upgrading project around the world, but it was one of its largest and most high-profile ones. In addition to generating voluminous reports and articles promoting the project, Habitat had facilitated many visits of international housing experts and donors to Kibera. Since Raila's ministry was responsible for the success of the project, Habitat did not

---

[41] Interview with OHR team member C, October 3, 2008.
[42] OHR Memorandum, May 7, 2005.
[43] OHR Memorandum, March 11, 2005.

want to jeopardize their relationship with him by complaining about one of his political allies, regardless of how many NGO staff complained about the councilor.[44]

As the councilor became increasingly brazen in his threats, a number of civil society actors whose staff were not physically present in Kibera tried to expose his corruption. For example, lawyers at KCS arranged for a journalist to expose the councilor's corruption in a newspaper article.[45] International housing rights lawyers from a Geneva-based housing rights group, the Center for Housing Rights and Evictions (COHRE) who were monitoring the unrelated issue of evictions, also published a report that highlighted the councilor's illegal and corrupt actions.[46] Neither the article nor the report elicited a response from KENSUP or UN-Habitat.

The Councilor Targets the Parish

At the start of January 2005, the councilor focused his threats directly against parish when he prompted a local vernacular radio station to run a story that the parish was trying to take advantage of the upgrade by purchasing land in Kibera and was evicting tenants without paying them compensation. The false accusations which were designed to provoke a violent retaliation against the parish were related to the parish's purchase of 10 structures located next to the chapel in the Lindi sub-parish. Two days later, the councilor brought a gang of NDP youth wingers in the middle of the night to destroy the security fence surrounding the main parish compound. Efforts by the parish priest to solicit help from the local government officials were futile. The DO, who was new, and the chief were both fearful of retaliation by the youth wingers and said they could not assist the parish in any way. The police told the parish priest it was a political matter and refused to take a statement. Two weeks later, the councilor returned with a gang of drunken youth wingers who tore down a different portion of the fence in broad daylight. The councilor's bold use of force sparked fear throughout the parish. Given the growing threats and insecurity, the OHR Team was forced to discontinue their nightly meetings in the SCCs and the priests could no longer visit SCCs for evening mass unescorted.

---

[44] Ibid.

[45] Maore Ithuia, "House Grab Fears Rock Slum Project," *The East African Standard*, Nairobi, March 28, 2005.

[46] Centre on Housing Rights and Evictions, *Listening to the Poor? Housing Rights in Nairobi* (Geneva: COHRE, 2005), 78.

When it was evident that the councilor intended to continue his campaign against the parish, the parish priest and the OHR coordinator met the new Nuncio's secretary to seek his advice and input. The Nuncio's secretary indicated that Archbishop Lebeaupin did not want to engage in local political issues, but that he was personally interested in the matter. He agreed to visit the parish and asked the Archdiocese's director of development office to attend the meeting so they could agree on how the parish should respond. During that meeting, the Nuncio's secretary reported that he had already met Mrs. Tibaijuka's undersecretary about the concerns concerning political manipulation of the project raised in the parish's memo provided to the previous Nuncio. The sister in charge of the development office expressed her concern that the Archdiocese had a very bad experience with violence in the slum of Mathare 4A and did not want another similar situation in Kibera.[47] Afraid that any action taken by the parish might ignite another explosive response from the NDP youth wingers, it was agreed that the parish would not act in the current volatile mood.

One week later, the Nuncio's secretary circulated the OHR's memo, which described the councilor's co-option of the SEC as well as the menacing role of the NDP youth wingers, to all the embassies in Nairobi. In response, the Ambassador of Poland, who was the chairman of the Committee of Permanent Representatives to UN-Habitat, sent letters of inquiry about the parish memorandum to Mrs. Tibaijuka, Kenya's permanent representative to UN-Habitat and the permanent secretary of the Ministry of Lands and Housing stating that he would raise the issue at the upcoming meeting of Habitat's governing council if the political interference in Kibera was not restrained. With their international reputation threatened by a high-level diplomat, the Habitat officials finally responded to the councilor's threats and corruption and immediately spoke with the Minister of Lands and the Director of Housing, both of whom publicly disavowed the councilor's actions. The Director of Housing also revoked the councilor's voting rights on the SEC and warned him to stay away from the SEC meetings. Days later, Raila accused the councilor of misusing his name and refused him entry to a meeting for the other area councilors.

After the councilor was removed from active participation in the upgrade, KENSUP implemented the house counting and enumeration exercise during March to May 2005. During that same time, the parish priest and OHR lawyers were invited to several meetings with Habitat

[47] OHR Memorandum, February 11, 2005.

officials, including Mrs. Tibaijuka, to provide updates on the community's concerns. In each of those meeting, the priest and lawyers in the OHR voiced their ongoing objection to the lack of information and community participation in the project. The UN-Habitat officials repeatedly stated that the communication strategy prepared by one of the donors was finished and would be implemented as soon as KENSUP held elections for zonal representatives that would give the community broader representation. Neither of these steps was taken. Once the enumeration was finished, there were no further meetings called by KENSUP or any other activities visible to the community in 2005. As of January 2009, six years and 500 million shillings later, KENSUP had managed to build a decanting site near the women's prison, but the project had yet to transfer any slum dwellers so that new housing construction could begin in Soweto.

Conclusion

This case study is another demonstration of how expectations that ordinary citizens can hold the government to account in a place like Kibera are not realistic. While the government's desire to improve housing in Soweto initially appeared to be well intentioned, when it became clear that neither KENSUP nor UN-Habitat wanted to spend the time or money to educate the community and create representative structures so the affected residents could participate in the project, its successful implementation became unlikely. This fact combined with the ethnically-based political agenda of the local MP and area councilor doomed the project to failure. Despite vocal concerns voiced by the Soweto community, the churches, housing NGOs and the OHR, none of the local civil society actors were equipped on a practical or political level to hold the project implementers to account.

Overall, the community affected by the upgrade in Soweto was not able to come together and promote its shared interest in having the government improve their housing. An inherent conflict of interest in the outcome of the upgrade as well as a long history of ethnic polarization that was manipulated by corrupt politicians made it impossible for structure owners and tenants to unite. The result was that the upgrade drove an even deeper wedge between the two groups and further polarized residents along ethnic lines.

Although residents viewed the churches as the most important advocates for the community's interests, the churches were not able to unite or effectively lobby KENSUP or UN-Habitat to implement the upgrade in a fair and inclusive manner. Within the FBOs, there were two distinct groups, the small Pentecostal and AIC churches and the Catholic Church. They had very different approaches, capacities and resources with respect to the upgrade. The pastors from the Pentecostal and AIC churches were divided along ethnic and political lines; others feared retaliation by the councilor and NDP youth wingers. They also did not have adequate leadership, competence, contacts and resources to undertake advocacy work.

The OHR was also limited in its ability to impact the upgrade, but for different reasons. Apart from the OHR Team members and a few active parishioners in Soweto, the parishioners were either afraid of or not interested in lobbying for a fairer and corrupt-free upgrade. The result was that the advocacy in parish was done almost exclusively by missionaries. Because they were expatriates and lacked full support from the local Archdiocese, the missionaries were limited in their ability to influence government officials. Without direct access, the missionaries were forced to rely on the intervention of international diplomats, especially the Papal Nuncio, to pressure UN-Habitat to respond to the concerns of the parish. The efforts of the two missionaries were not sustainable because they were personality driven, not institutionalized endeavors. The subsequent OHR coordinator and parish priest were not interested in pursuing the upgrade. As a result, by 2006, the parish ceased to play any role in the Soweto upgrade.

The most experienced and expert sector of civil society, the housing NGOs, turned out to be among the least effective advocates during the upgrade. Because of Kibera's hostile political environment, there were only a handful of active NGOs in Soweto that were involved in the upgrade and only one had significant experience in upgrading. Of those, most were struggling with reduced donor funds and weak relationships with the community. From the community's perspective, the NGOs did not have a significant role to play; most were viewed as more interested in earning money than advocating for the residents. Lacking political connections and a unified purpose and leadership, the NGOs also were not able to hold the government to account for the abuses and corruption rampant in the upgrade.

Chapter Six

Forced Evictions

The preceding two chapters were concerned primarily with the efforts of the parish OHR to hold low-level government officials to account for corruption and mismanagement in Soweto village. In this chapter, I examine efforts by the OHR to respond to a large-scale human right crisis that affected more than 300,000 slum dwellers in Nairobi including 100,000 people scattered throughout Kibera. In early February 2004, three government ministries revealed their plan to raze all slum structures built along the railway line, under power lines and in areas earmarked for future road construction. In violation of international norms governing forced evictions, the government had no plan to provide the affected communities with adequate notice of the evictions, consultation or alternative housing. I analyze here the efforts of the OHR to mobilize parishioners to protest and resist the government's planned evictions.

I argue that contrary to the hopes and expectations of civil society advocates, parishioners were limited in their ability to hold the government to account for its unlawful eviction plans. Even though tens of thousands of Kiberans stood to lose their homes and personal property, the community was too fearful, fractured and disorganized to resist the government's planned demolitions. Local civil society organizations were also ill-equipped to stop the illegal evictions. The Kibera churches lacked the leadership and resources to mobilize a grass-roots campaign and the housing NGOs declined to organize a public protest because of their close relationship with the NARC government. In the vacuum of an indigenous response, it was a group of expatriates, not the affected community, who took the initiative to stop the evictions. Faced with the impending crisis, the OHR coordinator along with a group of other missionaries mobilized a network of international human rights groups and high-level diplomats that reached all the way to the Vatican, which successfully lobbied President Kibaki to suspend the evictions.

Following the president's initial halt of the eviction plan, several housing NGOs in combination with a number of international diplomats and housing rights activists engaged in a campaign to persuade the government to implement a long-term political and legal solution to the eviction crisis. This chapter explains how fear and indifference led most residents to remain uninvolved. It also examines the role of the housing NGOs as well as the OHR and missionaries during the second phase of the eviction crisis. Despite some preliminary success in persuading the government to issue a permanent moratorium on the planned evictions, civil society's efforts were limited.

The Government's Threat of Evictions

At the start of President Kibaki's presidency, most Kenyans were optimistic that the NARC government would usher in a period of much needed reform. One of the government's central campaign pledges was to tackle corruption and restore the rule of law. Once in office, as one of its first acts of political goodwill, the NARC government declared its intention to repossess public land illegally grabbed during the Moi regime. In December 2003 Raila Odinga, as the Minister of Roads, Public Works and Housing, commenced an aggressive initiative to demolish structures built on government land that had been set aside for the construction of future public utilities. The government started by bulldozing houses in a wealthy Nairobi neighborhood including newly-built mansions, most of which were owned by former state officials.[1] According to Raila, the government had to forcibly to take over the illegally occupied land so that his ministry could proceed with the construction of a planned southern bypass road necessary to ease traffic congestion in Nairobi. Even though hundreds of families lost their homes and KANU politicians accused Raila of political retribution, the general citizenry, who viewed the spectacular demolitions on daily television news programs, hailed the demolitions as a valiant effort by NARC to restore the rule of law. Some human rights activists were even photographed with the bulldozers, naively unaware of the government's long-term plan for the slums.

On the morning of February 8, 2004, two government bulldozers demolished a small settlement located on the southwestern edge of Kibera known as Raila village. Since the tenants were not given notice of the demolition, most of them were attending Sunday church services in the main villages of Kibera and were unable to stop the eviction. The demolition of Raila village destroyed approximately 400 structures rendering more than 2,000 people homeless in less than two hours. In the

[1] Joyce Malumba, "Slum Upgrade a Tale of Later Rather than Sooner," IPS news service, April 30, 2004.

melee following the demolition, looters quickly stole the residents' household goods and personal property. In addition to the homes and businesses that were destroyed, a health clinic and part of a primary school were also razed.

Although Raila village was not located within the parish boundaries, about 20 parishioners were rendered homeless by the demolition. In the days following the demolition, members of the OHR met the acting parish priest to discuss the incident and what, if anything, the parish OHR could do to protest the illegal eviction. From the OHR coordinator's perspective, the eviction in Raila village was in clear contravention of the international standards governing forced evictions.[2] Unlike the well-to-do who had lost their houses in the wealthy neighborhood, the tenants living in Raila village were not given prior notice. In addition, the affected residents, the majority of whom were single mothers and their children, were one of the most vulnerable sectors in society and had no alternative housing.

Despite the coordinator's desire to protest the demolition, she recognized that the OHR's objections, standing alone, would have little impact. The coordinator therefore consulted individuals working in the housing NGOs to explore a possible joint-response. In contrast to their rapid responses during the Moi regime, the housing NGOs did not react to the demolition of Raila village. In October 2003 the new government had enacted a National Housing Policy denouncing slum evictions and declaring its aim to improve the slum through large-scale upgrading programs, evidenced by its highly publicized agreement with UN-Habitat to upgrade Soweto. A number of the NGO activists had participated in the drafting of the new housing policy and did not believe that the government was involved in the Raila demolition or that it would backtrack on its pledge to protect housing rights. In their view, the demolition of Raila village was an anomaly related to the local politics of the area MP.

As it turned out, the demolition of Raila village was just the first in a series of large-scale demolitions planned by the NARC government.

---

[2] In 1972, the Kenyan government signed the International Covenant on Economic, Social and Cultural Rights which mandates that a forced eviction can be implemented only if done in accordance with the protections of due process including providing the affected community with genuine consultation, adequate notice prior to the date of eviction, information on the proposed eviction, the provision of basic legal remedies and legal aid for those who cannot afford it. In addition, no eviction should render anyone homeless and alternative housing or resettlement must be provided for the evictees. See General Comment No. 7 on Forced Evictions found in Article 11(1) of the International Covenant on Economic, Social and Cultural Rights.

Several days after the demolition of Raila village, the DO visited the parish to finalize the security logistics for the arrival of Sir Edward Clay, the British High Commissioner, and the Manchester United under-Sixteen soccer club who had arranged to visit the parish and play a match with Kibera youth as part of their tour of the country. During the visit, the DO explained what had happened in Raila village and revealed that Raila intended to demolish all structures in the area set aside for the link road that would connect the southern and northern bypass routes. The exact location and measurements of the link road were still unknown, but it would likely cover a wide swath through the heart of Kibera. The DO also referred to two notices printed in the back of the daily newspaper the previous week. The notices said that the Kenya Power and Light Company (the KPLC), a public corporation administered by the Ministry of Energy, intended to clear all slum structures located under the power lines. The Kenya Railways Corporation, a public corporation administered by the Ministry of Transportation, also intended to repossess all land within 100 feet on either side of the railway line; all slum structures located in that area would be demolished. The evictions were scheduled to begin in two weeks on March 1, 2004.

In response to the DO's revelation, the OHR coordinator recognized the obvious need to move slum dwellers from dangerous areas, but objected to the lack of adequate notice. Most Kiberans did not have access to the newspaper and would be taken by surprise when the bulldozers arrived. In addition, no one from the government had consulted with the affected residents or offered alternative housing. The coordinator's protestations were futile. The DO indicated that the PA had been given orders "from the highest level" to undertake the evictions and that he and the chiefs faced immediate termination if they failed to implement the demolitions. The DO said the planned evictions would be the largest slum demolition exercise in Kenya's history and would affect tens of thousands of slum dwellers living in other slum areas such as Korogocho and Mukuru kwa Njenga and rural areas, but the impact would be greatest in Kibera. The safety corridor of the railway was densely occupied because it served a dual purpose; in addition to housing residents, it was the commercial spine of the slum. It was estimated that 5,250 structures were located along the five kilometers of the railway that passed through Kibera.[3] Although Kibera was only partially electrified, it was estimated that there were 3,255 structures located under low-lying power lines. Since the government did not identify the location of the link road, it was not

[3] See COHRE, *Listening to the Poor*, 35-36.

possible to identify the number of structures affected by this demolition order. According to rough estimates of the projected length and width of the road, it was believed that more than 16,000 structures would be impacted. In total, it appeared that approximately 100,000 people would be displaced by the three demolition orders in Kibera.

Although the notices said the demolitions were being done in the interests of public safety, the OHR later learned that the real reasons for the unplanned evictions were related to the NARC government's desire to privatize the KRC and KPLC. The Ministry of Transportation wanted to clear the rail corridor so it could enter into an agreement with the World Bank to concession the bankrupt KRC. The government was also in discussions with the World Bank and the Nordic Fund to expand and privatize the KPLC, which required the removal of people living under the power lines. The Minister of Roads, Public Works and Housing wanted the future bypasses cleared of human occupation because he was in the process of trying to raise international donor funds for the road construction.[4]

Visibly shaken during this meeting, the DO said it was the "worst moment in Kibera's history" because large-scale violence and chaos were inevitable. The DO also said that even though he had been instructed not to reveal the government's plan in advance of the demolition exercise, he wanted the parish to start making people aware of the unfolding situation to help reduce the level of shock and trauma that would accompany the evictions.

Parish's' Initial Response

Following their meeting with the DO, the OHR consulted members of the pastoral team and parish leaders for feedback on how the OHR should respond to the eviction crisis. During these meetings, a number of immediate concerns were identified; the greatest fear was that thousands of people would be rendered homeless overnight and there would be large communities of internally displaced slum dwellers. Contrary to the government's repeated mantra that Kiberans could just return to their rural homes, that was not a viable option for most Kiberans. The structure owners who lived along the railway line in Soweto and Line Saba were mostly second-generation Kikuyu who no longer had rural homes. The

[4] COHRE, "Civil and Political Rights in Kenyan Informal Settlements," (Submission to Human Rights Committee, New York, February 2005), 18.

Nubian population that occupied a large section of the area set aside for the link road also had no rural homes.

The majority of people living under the power lines were tenants who did not have the means to go elsewhere. Most were employed in the industrial area and earned less than $1 a day; they could not afford to move to another slum, let alone a long distance to rural areas where there were no jobs or opportunities to earn an income. Finding another room to rent in another part of Kibera was also a limited option; there were already high levels of overcrowding and congestion that worsened after the eviction plan was revealed. In many areas, rents doubled and tripled in response to the growing demand for rooms. Left with no other option for housing, the planned evictions would force thousands of people to migrate to other smaller slums or create new slum areas.

Of perhaps greater concern among the pastoral team was fear that the violence that would accompany the evictions would permanently destabilize Kibera. The evictions would be met with physical resistance by the structure owners as well as people fighting to occupy the limited space available after the government reclaimed the land. In addition to the short-term chaos, the long-term implications for the social and economic development of Kibera were very serious. Thousands of Kiberans would lose their businesses and jobs leading to greater impoverishment and hardship. The demolitions would also destroy the social fabric of the community; in addition to the displacement of families and neighborhoods, the demolitions would eliminate schools, churches and medical clinics. The parish itself also was at risk as the main parish compound was only a few meters from the railway corridor and would be affected adversely if bulldozers razed the structures contiguous to the church.

In developing a strategy for the OHR, the coordinator consulted numerous experts. Prior to coming to the parish, she had worked at the KCS providing legal services to slum communities faced with eviction threats during 1998-2001. Based on her personal experience, she knew the consequences of the forced evictions would be catastrophic. Aware that it was critical to sound the alarm immediately about the government's plan, the OHR coordinator first asked the OHR Team members to walk through the community to inform people of the few details gleaned from the DO so affected residents could have the option of pulling down their structures and salvaging the building materials and/or moving their household goods to another location. The coordinator also knew it was necessary to mobilize as many civil society actors as possible to pressure the government to suspend the demolitions, even if for a few days or weeks, to give the affected community a chance to prepare adequately.

Although the members of the pastoral team acquiesced to the coordinator's strategy, none of them, apart from the acting parish priest, got involved in the OHR's efforts to stop the evictions. Notwithstanding the urgent circumstances, the other ministry coordinators viewed the issue of evictions beyond the scope of their capacity and responsibility. The same was true for the parish leaders. As in the campaign against chang'aa and the Soweto upgrade, parishioners were not proactive in responding to the eviction issue; instead, they asked questions and waited for the OHR to distribute information about the situation.

Reaction of the Kibera Community

The residents' response to the news of the government's demolition plan covered a broad gamut depending on their status as a structure owner or a tenant. Most structure owners living along the railway line in Soweto and Line Saba expressed panic and fear about losing their homes and businesses. There was also concern that the demolitions would derail the planned upgrade for Soweto since a large section of the area to be upgraded was in the affected zone. Residents were confused as to why different ministries within the government were acting at cross purposes.

Despite their palpable worry, the affected residents did not mobilize an organized opposition to the state's plan. Given the urgency of the threat, most structure owners were concerned primarily with how to protect their financial investments. Virtually all the business people with market stalls encroaching on the railway line were preoccupied with moving their structures back 35 feet from both sides of the railway line in the hope that the government would call off the demolitions if they voluntarily moved from the immediate danger zone. A number of pastors as well as the Anglican priest also hastily dismantled churches located within the railway corridor. Some structure owners living along the railway line (around 10%) took down their houses and kiosks and moved from Kibera.

The majority of structure owners lacked the will or the desire to resist the forced evictions. Most were afraid the local chiefs would retaliate against them if they spoke against the government. One parishioner reported:

> During that first week we learned about the evictions, the chiefs moved around Kibera threatening us with physical harm if we tried to fight the

> government over the evictions. We knew what they were capable of doing to us, so many decided to keep off.[5]

Others did not take steps to resist the eviction because of a general attitude of apathy and resignation. In the words of one parishioner, "We kept quiet because most of us had just given up. We were tired and we let the government do what it wanted to do because there was no way we could physically stop the bulldozers."[6] Some residents remained impassive in the face of the threat because they were waiting for the NGOs to take action. Aware that KCS and Pamoja Trust had intervened to stop evictions in the past, there were many residents who assumed they would do the same thing in Kibera. The community's dependence on NGOs to act on their behalf was not limited to Kibera; it was also observed in Korogocho and Mukuru kwa Njenga. Also, most residents were not aware of their legal rights to protest the evictions. Unaware of the law and susceptible to manipulation by local authorities, most structure owners believed the propaganda spread by the PA that because they did not possess title deeds, they had no legal standing to object to the government's eviction plan. One parishioner explained, "We were afraid to do anything because we were on government land. We all knew that we were there illegally and we didn't think we could go to court. So we just lacked the will to do anything."[7]

Finally, there were numerous structure owners who did not take the threat seriously. Their attitudes were shaped by their prior experiences of eviction threats. One parishioner explained, "We didn't believe the railway evictions were real. The government had been threatening to evict us from the rail on and off for years. For many of us, the government was just talking and it would never happen."[8] Others did not believe the demolition threats were authentic because they had not been given eviction notices and there were no Xs painted on their doors; they thought the eviction threat was merely a rumor. Some thought Raila was just flexing his political muscle by showing his power to remove the Kikuyu from Kibera if they did not support him and had no intention of acting on his threats. Some structure owners were too busy managing their businesses and coping with daily survival. One parishioner commented, "I was fed up being called for meetings about evictions along the railway and nothing

---

[5] Interview with Saturday group member D, September 29, 2008.
[6] Interview with Saturday group member A, October 1, 2008.
[7] Interview with OHR team member A, September 22, 2008.
[8] OHR Memorandum, November 24, 2004.

ever happened. I could not close my shop every time someone wanted to call a meeting."[9]

In contrast to the structure owners, most tenants were not overtly concerned about the eviction threat. Many tenants viewed the evictions as a problem of the Kikuyu and Nubian communities since, as the structure owners, they had the most to lose. Given their long history of conflict and deep-seated resentment, most tenants were not sympathetic to or supportive of the structure owners' potential losses. Many were also reticent to question the agenda of their political patron, Raila Odinga, who had strongly advocated the need for the evictions in the middle-class neighborhoods and Raila village. Moreover, as temporary and transient residents, the tenants were focused on more imminent survival needs, not the long-term stability of the settlement. One Team member explained, "Evictions were not a priority for tenants because they knew they could just move. Almost everyone had at least one relative in other parts of Kibera or in other slums where they could stay in a crisis."[10]

Even if the affected residents had been able to overcome their fear and apathy, it would have been very difficult for the community to organize a grass-roots resistance to the evictions. The community was deeply divided along structure owner/tenant lines, a split that polarized people ethnically, religiously, socially and politically. In addition, there were no groups or individuals in the community with the capacity to mobilize a large number of people to resist the evictions. For example, most groups of Kikuyu structure owners in Soweto that had come together for purposes of opposing the move to Athi River were small and parochial by nature. They also lacked sufficient resources and contacts necessary to organize an effective response. They did not have money on hand to hire a private lawyer to file a lawsuit or pay a journalist to publicize their situation and there was not enough time to raise the money as they had during the upgrade. With respect to the tenants, there was only one recognized group, the Kibera Rent and Housing Association, a CBO created by ANPPCAN following the 2001 clashes to advocate shelter rights. This group, however, was too small and disorganized to mobilize a community-based opposition to the evictions.

The development CBOs that been created by the housing NGOs also were not able to mobilize a grass-roots response. There were only a handful of CBOs whose memberships ranged from 100 to 200 people and they were inexperienced in responding to socio-political issues; their

[9] Interview with Saturday group member C, September 24, 2008.
[10] Interview with OHR team member C, October 3, 2008.

primary focus was income-generation. They also lacked the organizational and leadership capacity to mobilize the community on complex issues related to land and housing.

The Muungano savings groups in Kibera similarly were not equipped to mobilize a community-wide response. In 2004, the Muungano savings groups in Soweto numbered less than 100 people. Not only were they too few, the majority of members were elderly Kikuyu women who were ill-equipped to organize an effective response. They also were not able to mobilize support from leaders in the other affected slums because the large intra-slum network created by the Muungano in the mid-1990s had shrunk considerably after the group's role in monitoring evictions was replaced with the savings methodology.

The fact that the SCCs and the Saturday group had learned their legal rights as they related to forced evictions did not cause them to take action. Just like the other residents of Kibera, parishioners were divided as structure owners/tenants, disorganized and afraid of possible retaliation. Church structures did not facilitate the OHR's ability to mobilize Catholics to resist the evictions. The issue of evictions was considered a political one and was beyond the scope of what parishioners in the SCCs and Saturday group were willing to address. One Team member explained:

> If anyone had tried to speak out on the eviction issue, they would have been rebuked by their fellow SCC members. People thought the issue of evictions was about politics because it involved land. The SCCs did not allow members to discuss political issues because they could divide people.[11]

The Saturday group also took no action. According to a Team member:

> The members of the group were very willing to talk about the eviction problem, but they were too afraid to raise the objections to the government in their SCCs. They were afraid the chiefs or youth wingers would find out and target them for harassment or arrest.[12]

The Housing NGOs

After learning about the government's plans, the OHR coordinator immediately informed individuals working at KCS, Pamoja Trust, ANPPCAN and Maji na Ufanisi, all of whom were shocked to learn about the planned evictions. A few days later, representatives from these NGOs

[11] Interview with OHR team member A, September 22, 2008.
[12] Ibid.

and the OHR plus Shelter Forum, the Kenya Human Rights Commission, ANPPCAN and the Basic Rights Campaign met to discuss a possible strategy to prevent the planned evictions. This meeting was the first time all the housing NGOs had gathered since the Land Caucus disbanded in 2002. Although some individuals within the NGO sector had continued to collaborate with one another, the NGOs as institutions had grown apart as the level of competition for funds and public profile increased during the first year of the KENSUP program.

In analyzing the unfolding crisis in the slums, the NGO personnel felt their options were limited. In contrast to their past strategy to oppose eviction threats through litigation, the NGOs did not want to file a lawsuit against the new NARC government. When Moi was president, the housing NGOs were united in their condemnation of the KANU regime when it violated the rights of slum dwellers, but the relationship of the NGOs to the state changed after the NARC government was elected. A number of human rights activist were appointed to high-level government positions and many who remained in the NGO sector were closely aligned with the NARC government and its officials. In the words of one NGO activist, "Civil society played such a key role in putting NARC into power; it was hard to distinguish NARC from the NGOs because they were so closely associated."[13] The housing NGOs that stood to receive lucrative contracts from the government, especially those related to the Soweto upgrade, were reluctant to confront the government publicly and risk jeopardizing their good relations. When discussing whether to file a lawsuit, the director of one NGO explained that she had a personal relationship with the Minister of Lands and had already begun behind-the-scene negotiations. The other NGOs agreed not to jeopardize the talks by suing the government.

The NGOs also discussed the other traditional alternative-mobilizing the Kibera community to resist the evictions physically-but this strategy was quickly rejected as an option. Mobilizing a community response would be nearly impossible not only because of the short time frame, but also because the housing NGOs did not have a collaborative relationship with the affected community. Despite efforts by Pamoja Trust and, to a lesser degree, KCS and Shelter Forum, to make inroads into Soweto during the initial phase of the upgrade, in February 2004 only two NGOs, Maji na Ufanisi and ANPPCAN, had a presence in Kibera. The handful of community organizers who worked for these entities did not have the capacity or networks to coordinate a Kibera-wide response to the eviction threat.

---

[13] OHR Memorandum, March 4, 2005.

Despite their decision to pursue negotiations with the Minister of Lands as their primary strategy, the NGOs also knew they could not ignore demands by slum dwellers to speak out against the unprecedented eviction threat. For years, the NGOs had held themselves out as advocates for the rights of slum dwellers and had raised donor funds on that premise. The NGOs decided to condemn the evictions publicly, but in the least confrontational approach possible; they took out a full-page advertisement in the leading daily newspaper to protest the evictions on human rights grounds.[14] The NGOs failure to act in a more substantive manner was a surprise to many slum dwellers. In their view, the advertisement appeared to be a public relations act designed to impress the NGOs' donors and had little ability to impact the crisis facing the slum dwellers. When the government did not react to the newspaper advertisement, the director of Maji na Ufanisi asked the OHR to prepare a written brief describing the impact of the eviction threat in the community for the Director of Housing and invited members of the OHR and lawyers from KCS and Pamoja Trust to meet the director personally.[15] Although the director listened to the presentation, she candidly admitted that she had no influence on the decision.

Faith-Based Organizations

Despite their prolific numbers and status as indigenous leaders, the religious leaders in Kibera were able to do very little to resist the planned evictions. On the day that the OHR learned about the demolition orders, members of the OHR asked the local pastors in Line Saba to organize an emergency meeting for the pastors in his fellowship because many of them had churches in Line Saba, an area that would be particularly affected by the railway and power lines demolitions. During the meeting, it was evident that the pastors did not know how to respond. Apart from a large eviction that took place in Toi Market in 1996, Kibera had been relatively free from large-scale evictions. Inexperienced in responding to a crisis of this size, most pastors admitted that they had no idea what they could do to stop the evictions; they did not know the law, their rights, or possible strategies that might stop the evictions. Also, they did not have personal contacts with any decision makers in the government including the area MP. The pastors reiterated their concerns that they were afraid to oppose

---

[14] See "Fight Poverty and Not the Poor: Stop Slum Evictions," *Daily Nation*, Nairobi, February 20, 2004.

[15] See OHR Memorandum, February 25, 2004.

the government publicly out of fear of retaliation. The evictions were being instigated by powerful cabinet members who had the support of the police, the local PA and NDP youth wingers. The pastors had invested a great deal in building churches and communities of faithful. Even though the demolitions threatened their very existence, many pastors preferred to keep silent in the hope that the eviction threat would pass. In their view, silence was a safer strategy than criticizing the government and risking retaliation for an event that might not happen.

Although some pastors expressed reservations in speaking out, the group agreed to send a letter from the religious leaders with churches and mosques in the affected areas to the area MP, the DO and the mayor articulating their opposition to the evictions. As they had during the upgrade crisis, the pastors asked the OHR to prepare the letter. However, when the OHR coordinator and one of the assistant parish priests visited the religious leaders to ask for their signatures, their response was mixed. The Anglican priest willingly signed the letter, but the imam in Lindi declined on the grounds that evictions would affect few, if any, Muslims. Efforts to explain that many Muslims living in Lindi would be affected by the bypass demolitions had no effect. The imam was not willing to sign the letter because the Nubian elders were in the process of negotiating for land in Kibera and he did not want to jeopardize those negotiations. A number of Pentecostal pastors who had initially been enthusiastic about the letter also declined to sign; they, too, were afraid to criticize the government out of fear of retaliation by the local chiefs. No government officials ever replied to the letter.

The OHR's subsequent effort to involve a large group of religious leaders also bore little fruit. After learning about the planned demolitions, the OHR asked the DO to hold an emergency meeting with the religious leaders to inform them of the government's plan so they could alert their followers about the impending demolitions; they could reach the largest number of people in the shortest amount of time and influence them to approach the eviction with calm and peace. The DO was initially reluctant to assemble the religious leaders; he did not know who they were or how to contact them. He was also afraid that if the pastors were organized for a meeting, they might mobilize in opposition to the government's plan. Despite his fears, the DO consented to the meeting because he was more afraid that a surprise demolition exercise would lead to uncontrolled violence, but he asked the OHR Team to mobilize the pastors and imams since he lacked the capacity.

On February 20, 2004, more than 70 religious leaders including Muslims and Christians from all the villages attended a meeting with the

DO for the first time in Kibera's history.[16] Recognizing that many Kibera residents did not believe the eviction threats were real, the DO confirmed the government's plans and urged religious leaders to talk to their faithful and convince them to accept the evictions.[17] Just as the Pentecostal pastors, the religious leaders who spoke out during the meeting were reticent to criticize the plan of the NARC government. Some feared possible retaliation by the local chiefs, while others believed NARC's promise that it had plans to improve Kibera and they did not want to undermine their potential to be given financial support during the hoped-for rehabilitation of the slum. Instead of uniting to resist the illegal evictions, most religious leaders pleaded for more time to help people relocate churches and mosques. The following comment by one pastor is illustrative:

> We know that NARC supports the rule of law and every Kenyan supports the changes the government is making. Kibera people are not economically strong and can't get money to move quickly. We are not against the government's plan. We pray for the government, but we beg this government to give more time.[18]

Although the meeting did not convince the DO to alter his planned course, it did help the religious leaders disseminate accurate information in advance of the government's actions. The DO ended the meeting with a promise to hold regular meetings with the religious leaders, but no further meetings were held.

The religious leaders also did not try to organize the group again. They were not able to act as a viable advocacy group on the eviction issue for several reasons. At a fundamental level, they were not an organized group with shared values and goals. Historically divided along religious, ethnic and political grounds, many of the religious leaders were more concerned about how the eviction would impact their individual church or mosque than the broader community. Some were reluctant to oppose the NARC government because they viewed it as a possible future benefactor. They were also afraid to speak out on political issues that might provoke a violent reaction form the chiefs or the youth wingers. Moreover, the pastors and imams reflected the general demographic in the community; many of them lacked the basic knowledge, expertise and resources to

---

[16] See "Thousands to Be Left Homeless in Slum Demolitions," *Catholic Information Services of Africa*, Nairobi, February 20, 2004.
[17] OHR Memorandum, February 20, 2005.
[18] Ibid.

influence government decisions. There were also no leaders in the group who had the ability to unite the different religious groups.

Advocacy by the OHR

During the early stages of the eviction crisis, the OHR coordinator did not expect the other churches to mobilize resistance to the eviction threat, but when the coordinator realized the NGOs would not act, she knew the situation was critical. The OHR coordinator decided to inform her network of international contacts about the threat. Relying on information gathered by the OHR Team, Saturday group and SCCs, the coordinator prepared a briefing memo that explained the government's illegal plans and the potential impact of the evictions and distributed it to a number of expatriate actors.

The OHR coordinator first contacted the missionary priests in the Kutoka network to inform them of the planned evictions and the possible impact in their parishes particularly St. Mary's Catholic Church in Mukuru kwa Njenga where the railway also passed. The conveners of the Kutoka network immediately prepared a letter for Archbishop Ndingi apprising him of the threat and requesting him to ask the government to delay the evictions until adequate notice and plans for a resettlement were made, but the Archbishop did not respond favorably. The missionary priest who tried to solicit the Archbishop's support described his reaction:

> When I went to see Archbishop Ndingi about the evictions to ask for his advice, he only gave me five minutes. He told me the Kibaki government was a Catholic government and that it was trying to develop the country. He said the slum people were choosing to live there and creating their own problems with the government.[19]

Despite his defense of the government's plan, the Archbishop eventually promised that he would write a letter to the government asking for a two-month delay on the demolitions, but he never did.

Despite the local church's refusal to get involved in the eviction crisis, a number of missionaries met frequently to exchange information about the unfolding situation and to protest the evictions. For example, the Kutoka conveners delivered letters that had been signed by all the network members to the mayor and the three ministers asking them to suspend the evictions. They also regularly sent e-mails to the local Catholic media and the daily newspapers to voice the network's protest against the evictions.

---

[19] Interview with missionary priest B, September 5, 2008.

However, the capacity of the missionaries to hold the government to account was limited by a number of factors–a weak structure and organization, few political contacts and a lack of a shared vision. From its inception, the Kutoka network was formed as a loose coalition to exchange information and discuss both spiritual and social issues that affected the slum communities; it was not set up to be an advocacy group. Even though there were a handful of missionaries who occasionally responded to emerging social justice issues, the majority were not in favor of the church playing a proactive role in the human rights arena, especially when the issue had a political overtone. Some of these missionaries were sensitive to their "foreign" status and were reluctant to confront the state about issues that could lead to their expulsion. Others felt the eviction issue was beyond the scope of their work; from their perspective, the primary role of the parishes was evangelization and attending to the spiritual needs of the Catholics, socio-political issues were best left to politicians and the government. Not surprisingly, the division in approach led to tension in the network. During the eviction crisis, apart from the three parishes directly affected by the eviction threat, only three other missionary priests were actively involved in the campaign to stop the evictions.

In addition to the competing interests and visions of the missionaries, the Kutoka network lacked formal structures and resources to hold the government to account. Although there were three conveners, these missionaries were essentially self-selected since no one else was willing to take on additional tasks given their already overwhelming workloads in the parish. All three conveners had limited time and access to government officials to undertake advocacy. Only one of the missionary priests had direct access to a high-level official, Vice-President Moody Awori, but the vice-president's response to the priest's request for assistance was irregular and unpredictable. Also, the network had no staff, office or financial resources; all activities were done on an ad hoc and voluntary basis by individual members.

Given the lack of an organized response, each parish affected by the demolition order responded to the eviction threat according to its own capacity. In Mukuru, it was estimated that 10,000 people would be displaced by the railway and power line demolitions. The missionary priest in that area had experienced some of the most devastating evictions in the mid-1990s and did not think it was possible to stop the evictions. He therefore voluntarily dismantled a sub-parish chapel, parish hall and toilets for the school which were located under power lines explaining:

> As the church we wanted to be an example to others to move before the government came. If they came with the bulldozer, they could destroy the iron sheets and timbers and other things. So we decided to salvage the material before they began the exercise.[20]

Many residents followed suit and took down their structures without voicing any objection to the government's illegal plan.

In Korogocho, it was estimated that 2,500 people lived under power lines. Although the number of affected people was much smaller, the missionary priest in Korogocho wanted to resist the evictions, but he did not want to collaborate with the housing NGOs. After leaving the Land Caucus, he remained firm in his belief that NGOs were not appropriate partners for the parishes given their track record for mismanagement and corruption. In his view, "The NGOs came into the community and offered a few services and then they left. The NGOs took advantage of slum communities for their own salaries and business. Many of the NGO leaders were corrupt and had no vision for the people."[21] Instead of working with the local NGOs, this priest helped an Italian housing rights group from his home country launch an e-mail campaign called "Viva Nairobi" to raise global awareness about the eviction threat. More than 9,000 thousand people sent e-mails to the government of Kenya, UN-Habitat and the European Parliament to register their protest against the demolition plan.

The situation was very different in Kibera. Approximately 100,000 people were potentially impacted by the demolition order including the main parish compound. Although the acting parish priest had been in the parish for only several months, he had been the parish priest of St. Michael's, the neighboring parish that included part of Kibera in the 1980s and was aware of the Kibera reality and the potential impact of the evictions. Unlike the other parishes in Kutoka, the parish had an OHR with a full-time staff and lawyer with experience in responding to evictions as well as contacts in other sectors of civil society. In his view, the OHR should use every available avenue to fight the evictions including collaborating with the NGOs and any other organization willing to resist the evictions.

Although each of the affected parishes adopted a different approach, they were in agreement that the Papal Nuncio needed to be apprised of the threat, especially since the local church had not responded. The Nuncio had not hesitated to support the parish during the upgrade crisis and the

---

[20] Kutoka Minutes, April 27, 2008.

[21] Interview with missionary priest B, September 5, 2008.

missionaries felt he would intervene again in light of the emergency situation. At the time the OHR coordinator learned about the planned demolition, she was in the process of preparing a written update on the status of the upgrading project requested by the Nuncio. She included the information about the demolition orders and requested a meeting with the Nuncio and the missionaries from the two parishes in Kibera. The missionary priest from Kangemi who assisted the Nuncio in representing the Holy See at UN-Habitat meetings also apprised him of the possible implications of the demolition orders and its international implications.[22]

The Papal Nuncio's response was immediate. The secretary to the Papal Nuncio invited the missionaries from the parish and Our Lady of Guadalupe, the neighboring sister parish, to update him on the planned evictions. He explained that Cardinal Renato Martino, the President of the Pontifical Council for Justice and Peace appointed by Pope John Paul II to oversee all issues of human rights and social justice, was arriving in Kenya on February 22 for a one-week pastoral visit. The main purpose of the Cardinal's visit was to preside over the 10th anniversary of the social ministry program at Tangaza College. The Nuncio's secretary also explained that the Nuncio had arranged for the Cardinal to meet Mrs. Tibaijuka about the Soweto upgrade as well as pay a courtesy call on President Kibaki. Prior to his appointment to the Pontifical Council, Cardinal Martino had been the Vatican's Permanent Observer to the United Nations for 16 years and was knowledgeable of and interested in issues of housing and evictions. The OHR coordinator asked the Nuncio's secretary to invite Cardinal Martino to visit Kibera before he met UN-Habitat in order to see first-hand the situation facing tens of thousands of slum dwellers. Several days later, the Papal Nuncio met a number of missionary priests in the Kutoka network to ascertain the impact of the evictions in their parishes. In agreement that the planned evictions were in violation of international law and would have disastrous consequences for the poor living in the slums, the Nuncio promised to address the issue at the diplomatic level.

Upon the Cardinal's arrival in Nairobi, the Nuncio briefed him on the demolitions planned for Kibera and other slum areas. Cardinal Martino agreed to see the situation himself and immediately went with the Papal Nuncio to visit the parish. During his tour, the Cardinal and the Nuncio met members of the Saturday group, the OHR and the acting parish priest for a briefing on the planned eviction exercise and its anticipated impact

---

[22] NGO Coalition Memorandum, February 24, 2004.

on the community. The Cardinal, visibly moved by what he saw, called upon the government to:

> Respect the human rights of the dwellers who will be affected...Every effort should be made first to provide alternative accommodation before proceeding with evictions and the demolition of illegal structures.[23]

After his visit to Kibera, Cardinal met Mrs. Tibaijuka and expressed his concerns that the planned evictions were an imminent threat to security and peace in Kibera. Two days later, he expressed those same concerns in a meeting with President Kibaki.

The OHR coordinator also contacted a number of other international organizations including lawyers from COHRE whose reaction to news of the planned evictions was very different from the local NGOs. Within hours of receiving the news, the COHRE lawyers, working closely with the OHR to gather accurate facts on the planned evictions and their impact at the grass roots, sent a letter to President Kibaki asking him to cancel the eviction plans because they were in breach of international laws binding on Kenya.[24] COHRE personnel also organized a media conference in Geneva targeting Kenyan and international media to highlight the eviction threat and the government's illegal actions. In addition, COHRE mobilized Human Rights Watch and numerous housing rights organizations in their network including NGOs from Turkey, Egypt, Pakistan, Philippines, India, South Africa and Brazil to issue statements to the Kenyan government objecting to the planned forced evictions.

The OHR coordinator also contacted officials at UN-Habitat. The Habitat officials were shocked to learn about the government's plans and recognized that the demolitions would impair their ability to proceed with the Soweto upgrade, but neither they nor Mrs. Tibaijuka publicly spoke out against the evictions. According to one official, Habitat refused to object to the planned evictions on the grounds that it was an internal issue for the government of Kenya.[25] But not everyone at Habitat agreed with the organization's official position of neutrality. Another Habitat official revealed that Habitat took a restrained approach because it did not want to antagonize Raila Odinga.[26] UN-Habitat was in the process of difficult

[23] "Cardinal Martino Concludes Pastoral Visit," *Catholic Information Services of Africa*, Nairobi, February 27, 2004.
[24] COHRE Letter to President Kibaki, February 24, 2004.
[25] OHR Memorandum, March 11, 2005.
[26] Rasna Warah, "Nairobi's Silent Majority Fight Back," May 11, 2004, available at http://www.peopleandplanet.net/doc.php?id=2217.

negotiations with the government for land to build a decanting site for the Soweto residents and did not want to jeopardize a project that it had already invested substantial time and money.

Habitat's refusal to denounce the government's demolition order came as a surprise not only because UN-Habitat personnel, including Mrs. Tibaijuka, had worked closely with several NGOs and the parish on the Soweto upgrade, but also because Mrs. Tibaijuka was hosting the first meeting of a much publicized group, the UN-Habitat Advisory Group on Forced Evictions, that assembled leading housing experts from around the world to inform UN-Habitat on how it could monitor, identify and promote alternatives to unlawful evictions. Ironically, that meeting occurred in Nairobi on March 5 just days after the demolitions were scheduled to start.

Other UN bodies were less reticent to criticize publicly the Kenyan government. In mid-February, at the invitation of the government, the Special Rapporteur on Adequate Housing to the UN Commission on Human Rights, Miloon Kithari, was in Kenya on a two-week mission to evaluate whether adequate housing was being realized in the country. Inexplicably, the government invited one of the most influential international human rights spokesmen on housing rights to be present in the country at the same time as it announced plans to undertake large-scale slum demolitions. The Rapporteur denounced the government's eviction of people living in Raila village and condemned its plan to undertake large-scale evictions in the slums deeming them a violation of international norms and procedures.[27] Promising to present his findings to the 61st session of the UN Commission on Human Rights in Geneva, the Rapporteur asked the government to halt the procedure and put a moratorium on all evictions until an evictions policy that complied with human rights standards was put into place.[28]

During the Kutoka meetings, the missionaries decided to notify other diplomatic contacts in the hope they would join the Nuncio in protesting the evictions. The OHR coordinator notified Sir Edward and his political advisors of the impending threats and provided them with detailed maps and data on Kibera, Mukuru kwa Njenga and Korogocho. She also sent briefings to the political advisors on the EU's land and settlements committee who had visited the parish in 2003. The acting parish priest

---

[27] "D-Day for Kibera's Derelict Structures," *Daily Nation*, Nairobi, February 29, 2008.

[28] Miloon Kithari, "Addendum Mission to Kenya," (Report presented to the 61st Session of the Commission on Human Rights, Geneva, February 2004), 18-19.

informed diplomatic contacts from Mexico and Spain while the priest in Korogocho contacted the ambassadors from Italy and Germany.

After the Rapporteur's report was publicized, the British High Commission tried to mobilize the diplomatic missions in the EU to present a diplomatic *démarche* addressed to Vice-President Awori asking that the necessary procedures required under international human rights law be put into place before effecting any further evictions in the slums of Nairobi. The diplomatic missions from four EU countries, the United Kingdom, Italy, the Netherlands and Sweden, signed the Aide-Memoire. The other diplomatic missions were reluctant to criticize the NARC government publicly because they had openly supported it, especially its purported pledge to restore the rule of law. Even though a number of diplomats privately said they wanted to dissuade the government from undertaking the evictions, they did not think it politically prudent to oppose efforts seen to reverse illegal land use after they had earlier urged the NARC government to be tough on corruption involving public land. Despite the reticence of other countries, after sending the *démarche*, Sir Edward and his staff continued to engage in diplomatic talks with a number of government officials.

While the Papal Nuncio and the diplomats pursued their lobbying efforts, the OHR coordinator in consultation with the COHRE lawyers decided it was necessary for the community to file a lawsuit against the government to try to stay the eviction, even if it was only for a short while, to give the affected communities more time to prepare for the eviction. Since the housing NGOs that had previously filed evictions cases did not want to sue the government, the COHRE lawyers offered to raise funds for a private lawyer to file the lawsuit. Given the short time frame, the OHR coordinator asked a Kenyan lawyer from International Justice Mission (IJM), an American-based legal aid NGO that regularly took referrals from the OHR, to file the case. The director of IJM agreed with the need to file a lawsuit but was initially reluctant to get involved because an eviction case was outside the scope of their expertise. However, because of the emergency situation, the IJM lawyers eventually agreed to prepare the pleadings if the OHR took responsibility for identifying the plaintiffs, gathering the facts and keeping the community informed of the case.

The OHR Team immediately told people living along the railway line about the need to file a case and asked parishioners and Kibera residents who lived and ran businesses along the railway to participate as plaintiffs in the lawsuit. The universal response was a resounding "no." In most circumstances, the legal process was an alienating experience for Kiberans; the law had been used as a tool of the rich to oppress them and had never been used to promote their rights as a community. Fears of using the legal system were heightened in the case related to the evictions. Kiberans were afraid of the certain retaliation that would be meted out by the area chief once they were known to have filed a case against the government.

The OHR Team then met several parishioners on an individual basis to try to persuade them to act as plaintiffs. During the course of a week, several parishioners agreed to bring the case only to disappear after learning that they would have to sign public documents attesting to the veracity of their claims. Eventually, a parishioner active in his SCC and the civic education program consented to sign an affidavit and provided a list of 88 residents willing to put their names on the case. According to the OHR Team member who visited the SCCs soliciting plaintiffs, "Njoroge agreed to be the lead plaintiff only because he knew the OHR would support him legally and financially if he was attacked or his house was burned down."[29]

In the course of preparing the pleadings, the lawyers at IJM consulted one of the senior lawyers at KCS experienced in filing eviction cases. Just days before the evictions were scheduled to start; the lawyers at IJM unexpectedly reported that their organization was no longer willing to file the case. With only two days remaining until the railway line demolitions, the lawyer at KCS agreed to file the case on behalf of the Kibera plaintiffs. He explained his last-minute decision:

> At that time, efforts were being made by some civil society organizations to negotiate with the government ministries, but it was becoming clear that we did not have the capacity to influence high-level people in the government. So we decided to put the legal system to use even though it was not likely to be favorable for the residents. It was a last desperate attempt to try to get an order. Other civil society actors had expressed reservations about the lawsuit, but time was running out and magnitude of the number of people involved caused us to file the case.[30]

On February 27, 2004, KCS filed a case in the High Court of Kenya against the Kenya Railways Corporation seeking an injunction to restrain it from forcibly evicting the plaintiffs on the grounds that the affected community had not been given adequate notice or adequately consulted in violation of the Railways Corporation Act and international laws that prohibit arbitrary forced evictions. The case specifically asked the KRC to

[29] Interview with OHR team member C, October 3, 2008.
[30] Interview with human rights lawyer B, September 28, 2008.

consult the affected community members and find an alternative place to settle them before undertaking any demolitions. Although the court found that there was no prima facie evidence of irreparable harm, to the surprise of many, the judge entered an order staying the notice of eviction and asked the plaintiffs to return in 10 days with concrete suggestions for the time frame needed for the community to move. The court's ruling was not a complete victory, but the case bought valuable time to try to resolve the matter before any evictions occurred.

Two days later, Raila Odinga announced at a rally in Kibera that he had been directed by President Kibaki to suspend the demolition exercise for the link road and that the government intended to look for alternative resettlement areas for the affected parties.[31] Although President Kibaki did not articulate the reasons or motives for his suspension of the evictions, it was widely believed to be the result of lobbying efforts led by Cardinal Martino and the Papal Nuncio in conjunction with the condemnation of the planned evictions by the UN Special Rapporteur on the Right to Adequate Housing and the British High Commissioner.[32]

During the last week of February, community organizers from ANPPCAN and the missionary priest from Korogocho organized an inter-denominational prayer rally for March 1 in Uhuru Park in a last-minute effort to urge the government to stop the evictions. Even though the evictions were called off, the NGOs and clerics continued with the prayer service to pray in thanksgiving for the reprieve. Although Archbishop Ndingi attended the rally, according to one of the event organizers, he agreed to participate at the last minute and only because the evictions been called off and his presence was specifically requested by the Papal Nuncio.

The government's stay of evictions only lasted one day. On the same day as the ecumenical prayer rally, Raila announced that the demolition suspension did not apply to the planned demolitions for the link road. Several days later, the Minister of Energy unilaterally excluded the power line demolitions from the presidential pronouncement and extended the eviction notice by 40 days. The vice-president confirmed these statements when he pronounced the decision to halt the demolitions was only temporary to allow time for the government to ensure proper planning.[33] Several days later, President Kibaki appointed Vice-President Awori to preside over an inter-ministerial committee to investigate how the

---

[31] Nixon Ng'ang'a, "Government Stops Demolitions," *East African Standard*, Nairobi, March 1, 2004.

[32] See John Mbaria, "Pope Stopped Kenyan Slum Demolitions," *EastAfrican*, Nairobi, March 15-21, 2004.

[33] "Demolitions to Resume Soon," *East African Standard*, Nairobi, March 4, 2005.

evictions should proceed in a coordinated manner. The series of conflicting statements issued by different government officials suggested that the suspension of the planned demolitions was only a temporary postponement and caused slum dwellers to believe that it was just a matter of time before the evictions would proceed.

Efforts to Secure a Permanent Moratorium

Once the evictions were temporarily delayed, the housing NGOs responded with a more vigorous effort to solve the eviction crisis now that their efforts were no longer viewed to be in direct opposition to the NARC government. On March 2, 2004, the KCS lawyer who filed the lawsuit convened a meeting of the housing NGOs to devise a coordinated strategy to secure a permanent suspension of the evictions. This group of NGOs-KCS, Maji na Ufanisi, Shelter Forum, Pamoja Trust and the Basic Rights Campaign-referred to themselves as the NGO Coalition against Evictions.

When the Coalition was formed, the convener invited the parishes in the Kutoka network to participate in their meetings. Apart from the OHR, none of the other parishes sent representatives to regularly attend the Coalition meetings. Some were consumed with pastoral responsibilities in their parishes. Others felt that they did not have the necessary expertise to contribute to the second phase of the eviction campaign; in their view, it was a matter best left to the lawyers and NGOs who had the financial resources and professional competence to influence the government's long-term policy making on the eviction issue. A few did not want to get involved with the housing NGOs because of the historical conflict relating back to the Land Caucus. The parish priest had reservations about the NGOs' financial motivations and bias in favor of the structure owners, but he agreed that the OHR Team should attend the Coalition meetings. The NGOs were not only an important source of information about the evictions; the Coalition was also the only civil society forum where the OHR could transmit the ideas and concerns of the affected residents to individuals negotiating on behalf of the community. This was especially important in light of the NGOs decision not to include community members in the Coalition.

The NGO Coalition

During the Coalition's first meeting, members divided tasks to respond to a variety of issues surrounding the eviction threat. KCS agreed to be responsible for the litigation and all legal matters. Pamoja Trust agreed to count and map the people affected by the eviction threat while Shelter Forum committed to profile the campaign in the media. In addition, three individuals from different NGOs who had contacts in the NARC government agreed to negotiate with officials from the relevant ministries to try to find a viable alternative to the evictions. The convener of the Coalition assigned the OHR the task of drafting a lobby document that described the historical background to the eviction threat, the impact on the affected communities and proposals for a way forward because it was the only participant situated in the slums with access to the community and up-to-date information from the grass roots.

During March and April, the Coalition met on a weekly basis to update one another on the outcome of their assigned tasks and brainstorm about the next steps necessary to secure to a permanent moratorium on the evictions. In early March, the OHR coordinator invited two lawyers from COHRE who were in Nairobi to attend the first meeting of UN-Habitat's Advisory Group on Evictions to attend a meeting of the NGO Coalition held at the parish. During the meeting, the parish priest asked the COHRE lawyers to undertake a fact-finding mission to raise the public profile of the eviction threat as they had done in other African countries such as Zimbabwe and Nigeria.[34] The COHRE lawyers agreed to the request so long as the Coalition secured donor funding for the fact-finding mission.

Throughout March lawyers at KCS along with four representatives appointed by the plaintiffs negotiated with KRC officials about the timeline for moving and possible relocations sites. Since the lawsuit was filed on an emergency basis, the KCS lawyers did not know the plaintiffs or have a personal relationship with them. The lawyers asked the OHR Team to organize the initial meetings with the plaintiffs and facilitate consensus among them on how much time they needed to move from the railway. Many of the plaintiffs could not attend meetings because they were working; they were also scattered throughout Kibera and many had no mailing address or telephone. The OHR Team kept the plaintiffs and the larger community informed of the case through individual and group meetings, church announcements and posters.

While the KCS lawyers were negotiating with the KRC, the Coalition sent the lobby document prepared by the OHR to numerous government officials and ministries. Even though the Kutoka network was not working directly with the NGO Coalition, the conveners of the network sent the lobby document to the vice-president and requested a meeting. Despite

---

[34] NGO Coalition Minutes, March 5, 2005.

numerous efforts by the missionaries to arrange a meeting, the vice-president never agreed to meet the network.

During this same time, the director of Pamoja Trust liaised directly with the Minister of Lands to find alternative land near Kibera to relocate the affected community living along the railway. Slum Dwellers International, Pamoja Trust's partner in India, facilitated an exchange visit of KRC officials to Mumbai to observe examples of successful railway relocations. The exchange visit yielded a positive outcome; the KRC agreed to withdraw its eviction notices and reduced the safety corridor from 100 to 50 feet on either side of the railway. Despite the positive progress made with respect to the railway line evictions, the NGO representatives tasked to meet the Minister of Energy and the Minister of Roads, Public Works and Housing lacked sufficient political contacts to gain access to these ministries. After several failed attempts to reach them, the NGOs quietly dropped the issue and focused exclusively on the railway line evictions. As a result, fear and uncertainty about how these ministries would act on their demolition orders was high among slum dwellers throughout the city.

In mid-May, Kenya Railways asked the Pamoja Trust to undertake an enumeration process of the residents living along the railway to assist in the formulation of a relocation plan. Because Pamoja Trust did not have a strategic presence in Kibera, the parish hosted the enumeration process in the church compound. The OHR Team mobilized 15 members of the Saturday group and other parishioners to join the enumeration team brought by Pamoja.

After the enumeration process started, NDP youth wingers working for the area councilor demanded to be included in the enumeration exercise. Every morning large groups of youth entered the parish compound and demanded that Pamoja Trust pay them to do the enumeration or else they would block the entire exercise. The community organizers at Pamoja Trust were relatively new to Kibera and unprepared to deal with the corrupt and violent tactics of the youth wingers. Left with no alternative, Pamoja Trust consented to the demands by the youth wingers. Parishioners who were involved in the enumeration process reported to the OHR that many of the youth wingers were demanding money from residents living along the railway line in exchange for including their names as affected residents. Parishioners also observed some youth wingers making promises to people living outside Kibera that they would get new plots from the KRC if they paid the youth wingers a fee in exchange for putting their names on the list. Fearful of the youth wingers and their tactics, most parishioners quickly stopped participating in the counting exercise. Unable to curtail the corruption, Pamoja Trust canceled the enumeration after a few days and focused its efforts in Mukuru slum.

Individual Efforts of the OHR

Members of the OHR attended most of the weekly Coalition meetings from March to May; but the coordinator soon realized that the Coalition's disconnection from the slum communities as well as its lack of shared motivation and coordinated leadership would limit its ability to secure a positive outcome for Kibera. The OHR coordinator therefore allocated the majority of the Team's time and efforts to keeping the Kibera community apprised of the situation and collaborating with a number of international actors within whom it had greater confidence and better relationships.

Following the suspension of the demolitions, the OHR incorporated the eviction issue into the civic education curriculum. In the Soweto and Shilanga sub-parishes where the residents were particularly affected by the threat, OHR members also gave regular inputs during Sunday masses. Although members of the Saturday group and SCCs welcomed lessons on their legal rights with respect to the evictions, parishioners were not interested in addressing the issue proactively or participating in events organized by the OHR. For example, in March 2004 the NGO Coalition distributed copies of a petition protesting the evictions and demanding the government resettle the affected communities before the demolition orders were put into effect. The goal was to generate 500,000 signatures not only to apprise the community of the situation, but also to demonstrate to the government the strength of the slum dwellers numbers and unity. The OHR invited the Saturday group members to staff tables after Sunday masses where parishioners could sign the petition. For three Sundays in a row, only a handful of people from the Saturday group turned up to collect signatures and their efforts produced fewer than 50 signatures. Parishioners were reluctant to sign the petition out of fear and confusion; most were afraid that the local chiefs and youth wingers would get a copy of the petition and target anyone who complained about the government. In addition, many parishioners thought the NGOs were collecting their signatures to sign them up secretly for the NARC party.

Members of the OHR also met other local religious leaders to see if they could build a local ecumenical response to the evictions. Following several meetings, the OHR joined by the Anglican priest and a handful of Pentecostal pastors, organized a prayer service along the railway line for March 24th to raise awareness about the on-going threat of evictions and to pray for a peaceful solution to the crisis. But on the day of the prayer service, to the surprise of the organizers, only about 100 people attended. Most parishioners were afraid to attend because they thought they would be targeted by the area chief. In addition, once the immediate threat had passed, the majority of Kiberans lost interest in the issue. According to one Team member, "Most of the structure owners along the railway line were business people focused only on their commercial interests; they did not want to spend time on events that would not give them something financially in return."[35] The tenants generally approached the eviction issue with ambivalence and a lack of interest. "The tenants didn't attend eviction events because they were busy finding their daily bread and they knew they could live elsewhere if they had to, so it wasn't a priority for them."[36]

The OHR's inability to mobilize Catholics was not unusual; the same scenario occurred in the other parishes affected by the demolition. For example, the missionary priest who tried to mobilize SCC members in Korogocho slum to attend the March prayer service was able to convince only 50 people to attend. In his view, there were two main obstacles to mobilizing Catholics. First, he blamed the NGO practice of paying slum dwellers to attend events.

> NGOs have inculcated a mindset in the slums that a person should be paid transportation costs if they go somewhere outside the slum. This has created a situation where if the church tries to organize an event without paying, it is doomed to fail because the people will not attend unless they are paid."[37]

Second, Catholics did not attend because priests and religious sisters, both local and expatriate, were not mobilized to attend.

> In Kenya, our bishops do not want to see priests and nuns behaving as activists because it looks like we are trouble makers. They have no problem for us to discuss the issues, but we cannot take any public action and if the parish priest is not active, the Catholics similarly will not take any action.[38]

In his view, efforts by the parishes to mobilize Catholics would never be successful unless the church first played a role in building up leaders

---

[35] Interview with OHR team member B, September 20, 2008.
[36] Ibid.
[37] Interview with missionary priest B, September 5, 2008.
[38] Ibid.

grounded in Christian values, especially a spirit of service and volunteerism.

In addition to raising awareness in the community, the OHR continued to collaborate with the Papal Nuncio who remained personally committed to ensuring that further evictions did not happen. Using his influence as the dean of the diplomatic corps, he continued to meet members of the diplomatic missions and Kenya's permanent representative to UN-Habitat who was working behind the scenes to influence the government because he was embarrassed that large-scale evictions would be sanctioned by the government in Habitat's host city.[39]

In April 2004 the Nuncio asked the OHR coordinator and the missionary priest from Korogocho to partner him in preparing a 30-minute video about the threatened evictions to be used as tool in the on-going lobbying efforts. The video entitled, "For Love of Neighbor, Evictions in Nairobi, Kenya," was launched on June 24, 2004, at the Nuncio's residence where he reiterated his plea to the government to suspend the evictions until a resettlement plan was put into place. At the Nuncio's invitation, the launch was attended by numerous ambassadors, missionaries in the Kutoka network and representatives from UN-Habitat and the housing NGOs. Members of the Kutoka network distributed the video to all government ministries involved in the eviction threat, key members of the PA, all embassies, UN-Habitat officials, housing rights NGOs and the media houses. The priest from Korogocho showed the video at the 2nd Session of the World Urban Forum held in September 2004 in Barcelona and NGO Coalition members circulated it during a session of the UN Human Rights Committee in New York City in October 2004.

The British High Commissioner also personally continued to lobby for a permanent moratorium on the eviction plan and a long-lasting solution to the slum problem. The intervention of the British government was significant because it was a key donor in the on-going land policy review process being undertaken by the Ministry of Lands that included a review of how to respond to the slum crisis in the country. Throughout 2004-2005, the High Commissioner and his staff met and corresponded regularly with the OHR about events unfolding in Kibera in order to inform their lobbying efforts with the different ministries involved in the evictions.

The OHR Team also took the lead in assisting COHRE in the fact-finding mission. Although the NGO Coalition had initially agreed to

---

[39] NGO Coalition Minutes, March 29, 2004.

support the COHRE lawyers, some individuals in the Coalition withdrew their support after COHRE formally agreed to do the mission. Some of the NGOs argued that local Kenyan NGOs, not foreign organizations, should be the ones to investigate evictions in Kenya; implicit in their argument was the fact that donor money should benefit them, not outsiders. It turned out the most vocal opponent, unbeknownst to the other NGOs, was lobbying for a separate fact-finding mission with UN-Habitat's Advisory Group on Forced Evictions and did not want the mission of COHRE to overtake its chances of securing the Habitat contract. During a Coalition meeting, a low-level employee from that NGO inadvertently revealed that their director had sent secret letters to a number of donors expressing its objection to the COHRE mission.[40] The NGO's efforts to undermine the COHRE project did not succeed because another donor had already agreed to fund the mission.

In July 2004 COHRE sent a team of five international lawyers who were experts in housing rights and resettlement programs in Africa to collect information and analyze the eviction threat in Kibera. However, as a result of the conflict about the mission, apart from the KCS, most of the NGOs did not participate in the mission. Since the KCS had limited contacts in the Kibera community, COHRE liaised primarily with the parish OHR Team who arranged for the COHRE lawyers to meet and interview community representatives including religious leaders, CBOs and groups of structure owner and tenants. In March 2005, COHRE published the findings of the mission in a 128-page report entitled, "Listening to the Poor? Housing Rights in Nairobi, Kenya." COHRE distributed the report, which detailed the legal and human rights violations associated with the threatened forced evictions, to government officials, donors and diplomatic missions, UN-Habitat and media houses. No official response was ever issued by the government.

Collapse of the NGO Coalition

Although the Coalition made significant progress in negotiating with the Kenya Railways to find an alternative to forced evictions, the NGO Coalition fell apart before the NGOs could persuade the government to adopt a permanent solution to the eviction crisis. After meeting on a weekly basis during March and April 2004, NGO attendance at the Coalition meetings was sporadic in May and stopped altogether in mid-June after one of the NGOs was told by NARC insiders that the political

[40] NGO Coalition Minutes, May 18, 2004.

environment did not favor the evictions and they were unlikely to occur before the government prepared eviction guidelines. No longer faced with an emergency situation, the Coalition's goal of finding a long-term solution dissipated. According to one human rights lawyer, "The NGOs were only active when there was a crisis because that was when it was easier to galvanize resources and supporters. Once the crisis passed, so did the NGOs' interest."[41] In addition, the Coalition's goal of finding a long-term solution to the evictions was gradually overtaken by internal conflicts related to methodological differences and competition for money, power and influence.

Key among the NGOs' differences was disagreement about the role of the slum communities in the advocacy process. Throughout the four months that the Coalition met, complaints about the lack of community participation on the Coalition was raised at virtually every meeting. Despite this continual objection by some NGO personnel, community representatives were never invited to attend the Coalition meetings. Disagreement on this issue related to prior experiences with the Muungano and other slum communities. The NGOs knew that it would not only be a timely and difficult process to select legitimate leaders, but also their presence at the meetings would make meetings substantially longer and more contentious; each person would want to speak and there would be many disagreements on how the community should proceed. Aware of the urgency of the situation, the majority of NGO personnel felt the Coalition needed to build consensus and act quickly before the eviction threat was carried out and, therefore, excused the Coalition from including the affected community. There was also an implicit assumption among some of the NGOs that they knew the reality and needs of the slum dwellers and had the authority to speak for the community. Although a number of NGO personnel took issue with this assumption and argued that the NGOs were self-appointed and operated with no mandate from the affected community, they were the minority and had little sway with the group. As a result, apart from the four plaintiffs chosen to negotiate with the KRC, the affected residents had no voice in the negotiations carried out on their behalf.

The Coalition also never agreed on a long-term strategy for how to respond to the recurring eviction threat in the slum. Most members were stuck in a historical mentality of firefighting the immediate eviction threat and then stopping to wait for the next eviction threat. In meeting after meeting, a handful of individuals reiterated the need to devise a policy

---

[41] Interview with human rights lawyer B, September 28, 2008.

position that did more than assuage the immediate eviction threat, but the strategy paper never materialized. In a later evaluation of why the Coalition failed in this area, one member commented:

> As NGOs, we were part of the middle class. We did not do it objectively, but the majority of us had no objective intention to get at the root causes of the eviction problem. We were much better able to deal with its visible manifestations. But when the visible manifestation of the crisis appeared to be resolved, we had no agenda beyond that. This was one of our greatest limitations.[42]

A number of Coalition members also complained about the failure of the community organizers to mobilize a community response to the evictions either through the Muungano or some other groups. He further lamented:

> The community is not involved in this campaign. This was initially excusable because we were seen as the rescuers, but now we need to change this situation. The organizations that have community organizers need to come together and mandate them to organize this campaign at the grass-roots level. If the evictions go forward, we will have no community to work with at all.[43]

Although the Coalition members agreed about the need to include the affected residents in the campaign and develop a community organizing strategy, a common strategy was never developed. Two key reasons explained why. First, community mobilizing is a slow and labor-intensive process under the best of circumstances. In a community as deeply divided as Kibera, it would be even more time consuming. Most of the NGOs were restricted by their donors to pursue planned-for activities within designated time frames and approved budgets. As a result, many of the NGOs did not have the financial resources, time or personal motivation to dedicate to community mobilization. Second, in a follow-up evaluation of the Coalition's activities, it was evident that the different NGOs were in competition and did not want to pursue a joint approach.[44] According to one NGO activist, "The NGOs were not just competing for funds; they were also under growing pressure to show their donors that they had

---

[42] Ibid.
[43] NGO Coalition Minutes, April 14, 2004.
[44] Ibid., May 5, 2004.

community connections."[45] Thus, the NGOs that had a relationship with residents did not want to share their contacts.

In addition to intractable disagreements about methodology, the Coalition was plagued by a low level of commitment and accountability among Coalition members. For example, tasks were frequently assigned during meetings, but attendance at the meetings was sporadic and inconsistent making long-term planning and follow up difficult, if not impossible. When the potential for media coverage or donor financing emerged, numerous NGOs suddenly appeared, agreed to take on tasks and then disappeared without fulfilling their assignments. Some also put their names on the briefing paper prepared by the OHR, but did not attended meetings. According to one member, "A lot of organizations came into the Coalition only because they wanted to be seen by their donors as being on the side of the people."[46] Some of the NGOs were also not accountable to the group, especially those engaging in the behind-the-scenes negotiations with NARC officials. As an example, one NGO worker observed:

> The NGOs that had a close relationship with NARC deliberately did not invite other NGOs to attend the meetings because they knew that if the meetings were opened up, the presence of others would dilute their monopoly over government contracts. That meant that most of their interventions were done secretly and not fully shared with the Coalition. These NGOs always gave the excuse that there was no time to invite the rest of us, but we knew they were pursuing their own business interests with the government.[47]

The Coalition, although inclusive of some of the most informed and influential NGO personnel on the issue of slum evictions, was not able to promote a long-term solution to the eviction crisis due to a fundamental lack of collaborative spirit among the NGOs. A senior NGO activist noted:

> The NGOs in the Coalition did not trust each other. Certain NGOs used the briefing paper prepared by the OHR to raise donor funds to secure their own survival. They wanted to source money for their own implementation not for the Coalition's efforts or the benefit of the slum communities.[48]

Ultimately, any successful efforts attributed to the Coalition reflected the personal commitment of a small number of individual human rights

[45] Interview with housing NGO community organizer B, September 29, 2008.
[46] Ibid.
[47] Ibid.
[48] Interview with housing NGO community organizer C, September 26, 2008.

activists, not a coordinated effort of the housing NGOs dedicated to promoting grass-roots participation, consensus and accountability.

Even though the Coalition fell apart, the lobbying efforts of the international diplomats, the Special Rapporteur and the COHRE lawyers as well as a number of individual NGO personnel continued throughout 2004 and 2005, which unexpectedly led to the government's announcement of its permanent moratorium on the eviction threat in March 2005. After more than a year of uncertainty, the Attorney General of Kenya formally announced during his appearance before the UN Human Rights Committee in New York: "The government of Kenya has stopped evictions in Kibera and other informal settlements and future eviction, if necessary, will be done according to the established international and UN standards on evictions."[49] Notwithstanding the end of the immediate threat of evictions and the collapse of the NGO Coalition, two NGOs continued with their singular efforts to establish a long-term solution to the eviction crisis. Neither of these NGOs, operating in isolation with little support from the other NGOs or the affected communities, was able to resolve the multiple problems related to the evictions.

In the first initiative, lawyers from COHRE wanted to continue their intervention in Kenya by supporting the KCS lawyer who filed the case against Kenya Railways start HakiJamii (Economic and Social Rights Center), a new NGO that would focus primarily on the eviction issue. With financial and technical support from COHRE, HakiJamii organized several workshops in 2005 to solicit input from housing experts and representatives from the affected communities on eviction guidelines consistent with international human rights standards. Members of the OHR and several Kibera pastors attended these meetings. In January 2006 the Minister of Lands announced his intention to develop guidelines on forced evictions and published a draft housing bill that contained a provision for eviction guidelines. In response, HakiJamii organized representatives of several affected slums to draft a set of guidelines to reflect the communities' views. A few months later, the government created a government task force made up of key government ministries and several community representatives, but hopes for government-endorsed eviction guidelines were disappointed. Although the group held several preliminary meetings in 2007, it did not did not develop eviction guidelines and discontinued meeting in 2008.

---

[49] Odindo Opiata, and Odenda Lamumba, "Breach of Human Rights," *East African Standard*, Nairobi, June 26, 2005.

In the meantime, although the government did not carry out the slum evictions announced in February 2004 because of the international spotlight focused on the issue, during 2006-2008, the government continued to evict thousands of Kenyans in violation of international laws and its own pronouncements. Most of the people rendered homeless by these evictions were forest dwellers living in remote areas far from Nairobi. In contrast to the campaign to stop the slum evictions, there were no civil society actors interested in assisting the affected communities apart from HakiJamii, but as a new NGO with only two staff and limited funds, it was not able to stop the evictions. As a result, the evictions of these people went relatively unnoticed except for periodic newspaper articles and reports.

The second initiative was undertaken by Pamoja Trust. In the aftermath of the eviction crisis, the KRC entered into a contract with the International Finance Corporation (IFC), the financial arm of the World Bank, to develop a relocation plan for Kibera residents living within the railway corridor. The international consultants hired by the IFC were directed by the Ministry of Lands to contract with the Pamoja Trust to undertake the enumeration of the affected area and assist in the design of the relocation plan. In December 2004 Pamoja Trust returned to Kibera accompanied by the IFC consultants to count the structures located within the safety corridor and identify their occupants, a process that was once again marred by interference and corruption by the NDP youth wingers. In October 2005 Pamoja Trust and the IFC consultants submitted a relocation plan to the government that recommended all structure owners with structures located within 5.2 meters of the railway be compensated for their loss and relocated either within Kibera or a location to be designated in the future.[50] When a small group of businessmen who had shops along the railway gained access to the relocation plan, they objected to the plan with respect to how much they would be compensated. This group of businesspeople documented their complaints and then submitted an alternative proposal to the KRC in March 2006.[51] Unfortunately, the disputes about the relocation plan were not addressed by the KRC because the process permanently stalled in 2007 when the South African company awarded the concession experienced major financial difficulties.

---

[50] See Pamoja Trust, and Tecta Consultants, "Relocation Action Plan for Improving the Safety Along Kenya Railway Line," (Report prepared for the Government of Kenya, Ministry of Transport and Communication and Kenya Railways Corporation, Nairobi, 2005).

[51] Interview with HakiJamii program officer, September 29, 2008.

Conclusion

In this chapter, I have analyzed the OHR's response to the government's illegal plan to demolish a significant portion of Kibera. The affected community played a very minor role due to their fear, resignation and apathy. The housing NGOs and, to a lesser degree, the churches, two groups that civil society advocates typically portray as the key actors in holding the government to account, also did not adequately perform this role. Contrary to the expectations of the civil society advocates, the presence of the housing NGOs did not guarantee that the interests of the slum dwellers would be represented. After NARC came into power, many NGOs no longer acted independently from the government; rather, they were insiders with a vested financial interest in supporting the government's actions. Since it was not possible for the NGOs to play a watchdog role while they were simultaneously vying for government contracts, the housing NGOs were conspicuously absent from the first phase of the eviction crisis. Local church leaders were similarly absent. The local hierarchy was too closely aligned to the government to hold it to account during the eviction crisis. Parishioners were just as afraid of the government as the rest of the affected community. The initial steps to stop the evictions in February 2004 were orchestrated and implemented primarily from outside Kibera by high-powered expatriates who were part of the church hierarchy, diplomatic corps and international human rights sector.

The role of the OHR and other Kutoka missionaries was much less significant in the second phase. The OHR managed to play an important role in gathering and disseminating information, but lacked the contacts and capacity to engage in the lobbying activities of government officials. The OHR therefore provided information to a network of diplomatic contacts that exerted influenced on the government.

The NGOs managed to exert greater influence during the second phase of the eviction crisis. They brought the issue of evictions into the public debate and raised the profile of the slums in the media and at a national policy level, but they were not able to persuade the government to adopt long-hoped-for solutions to the problem. Unlike during the late 1990s when the NGOs had no way to access government officials, a number of NGO personnel had personal relationships with officials in the NARC government, but they were not able to influence decision makers to change the government's policy. In addition, as donor money shrank, many of the NGOs had become divided and isolated as they competed for shrinking sources of money. The prioritization of money and profile by some NGOs had also estranged the NGO sector from the very community they purported to represent. Moreover, the NARC government apparently did not intend to live up to its promise to adopt eviction guidelines. Like the Moi regime, the NARC government wanted to retain the ability to evict slum dwellers without any restrictions because they occupied some of the most valuable land in Nairobi.

CHAPTER SEVEN

CONCLUSION

Summation

In this study I have tested the theory of the civil society advocates who celebrate the potential of civil society to promote democracy, human rights and the rule of law in Africa by examining whether the parish human rights ministry was able to help consolidate democracy at a grass-roots level in Kibera during 2002-2005. After explaining the two distinct perspectives concerning the role of civil society in chapter one, I described the context for my study in chapter two. Chapter three focused on the efforts of the OHR coordinator and a team of volunteer Kenyan lawyers to provide parishioners with civic education in order to inculcate them with democratic values and habits. Unlike the civic education frequently glorified by the advocates for its political empowerment of ordinary citizens, the impact of OHR's civic education program was more limited and did not produce a similar outcome in Kibera. While the classes helped instill participants with democratic values and skills, the democracy education did not empower parishioners to hold the state to account at a local level. The social, economic and political dynamics in Kibera as well as the internal functioning of the local Catholic Church and the parish undermined ordinary Catholics' ability to confront government functionaries about their abuse of power and corruption. Instead, parishioners used their new knowledge and skills to help family and friends solve personal legal problems that frequently arose in Kibera. Another benefit was that they debated and discussed issues related to the government and political system, something they had not been allowed to do during the repressive Moi era.

In chapters four, five and six, I analyzed three different human rights issues that arose in Kibera to determine whether the response of parishioners and the OHR was in keeping with the expectations of the civil society advocates. Specifically, chapter four looked at the campaign against chang'aa started by the OHR in 2003 and later adopted by the Soweto sub-parish. Despite genuine concerns about the impact of the sale and use of the illicit brew, the vast majority of parishioners in Soweto were not willing or able to pressure low-level government officials to enforce the law prohibiting it because they were afraid of retaliation by the police and the chang'aa sellers. The small handful of parishioners who were not afraid lacked the time, capacity and resources to change the situation. As a result, the OHR played the dominant role in implementing the campaign and lobbying local officials, efforts that were not successful for the long-term.

Chapter five examined the OHR's response to the government's plan to collaborate with UN-Habitat to upgrade the village of Soweto. From the start of the announced upgrade, the area MP and local councilor misused the project to promote the interests of their ethnic community. This chapter described how parishioners in Soweto were not willing to confront the politicians, the government or UN-Habitat about the corruption and malfeasance of the project due to a combination of fear, disunity and limited resources. The local churches and housing NGOs also were also not equipped to stop the local politicians from hijacking the project for their personal and political benefit. Some of the pastors had been co-opted by the politicians; others were either too afraid or uninterested to get involved in the upgrade issue. The housing NGOs fared no better; they lacked sufficient numbers, information, networks and political access to influence the project implementers. In the absence of other avenues, the OHR coordinator and the parish priest used their personal network of international contacts to lobby UN-Habitat officials to reduce political interference and enhance the project's level of community participation and information flow. Although the lobbying efforts had some success in reducing overt corruption on the part of the councilor, they did not lessen the political interference or lead to a more fair and participatory upgrading process in Soweto.

Chapter six analyzed the OHR's response to the government's plan to implement the country's largest forced evictions in the slums of Nairobi. Apart from some structure owner organizations, the community lacked both the will and capacity to mobilize a grass-roots resistance to the planned evictions. The local civil society organizations were equally ill-equipped to stop the planned evictions. Most housing rights NGOs did not vigorously oppose the illegal plan because they were closely aligned with the NARC government and did not want to jeopardize their relationship. The local churches were not capable of mobilizing a grass-roots resistance because they lacked sufficient leadership, networks and resources. Faced with a pending crisis, the OHR coordinator and the parish priest, with support from other missionaries in the Kutoka network, lobbied a number of international diplomats to pressure President Kibaki to suspend the evictions. Subsequent efforts by a network of diplomats, international human rights activists and local NGO personnel caused the government to suspend the slum eviction plan permanently, but failed to secure a long-term political and legal solution. The NGOs were limited in their efforts because of internal divisions, power struggles and competition. The NARC government was also not sincere in its promise to reform its eviction policy.

Summary Analysis

Civil society has been romanticized by many scholars and donors who maintain that a strong civil society is the most important and effective way to deepen democratization in Africa. The expectations of the civil society advocates have been particularly high when it comes to the role of Christian churches in the promotion of democracy, human rights and the rule of law at the grass-roots level. A number of scholars assert that because the churches are immersed in the community, they are in daily touch with the people and aware of the reality at the grass roots. They are therefore in a position to make the greatest difference in democratic transformation. In this study, I have tested the civil society debate as it applies to a Catholic parish in a slum environment to determine whether it was able to perform the two key functions assigned to it by the civil society advocates: (1) inculcating individuals with democratic values and behavior and (2) mobilizing citizens to hold the state to account for its abuse of power and corruption. Although many scholars address only the opposition role played by civil society, in this study both functions are given equal consideration because of their interconnected nature.

The findings in this study show that the civil society advocates are only partially right in their argument. Data from the civic education case study shows that with organizational assistance and funds provided by an expatriate missionary combined with the professional expertise of a team of Kenyan lawyers, the civic education program was able to inculcate a small percentage of parishioners with democratic values and principles in a modest, but significant way. The civic education program not only raised awareness and enhanced the participants' communication and participation skills; it also improved their ability to resolve personal and local conflicts. However, only about 15% of the parishioners participated in the program. The majority of parishioners were either not interested or not available to learn about democracy and human rights. The overall impact of the OHR's efforts does not match the scale of change envisioned by advocates who assert that civil society is capable of habituating the masses into democratic attitudes and behavior.

The findings also run counter to the advocates' presumption that a church is able to mobilize its followers to hold the state to account for its abuse of power and corruption at a grass-roots level. Although the circumstances surrounding each of the OHR's interventions varied considerably, there are key themes that demonstrate that it is not realistic to expect that the OHR or any other civil society actor can mobilize citizens to hold government officials to account in a place like Kibera. The advocates' expectations overreach because their discourse fails to consider the reality of the social, economic and political environment in which much of Africa's civil society exists. Instead of addressing these factors, the advocates tend to focus exclusively on the normative dimension of their argument; those who do address the issue typically do so in relatively neutral terms or with the mistaken presumption that circumstances facing civil society in Africa are the same as in the West.

Data from this study show that the way the parishioners responded to the human rights violations was significantly different from the manner in which civil society advocates contend civil society works. Apart from the OHR Team members who were paid by the OHR to work full-time on human rights issues, only a handful of Saturday group members regularly participated in human rights advocacy. Contrary to the expectations of the civil society advocates, it was not the Catholic community, but rather two expatriate missionaries who drove the human rights agenda in the parish. In each intervention, the role of the parishioners was limited primarily to monitoring human rights abuses and gathering and disseminating information about those abuses. Most of the advocacy was done by the OHR coordinator and parish priest who had greater immunity from local retaliation. They were also educated professionals with access to funds and a network of high-level church officials and diplomats to assist them.

In drawing this conclusion I do not mean to suggest that individual parishioners, especially some members of the OHR Team and the Saturday group, did not play an important role in promoting human rights both within the parish and in the broader community. To the contrary, numerous parishioners taught others about their legal and human rights and helped them resolve personal legal problems. Similarly, during the chang'aa campaign and the crises related to the upgrade and eviction threat, it was the OHR Team and the Saturday group members that provided guidance and leadership to other parishioners. In addition, they regularly attended community meetings and spoke out for the interests of the community.

Parishioners also created an important communications network that gathered and disseminated information about numerous human rights issues, especially the Soweto upgrade and eviction plan. The OHR was able to document this information and circulate it to interested parties such as the Papal Nuncio, the Archdiocese, diplomats and donors for use in lobbying efforts; no other organization in Kibera provided this kind of detailed information. Besides supplying information about how these issues were affecting the community, parishioners also disseminated information and advice to their SCCs, sub-parishes, friends and neighbors about how to respond to these issues. This was important because the state's failure to provide the community with information had created an environment rife with rumors, lies and speculation.

In addition to improving the flow of information internally, the Saturday group played a key role in transmitting the viewpoints of the community to outside decision-makers. For example, there were numerous individuals and groups whose interest in Kibera grew following the announced upgrade. These interested parties ranged from academics and human rights lawyers to high-level international officials from donor countries such as Finland. Many of these individuals and organizations were afraid to enter Kibera alone. They also were reluctant to engage too closely with the housing NGOs because of their high degree of government co-option and donor influence. The Saturday group was asked on a regular basis to participate in discussions with these constituencies about the issues arising in Kibera. The process of dialogue and exchange with high-profile decision makers enhanced the quality of information received by the visitors and raised the confidence and self-reliance of the parishioners involved in the discussions.

The Saturday group also produced several leaders in the broader Kibera community. As an example, one of the parishioners, an illiterate woman from Soweto, was elected as a representative for the structure owners in the Settlement Executive Committee addressed in chapter five. Explaining her decision to stand for office she said:

> I was willing to be the SEC representative because I was not afraid. It was not easy for a woman to stand in public and speak but I got used to standing in front of men in civic education classes and I spoke out my own ideas so I wasn't afraid to be in the SEC.[1]

Two OHR Team members also assumed leadership roles. After four years of facilitating civic education, they learned skills in planning,

---

[1] Interview with Saturday group member F, September 28, 2008.

participatory methodologies, documentation and record keeping and organizing meetings. They also learned how to assist parishioners to resolve personal legal problems. As these two team members grew in confidence and skills, they became the primary liaison between the parish and the PA. For the first time, they started initiating meetings with the chiefs and DO to resolve problems in the community which was an important step in reversing a long-term pattern of obeisance and capitulation to the PA. In 2006 one of the OHR Team members joined the People Settlement Network, a grass-roots group representing all slum dwellers in Kenya and was elected the regional chairwoman to represent Kibera. In that capacity, she presented the People's Budget to more than 5,000 people including NGO personnel, diplomats and other slum dwellers gathered for a national forum to expose the shortfall of the country's national budget. Publicized on national television and in the daily newspapers, her analysis presented Kibera's economic reality to the whole country. In 2007 another team member established a human rights ministry similar to the OHR in the Our Lady of Guadalupe parish.

Despite the accomplishments of these individuals, the parish as a church body did not live up to the expectations of the civil society advocates who claim churches are important advocacy groups for democracy and human rights. Indeed, much of recent civil society literature suggests that the church is primarily about socio-political issues. That was not the case in the parish. But the parish did not so much fail as it prioritized traditional church functions more than human rights issues. The parish was primarily a religious and spiritual organization focused on evangelization and sacraments. Priests and pastoral workers in the parish responded to the spiritual needs of more than 3,000 Catholic members, which included the usual cycle of baptisms, marriages and funerals in addition to the training of catechists, teaching Bible school and visits to the sick and dying as well as daily mass in the main parish compound and the SCCs.

The parish also had a significant impact on the social landscape of Kibera, but in ways unrelated to the advocacy interventions of the OHR. Members of the pastoral team met the social needs of thousands of destitute Kiberans seeking food, medical care and emergency relief. The parish also provided primary and secondary school, vocational training and assistance with job searching and skills. Thus, if the parish was to be analyzed from its efforts to evangelize and address the social needs of the Kibera community, it would score high. However, civil society scholars are not concerned with this function of the church; they focus on something else, promoting democracy and human rights as a member of civil society. With respect to this aspect of the church, at least in the parish in Kibera, some of the civil society advocates' claims were not achieved.

I also do not suggest that the OHR failed to promote democracy and human rights in Kibera. I argue here that the way in which the parish OHR approached these rights issues was in a manner different from what the literature claims. Instead of mobilizing Catholics at the grass-roots level to unite in protest against government abuses, the OHR coordinator and parish priest primarily used informal diplomatic channels and elite social networks to confront the government's abuse of power and corruption in Kibera. In fact, it was precisely because of the missionaries' expatriate status and access to international diplomats that they were able to hold the state to account in a way that other civil society actors could not accomplish.

The OHR's response to the threat of evictions is a good example of how the parish's distinctive attributes allowed it to play a key role in addressing human rights abuses in Kibera. Unlike most of the housing NGOs, the OHR had a personal relationship with many Kiberans. The office was located physically inside the community and was staffed by parishioners, with the exception of the lawyers. The OHR's immersion in the community provided it with a thorough and nuanced understanding of how social and political issues affected the residents. Also, through day-to-day encounters with Kiberans in community meetings, religious services, SCC meetings or one-on-one encounters, the members of the OHR had built relationships of trust and confidence with many Kiberans who consistently provided the OHR with accurate and timely information. The OHR members had also developed a personal relationship with the DO and other local officials and, therefore, were the first civil society actor to learn about the government's plan. Moreover, unlike the housing NGOs, the OHR could criticize the government freely and quickly because the missionaries had no personal relationships or ethnic ties to it. They also had no interest in acquiring government funds, contracts or jobs. In addition, although the parish was not completely immune from retaliation by the local chiefs and youth wingers, it had far more immunity than other local groups; the parish possessed a title deed, which gave it greater protection from a forced eviction and the presence of expatriate missionaries, including a lawyer, deterred local actors from interfering overtly with the parish OHR. Finally, due to the active participation of the OHR coordinator and parish priest in the Land Caucus and Kutoka network, they were able to tap diverse networks that quickly brought together high-level diplomats and international human rights activists in a collaborative fashion that maximized their ability to stop the evictions before they started.

The fact that the parish OHR had the power to influence the political arena in Kibera, but not in the way imagined by the civil society advocates, corroborates some of the conclusions reached in Ronald Kassimir's 1998 study of the Catholic Church in Uganda.[2] In Kassimir's view, the civil society advocates mistakenly assigned the church a leading role in civil society before they determined whether or not it had the internal organizational capacity to promote political participation and efficacy among its members. According to his research, he found that the church lacked proper linkages with its lay members to mobilize them for political action. The church's key mechanism to socialize and mobilize its members, the SCCs, failed to take root in Uganda.[3] Catholics who were not members of a SCC relied on the church for social support, but chose to be politically active outside the parameters of official church organizations. Unable to mobilize Catholics, church leaders promoted democratization in the country through formal and informal diplomatic channels, elite social networks and economic development projects. Since these interventions were performed by church leaders in isolation from the laity, Kassimir questioned the utility of using the civil society approach in accounting for the church's capacity to effect social and political change.[4]

Although the reasons why the OHR was limited in its ability to mobilize Catholics in the parish vary somewhat from Kassimir's findings, his observations are applicable here. In my final remarks, I want to summarize the factors that demonstrate why it is not practical or realistic to expect the OHR to mobilize parishioners to challenge corruption and abuses perpetrated by government functionaries in Kibera. These factors falls within two categories: (1) the social, economic and political reality of Kibera and (2) the internal functioning of the local Catholic Church and the parish. Often overlooked by civil society advocates, these impediments shed considerable light on why a Catholic parish located in a slum was limited in its ability to empower Catholics to hold the state to account.

---

[2] Kassimir, "The Social Power," 55.
[3] Ibid., 70-71.
[4] Ibid., 76.

Impediments within Kibera's Environment

Lack of Rule of Law

For civil society to be able to hold local government officials to account for corruption and the abuse of power, it is necessary for the rule of law to function. Since that fundamental feature was generally absent in Kibera, most parishioners were reluctant to get involved with human rights issues because their actions could expose them to retaliation by corrupt chiefs and police, most probably in a violent manner. Under the Moi regime, the PA had been a shadow government in Kibera wielding far-reaching and illegally-gained executive and judicial powers. Protected by their political barons, the chiefs and their assistants were not accountable to the governed or to their superiors. Low-level functionaries routinely ignored their responsibilities and used their power to enforce the political agenda of certain powerful individuals in the government and for rent-seeking purposes. Residents knew that if they exposed corruption or abuse by a local official, their actions would be met with swift reprisal; they could be harassed, beaten, evicted or even arrested and detained. The PA's use of force and corruption did not change when Kibaki was elected president. During the constitutional reform debates, faced with pressure from the politically-connected PA, Kibaki backtracked on his campaign promise to dismantle the PA and replace it with elected local leaders. The chiefs and village elders continued to administer Kibera, albeit less ruthlessly than under Moi, but with the same domination and control. Community members were not the only actors in Kibera who feared the threats of the chiefs and their assistants. All who worked or lived in Kibera were vulnerable to retaliation including the pastors, NGO workers and the parish.

The corrupt and brutal system perpetuated by the chiefs and police has gone unchecked for years, in part, because the residents of Kibera have no venue to take their complaints about government corruption. Since the appointed and elected custodians of law and order are the primary perpetrators, they are not an option. The regular legal process is also not feasible for the vast majority due to costs and distrust. For those that can raise the fees, many fear that lawyers will defraud them; a common experience for slum dwellers who do not understand the legal system and its incomprehensible jargon. Many view the legal process as a tool for the wealthy and well-connected; especially since many court clerks and even judges typically demand bribes. As a consequence, Kibera residents who want to protect their rights do so primarily through self-help or mob justice; tactics that only contribute to the on-going spiral of violence in Kibera.

Political Exploitation

In addition to the endemic corruption of low-level government functionaries, there was a great deal of political interference and manipulation perpetrated by local politicians eager to win the support of their ethnic constituency. The level of political interference in Kibera increased significantly after Raila Odinga was elected MP for the Langata constituency, which contains Kibera. To secure his reelection, Raila needed to garner the majority of his votes from Kibera, which he accomplished through a well-planned and executed strategy. A skilled orator, Raila regularly visited Kibera to promise the Luo tenants a wide range of patronage and favors. He also recruited and organized a group of NDP youth wingers to promote his political agenda, deter opposition and punish people who objected to him or his platform. The efforts of the well-organized youth wingers were supplemented by the area councilors who also regularly threatened and abused Kiberans out of loyalty to Raila and to secure their own political futures. In the early 2000s, as Raila's national profile in NARC grew, the youth wingers and councilors became more powerful and brazen in their use of force than the PA.

Despite the menacing tone and illegal nature of much of the NDP youth wingers' and the councilors' behavior, Raila and his retinue of supporters routinely acted above the law. As discussed in chapter five, due to his large and loyal Luo constituency, Raila was an important political ally of President Moi who readily turned a blind eye to his political machinations in Kibera. Under Kibaki's NARC regime, Raila's power grew. As the head of a powerful ministry, Raila used his official authority to further exploit his political interests in Kibera. Given the degree of his power in the government, it was not practical to think that the ordinary people of Kibera could confront him or his followers including the councilors and NDP youth wingers.

Lack of a Rational Government Policy

Even if ordinary Kiberans had been able to overcome the fear of corrupt governance officials, they could not influence the government's policy on the slums because the government did not have a rational plan or strategy for the settlement. Despite frequent campaign promises and public pronouncements to provide slum dwellers with secure tenure, infrastructure and housing, President Kibaki's approach to the slums did not substantively change the policy of neglect he inherited from President Moi. Kibera remained an illegal settlement that was denied basic services. Just like his predecessor, Kibaki viewed the residents of Kibera as illegal squatters who could be evicted at any time. President Kibaki went even further than Moi in perpetrating illegal forced evictions when he allowed three of his ministries to plan what would have been the largest forced evictions in the country's history. Notwithstanding unprecedented international censure by the UN's Special Rapporteur on Housing, the NARC government refused to adopt eviction guidelines that might restrict the government's ability to later demolish slums located on valuable urban land. Nor did the Kibaki government show a sincere desire to upgrade the slums; from the outset, the KENSUP project was mired in political and ethnic manipulation perpetrated by Kibaki's own minister and officials.

The NARC government's failure to improve Kibera was tied, in large part, to its lack of political will to confront the cadre of influential people who profited financially from the growth of slums. A 2004 study on slum housing in Nairobi calculated that slumlords in Nairobi earned more than $31 million annually;[5] a significant portion generated by Kibera tenants. In addition to generating lucrative revenue for the structure owners, many individuals and businesses also made substantial profits selling services like housing and water that the state did not provide. The government benefited because it spent nothing on housing, infrastructure and basic services for the poor living in slums. In addition, low-level government officials, the police and private individuals profited through an elaborate system of extortion and corruption. Private businesses also profited; slums kept housing costs down which, in turn, kept wages low for employers. Businesses benefited from the pool of cheap labor that slums provide and the low-cost goods and services produced in the informal sector.

Limited Interest and Capacity

There is also a presumption among most civil society advocates that ordinary citizens have the requisite desire and resources necessary to influence government decision-making processes. That presumption did not fit the reality of Kibera. In addition to their pervasive fears of retaliation, most Kiberans were young, transient and concerned primarily

[5] See Sumila Gulyani, and Debabrata Talukdar, "Slum Real Estate: The Low-Quality High-Price Puzzle in Nairobi's Slum Rental Market and its Implications for Theory and Practice," *World Development* 36, no. 10 (2008): 1933.

with earning an income. Preoccupied with meeting basic survival needs, the vast majority did not have extra time for promoting democracy and human rights. Moreover, most Kiberans were not interested in the change process because of a general attitude of apathy, resignation and dependence; feelings that were a reflection of their personal experience in Kibera. NGOs and donors had spent millions of dollars in Kibera to improve the lives of the residents and yet there were few tangible results. As a consequence, many Kiberans felt betrayed by decades of broken promises and were cynical about the real motives and purposes of civil society's interventions. There was also a high level of fatalism. Many Kiberans felt that since they were illegal squatters, they did not have a right to question the government. For some, their illegal status bred a sense of guilt that led them to feel that they were the ones to blame for their situation, not the government's neglect and corruption.

Most Kiberans had never participated in community-led initiatives to demand change and, as a result, many did not see that they had a role to play in changing their environment. In their experience, lawyers and clerics changed unjust situations, not ordinary citizens. There was also a deeply-ingrained culture of dependence. In light of the state's failure to provide services in Kibera, local NGOs, missionaries and organizations from all around the world had distributed charitable handouts to the community for almost two decades, with little consideration to the long-term negative consequence of their benevolence. This pervasive charity had created an environment of passivity and malaise. In addition, the NGO strategy of paying slum dwellers a monetary allowance as an incentive to participate in community meetings exacerbated the dependency problem. Paying slum dwellers inducements may be among the most negative long-term impacts of civil society's interventions because this practice eroded the little voluntary spirit that existed, diminishing residents' sense of responsibility for their own future and their initiative in gaining that future.

For an organization to carry out advocacy effectively, the members of the group must understand the issues and how they link to their reality before they will get involved. That understanding was largely absent in Kibera. The majority of the adult residents had not finished secondary school and had only a rudimentary understanding of how the government worked. They did not know how policies were made, their implications for the community or how they could influence policy making. The issues taken up by the OHR were complicated especially those related to land and housing, which were tied to a long-standing ethnic and political struggle about ownership and control of Kibera. The community's basic lack of knowledge was exacerbated by the fact that there was a serious dearth of information on issues that affected Kiberans. In many instances, the government deliberately withheld vital information on its plan for Kibera as a means to control the community's behavior and activities. Outside sources did little to make up for the government's shortfall; news coverage was scarce and documents prepared by NGOs, donors, academics and UN-Habitat were rarely circulated to the community.

Even if the Kibera residents had been able to secure a firm grasp of the issues, they lacked the competencies and resources to mobilize the community. Most Kiberans did not possess basic organizational and communication skills; as a result, few were able to organize meetings, facilitate discussions or keep records. The primary means of communication was word-of-mouth, a time-consuming and ineffective method. Fewer than 15% of parishioners had a mobile phone and those who did could afford only to send short text messages, making it difficult to spread community information. Venues to hold meetings were scarce. Apart from churches, most of which charged a fee, there were no meetings halls in Kibera. Limited electricity and few computers meant that documentation had to be typed and photocopied outside Kibera, another timely and costly endeavor. Kiberans had limited financial resources to dedicate to community interests; most were struggling to make ends meet and there was little surplus for expenses outside the family. Accessing donor funds was not a viable option for most residents since international donors were generally not willing to fund grass-roots groups that lacked formal structures including bank accounts and systems of accountability. Without the basic tools and resources to organize people and communicate ideas, it was not practical to think Kiberans could promote the interests of the community.

In addition to their lack of resources, most Kiberans did not view the state as a partner with whom they could discuss and debate matters affecting them. To the contrary, most Kiberans were alienated from the state; they had grown up under the repressive Moi regime and had never been exposed to a form of government that was not dictatorial. In their experience, the state was all-powerful and they had no choice other than to submit to it. Most Kiberans did not know their rights or the laws that protected them, which made them vulnerable to the rumors, lies and political propaganda spread to maintain the status quo. To complicate matters, the situation in Kibera was in constant flux as local officials and politicians came and went with frequency and unpredictability. The community also was inexperienced in voicing their opinions because of the lack of institutionalized mechanisms for community participation.

Except for a few local issues, most decisions in Kibera were under the exclusive purview of the chiefs and village elders who did not include the community. As a result, most Kiberans were accustomed to being told what to do in a top-down and paternalistic manner. In light of their history, most Kiberans were afraid to verbalize their viewpoints; some did not even know how to go about it.

Lack of Organized Community Groups

Parishioners faced another significant impediment to entering the political arena in Kibera. Unlike many of the other Nairobi slums, the Kibera residents were not organized into groups at the village level. Even though the residents faced the same harsh conditions, corruption and abuse, they were not inclined to mobilize to promote their common interests. Their inaction was driven more by fear than any other factor. The tactics of the PA in Kibera were particularly repressive during the Moi regime which is why many NGOs sent community organizers to other slum areas and avoided Kibera. Kiberans who tried to meet and form groups to discuss issues around land, housing or governance were harassed, intimidated and even arrested. Even though there was a loosening of strictures on group formation under the Kibaki government, the effects of two decades of repression remained potent; an entire generation of Kiberans grew up afraid to start or join groups that advocated for improved living conditions. In addition to fear of the PA's repressive tactics, Kiberans were also afraid of retaliation by the NDP youth wingers and local politicians, who frequently were even more violent than the PA.

The lifestyle in Kibera was also antithetical to building community groups and networks necessary for promoting cooperation and collective behavior. The most basic unit for building community, the family, was largely absent. The majority of households were headed by single mothers mired in chronic poverty. Men lived in Kibera because of the cheap accommodation and easy access to the industrial area; they stayed in the settlement only to eat and sleep. The unstable family environment caused many youth to leave home and form their own sub-groups often joining groups of youth wingers or criminal gangs. In addition to the unstable family life, there was a low level of shared identity and unity among residents. The only time that people had to attend meetings, talk and build personal relationships was late in the evening when most people were too tired and worn out to meet and associate. As a result, there was not a strong sense of community; some people did not even know their neighbors. Since many people, especially the tenants, followed a transitory like lifestyle, it was difficult to build a sense of belonging and commitment to a particular group in a constantly changing environment.

The formation of community groups was also inhibited by the lack of cooperative spirit and harmony in Kibera. Many researchers have confused the visible signs of generosity and hospitality as indicators of solidarity. The fact that Kiberans were united during times of trouble such as death, fire or eviction did not translate into cohesive groups that shared values, motivations and aspirations. These components were largely missing because of a fundamental lack of trust. The most pronounced reason for the pervasive mistrust was the lack of ethnic homogeneity. Kibera contained people from every ethnic group in Kenya, a situation very different from their life in the rural areas where there was shared ethnicity and cultural practices. Although they were living together in close proximity, in their daily activities most Kiberans interacted primarily with people from a shared ethnic community using their indigenous language, customs and practices. As a result, it was difficult for people to identify with the same cooperative ethos generally found in homogeneous groups.

Unscrupulous politicians in Kibera manipulated ethnic divisions to advance their political agendas without regard to the impact on the long-term stability of the community. The most visible manifestation of the ethnic conflict in Kibera was the division between the structure owners and tenants. In addition to their division along ethnic, political, religious and socio-economic lines, the structure owners and tenants had inherently conflicting interests in Kibera. As long-term residents who had financial investments in the community, the structure owners had a strong incentive to resist any actions that might threaten their investments such as an upgrade or eviction. In contrast, the tenants had much less at stake and were less concerned about what happened in Kibera so long as their rents were not raised. Their fundamentally different agendas and long history of antipathy toward one another made it difficult to bring the two groups together.

Fractured Housing NGOs

Parishioners also received little support from the housing NGOs who purported to represent their interests. Contrary to the hopes of many civil society advocates, the presence of a large number of NGOs did not guarantee that the interests of the poor were represented. In the new political era of NARC, the role of the NGOs was frequently confused and ambiguous not only to Kiberans, but also among the NGOs themselves. In many circumstances, the housing NGOs could not be counted on to hold the government to account for its corruption. A number of NGOs were so closely tied to NARC that it was difficult to distinguish between the two. No longer united in their mutual endeavor to rid Kenya of Moi's hegemonic control, the many fractures that had been invisible became much more pronounced. The housing NGOs became increasingly divided along the lines of ethnicity, political affiliation and commercial interests; divisions which occasionally eclipsed the NGOs' vision for the slums.

A good example of the fractured state of the housing NGO sector was the NGO Coalition that tried to respond to the eviction and upgrade issues. Even though the housing NGOs working in Kibera identified themselves as the NGO Coalition to donors and government officials, their name belied the reality. The Coalition was not a coordinated network working together with common strategies and goals. In truth, the Coalition was a group of individuals who worked independently from one another and sometimes in direct contravention, each in pursuit of its own agenda most often directed by a donor, not the community. Forced to compete for an increasingly smaller pot of funds from the same donors, many of the NGOs were mired in divisive competition, personal jealousies and turf battles.

The Coalition was also ineffective because it did not work closely with the community. Many Kiberans did not want to collaborate with the NGOs due to concerns about the NGOs' co-option by the government, their overriding commercial interests, top-down approach and general lack of accountability to the community. In the early 2000s, fewer than 500 Kiberans regularly collaborated with the housing NGOs including the fledgling Muungano savings groups. If they did participate, it was often because they were paid allowances. Since many NGO workers were far removed from the community and the daily reality of Kibera, they did not know or understand the local political and ethnic dynamics. Consequently, the impact of their interventions was often limited and, in some instances, worsened the situation.

Ill-Equipped Religious Leaders

Even though most Kiberans identified the pastors and imams as the key local leaders, the religious leaders could not overcome the internal divisions within Kibera to promote the common good of the community. There was no single religious leader or group of leaders to bridge the underlying divisions in the community. The churches and mosques were divided along the same ethnic and political fault lines that divided the broader Kibera community. Although the Catholic parish had the most ethnically mixed following, it was not a unifying force. Separated from other churches on spiritual matters as well as its missionary status and financial resources, the parish had a history of operating independently. Even if the churches had operated as a unifying force, the generally-accepted assumption by civil society advocates that church leaders act in a way that benefits the poor and voiceless did not always hold true in Kibera. The majority of religious leaders played a very small role in the broader social justice issues. Not only did the majority lack expertise, resources and political clout to lobby for change, they also were afraid to raise human rights issues out of fear of possible retaliation. The pastors were not immune to local ethnic and political machinations; some of the pastors were even co-opted by the area politicians.

Impediments within the Local Church and Parish

Limited Leadership and Support from the Local Church

There were several significant obstacles to the OHR's efforts to mobilize parishioners that were part of the internal functioning of the local Catholic Church and the parish. I have discussed them in the previous chapters and I summarize them here. Key among those impediments was a lack of leadership and guidance from the leaders in the Kenyan church. For example, the bishops were not consistent in their implementation and interpretation of the church's teachings on social justice. On repeated occasions in the 1990s, individual clerics including the KEC bishops criticized the repressive tactics of the Moi regime in a manner that had never before occurred. Church leaders, however, played a much more ambiguous role in the post multi-party era of Kenya. In the 2000s, firmly rooted in the Roman orthodox agenda, the bishops as a group pulled back from the national debate on democracy and political reform and focused their public attention on issues such as individual salvation, personal devotion and sexual morality. Moreover, despite their pointed public statements in the 1990s, the bishops did not mobilize ordinary Catholics at the grass-roots level to join them in demanding reform; the people were involved indirectly only through the voice of their religious leaders.

In addition to their shifting positions, unlike the church in South Africa, Latin America and the Philippines, theologians in East Africa did not develop a critical political theology to help the churches respond to the deprivation, corruption and repression that are commonplace in the slums. Since the early 1970s, church leaders in East Africa were urged to study urbanization in a systematic matter (economically, politically, culturally, religiously and morally) and develop a particular theology to support an urban slum apostolate.[6] The church leadership in Kenya, in both its documents and actions, did not heed the call to offer guidance. In the nearly 50 years that the Kenya bishops have issued pastoral letters, apart from a number of cursory references, it has never addressed the issues of slums or urbanization.[7] Nor have most theologians in East Africa. Instead of developing a theology that promotes an option for the poor, theologians have focused almost exclusively on an on-going debate as regards African culture and its relationship to Christianity.

The Archdiocese of Nairobi, which is home to the vast majority of the country's slums, has similarly provided little direction. For a brief period during the early 1990s, the Archdiocese's JPC became a meeting place for church members to discuss and organize around issues facing slum dwellers, but the Archdiocese's attention did not last long. By 2000, the Archdiocese's priorities had shifted to economic development. Unable to generate funds for the Archdiocese, the JPC was given little attention and eventually the JPC director was dismissed and the JPC office subsumed under the development office where it has remained moribund.

Archbishop Ndingi's reluctance to address the human rights abuses in Kibera revealed the level of ambiguity surrounding the church's desire to address social justice issues. Although the mission of the church and its social teachings were well pronounced by the church hierarchy, the local church did not always follow the statements with concrete actions. The sizeable gap between the teachings of the church and their practice at the local level was best evidenced during the eviction crisis. Even the personal involvement of the Nuncio and the highest-ranking Vatican representative on justice and peace issues did not compel the Archbishop to protest the government's illegal plans. As a result, parishioners did not follow the pronouncements of the Nuncio or the visiting Cardinal because they were not supported by Archbishop Ndingi, whose views and actions held much greater sway than those of expatriate dignitaries. From the parishioners' perspective, the Vatican's representatives were unknown to them and far removed from their daily lives. The Archbishop's failure to heed the example of the Vatican's representatives created a disincentive for

---

[6] John Mary Waliggo, "Urbanization in Africa: Challenges for the Church," (Mimeo, Nairobi, April 1994), 3.

[7] There are only three references to slums and they are in context of poverty generally. See Stanlaus Muyebe, and Alex Muyebe, *The African Bishops on Human Rights: A Resource Book* (Nairobi: Paulines Publications Africa, 2002), 234.

Catholics at the grass-roots level who wanted to voice opposition to government corruption in Kibera but felt constrained by the Archbishop's position. The Archbishop's inaction also highlighted the fact that even bishops were vulnerable to political pressure and patronage.

The church's avoidance of social justice issues in slums was not limited to the hierarchy; the same attitude and approach percolated down to the diocesan and parish levels. This was true for parishes administered by local Kenyan priests as well as missionaries. With respect to local diocesan priests, there tended to be a low level of awareness and understanding of many complex socio-political issues because of a historical lack of attention to and formation on social issues for seminary students. Moreover, in keeping with strict hierarchical practices, most local priests were not willing to take a position counter to their local bishop regardless of the curia's pronouncements. Although the expatriate missionaries typically had been more vocal on socio-political issues in the slums because of their autonomy and independence from the state, apart from a handful of activists, most opted not to speak out on social justice issues. This division among the missionaries was evident in the Kutoka network. The majority of missionaries, particularly those of African origin, felt issues related to human rights and social justice were beyond the scope of their primary mission which was evangelization. Others were afraid of being labeled as a radical or trouble maker by their religious community or suffering retaliation by the government in the form of deportation or bodily harm.[8]

Not only did exhortations by the church hierarchy not inspire or empower ordinary Catholics to respond to human rights issues, regular pronouncements by the parish priest and the OHR coordinator also had limited impact. Parishioners did not view the statements of the expatriate missionaries as a substitute for the local bishop or clergy. The missionaries were viewed by many parishioners as Western outsiders who represented a more liberal Catholic thinking about human rights than the local church. They also did not have the same degree of credibility and influence as the local church because of their transient nature. Parishioners knew the missionaries would inevitably leave Kenya and return home or be assigned to another country.

---

[8] During the Moi regime, a number of religious active in the area of human rights especially on land matters died under mysterious circumstances. The most recent incident was the politically motivated murder of Mill Hill missioner Father John Kaiser in August 2002.

Structures of the Parish

In addition to the attitudes and practices within the church hierarchy in Kenya, there were a number of limitations within the parish structure and practices that inhibited Catholics from promoting human rights in Kibera. In 2004 the model and operating style of the parish was changed from a top-down centralized model to a more horizontal one. The parish priest did not want to be a traditional "father in charge" who made most decisions and planned the parish activities; instead, he wanted the ministry coordinators to take full responsibility for the different departments including the plans, activities and fund raising. Although the shift was viewed as a positive step by most parishioners, it was not fully executed or synchronized. Instead of planning together as a whole parish, each individual ministry made its own individual plans without input from other departments, SCCs or parishioners, resulting in activities considered by parishioners to be the exclusive project and responsibility of individual coordinators, not the parish generally. Consequently, OHR interventions were often implemented in an isolated manner with little support from other actors in the parish. The ministries were driven by the personality of the individual coordinators, not a unified commitment by the parish.

The SCC model also had an impact on the OHR's efforts. Even though the SCC offered a convenient venue for the OHR Team to teach civic education and inculcate democratic values and behavior, on other levels, the SCCs prevented parishioners from mobilizing concrete actions to promote and protect their rights. SCCs in Kenya were not active in socio-political life, let alone radicalized to lead mass protest against the government. SCCs in East Africa were formed to promote prayer and mutual assistance, not to pursue a political agenda as in Latin America and other parts of the world. Church protocols in the parish and elsewhere in Kenya restricted SCC members in their ability to speak about any issues that could be characterized as "political," which included most issues other than those directly related to spiritual and religious matters. Those few parishioners who addressed political matters (such as the structure owners who filed a lawsuit to stop the move to Athi River) did so by using alternative channels located outside the church. In addition, authoritative leadership structures in the church prevented parishioners in the SCCs from taking initiative to mobilize their members around socio-political issues.

The low functionality of many SCCs in the parish was also an inhibiting factor. Although the number of SCCs in the parish grew and some improved in their operations during 2002-2005, the improvements were too little to alter their impact in the parish. The reasons for their failure to thrive in Kibera bear brief mention. Despite efforts by the founding parish priest to promote spiritual formation and training for the SCCs, subsequent clerical support for the SCCs had been low, which meant the basic formation and development of the SCCs had not been fostered. Many of the SCCs lost their original identity and purpose. Instead of forming groups of neighbors to engage in prayer, worship and service to the community, many SCCs were groups of friends who shared the same regional and ethnic identity and met primarily for the purposes of generating savings or starting an income-generating project. In light of the members' pervasive poverty, spiritual formation was less important than generating revenue of some sort. In addition, the different SCCs had received different kinds and levels of spiritual formation depending on their place of origin. According to one catechist, "Parishioners had different experiences from their rural homes and what they experienced there had a bigger impact on them than the formation they received in the parish."[9] Given the variations in their spiritual orientations and backgrounds, it was difficult to develop a common plan for the SCCs.

Life in Kibera was also counter-productive to building strong SCCs. Members were constrained by time because most parishioners worked during the daytime and the majority of SCCs met at night. This excluded many women because it was not safe for them to walk after dark. Although some women formed a handful of SCCs to meet during the day, they were frequently too busy with household and business obligations to attend the meetings. It was even more difficult for the men. After working 12-hour shifts in the factories, most were too tired to attend their evening SCC meetings consistently. The high degree of mobility combined with the temporary lifestyle commonplace in Kibera also undermined efforts to facilitate unified and cohesive SCCs. Like most Kiberans, many Catholics followed a transitory lifestyle. Viewing their home to be their rural homestead, they moved back and forth to Kibera only when it was necessary to find work in Nairobi. Others lived in Kibera only as a stop-over residence while looking for a job or better housing.

Not only did many of the SCCs function poorly, they also attracted very few Catholics. Notwithstanding the fact that the SCCs were the church's official pastoral priority, they were not effectively established in the Kenyan church. In the parish, as in most other slum parishes, the vast majority of Catholics were not interested in joining a SCC; membership in the SCCs hovered around 10%-15%. The low level of interest was attributed to several factors: membership required time, commitment,

[9] Interview with parish catechist, September 29, 2008.

financial contributions, a spirit of volunteerism and initiative, attributes all in short supply in the slums. In addition, there were many Catholics who viewed the SCCs as exclusive ethnic clubs. There were also many Sunday Christians who were not necessarily practicing or committed Catholics. It was common practice for Kiberans to attend several churches in order to maximize the scope of their social networks. As a well-resourced church, the parish naturally attracted many people whose primary aim was to access food, medicine and financial assistance.

In addition to the SCCs, the other parish groups-Saturday group, the JPC, PPC and sub-parishes-also lacked the capacity to promote human rights in Kibera. The OHR coordinator's aim to build the capacity of the Saturday group so that it could confront the broader structural injustices and promote more democratic processes in Kibera was, in large part, not met. Although the JPC had ceased to function by 2004, the Saturday group did not become its substitute. The Saturday group monitored human rights abuses and assisted parishioners in their individual problems, but it was a loosely knit group whose members were not elected leaders. The Saturday group had no official standing in the structures of the Archdiocese or the parish and, as a result, no power or authority to pursue human right issues on behalf of the parish as had the JPC. In addition, contrary to the expectations of the OHR coordinator, most of the members of the Saturday group did not want to play an advocacy role.

Leaders in the PPC and the sub-parishes were also limited in their interest in and capacity to promote the rights of parishioners. The overall quality of the parish leaders was low. Many wanted to be in positions of authority in the SCCs and PPC to gain priority in the distribution of parish resources either through direct handouts or a personal relationship with the parish priest. Others were motivated more by the desire to be viewed as a powerful leader rather than a sincere commitment to serve. Moreover, the leaders were separated by ethno-regional lines, education and competency levels making it very difficult for the group to work together for the good of the whole parish. They also were not given adequate formation or training on organizing, communication and human rights issues, which meant they were not equipped to deal with complex socio-political issues in Kibera.

The Missionary Factor

The missionary status of the parish also had an impact on the ability of the OHR to empower parishioners to take action on human rights issues. First, the fact that the parish priests and OHR coordinator were missionaries meant that it was Western, liberal-minded expatriates, not the parishioners or the local church, who determined what issues to follow and, more importantly, how to intervene strategically. As a result, it was unclear how much, if any, local interest in issues like chang'aa, slum upgrading and evictions, really existed on the part of the Catholic community in Kibera. The missionaries also had access to financial resources without which none of the activities in the OHR would have been possible. This situation was not unique to the parish. There were several other missionaries in the Kutoka network whose emphasis was social justice and human rights and who similarly had access to international resources. In addition, the missionaries who pursued a human rights agenda were often on parallel or even contradictory paths from the local Kenyan church that was more focused on development issues. The different priorities of the local church and the missionaries combined with uneven access to resources inevitably led to periodic tensions and resentment between the local church and the missionaries and, in some instances, the local church's reluctance to get involve inhibited the missionaries' efforts.

Second, the foreign status of the parish priest and OHR coordinator limited the scope and quality of their advocacy efforts. Not only did the missionaries have limited knowledge of the complex issues related to Kibera's culture and politics, they also were viewed as unwelcome outsiders by some Kiberans, especially the pastors. The coordinator and the parish priest had few relationships with government officials apart from the local chiefs and DO in Kibera, which meant they could not directly influence decision makers in the government. As a result, they had to rely on diplomatic intermediaries such as the Papal Nuncio and the British High Commissioner. These expatriates had temporary assignments and their interactions were based on personal relationships and commitments, not institutional ones. Although Archbishop Tonucci was personally interested and committed to assist the parish in human right matters, his successor was not; nor was the successor of Sir Edward Clay. The change in personnel and lack of institutional support made it difficult to count on the important support of these political allies in future human rights crises.

Third, the missionaries' relationships with other civil society actors were affected by their foreign status. For example, many of the small Pentecostal churches in Kibera were not willing to work with the OHR because they felt overpowered by the status and resources of the missionaries. The missionaries also had difficult relationship with some of the NGOs who felt the parish was competing with them for the same donor funds and the trust and confidence of the slum communities. Some of the NGOs thought the parish had over-stepped its boundaries when it entered the human rights arena, a venue they felt was exclusively within their purview and expertise. As a consequence, it was often difficult for the OHR to build collaborative relationships with other local civil society actors.

Fourth, the fact that the parish was administered by missionaries meant that its key personnel were, by definition, transitory and non-permanent. The inherent transience was exacerbated by the frequent changes in the priests; between 2001 and 2006, four different priests were assigned to be the parish priest. Each new priest introduced a new organizational structure and methodology, a situation that caused confusion among the parishioners. It made it difficult for the OHR to plan and implement activities on a consistent basis because each new parish priest had a different view how the parish should approach social justice issues. For example, the parish priest during 2001-2005 was personally supportive of the OHR and its efforts to pursue a human rights agenda in the parish, but his views did not reflect the consensus of his missionary congregation. Most of his fellow priests followed a more conservative approach common in Mexico that discouraged human rights activism. As a result, after he was reassigned from the parish, it was necessary to convince each subsequent parish priest of the value of the OHR, a situation that created instability and threatened the OHR's long-term sustainability.

In conclusion, I want to point out that civil society in Kenya is not homogeneous and the parish OHR does not mirror most civil society organizations including those traditionally found in the Catholic Church. It is one component of civil society and has particular characteristics related to its origin, location, vision and missionary orientation. One cannot over-generalize to other religious actors or sectors within civil society. The research in this study is also limited to a four-year period. It is quite possible that an analysis of the OHR's efforts over an extended period of time might show a different result. Moreover, in a more middle-class milieu, research might very well reveal another dynamic. That said, however, a Catholic missionary parish in Kenya's largest slum is a revealing study to explore the capacity and ability of civil society organizations to promote democracy during a country's consolidation of democracy for a number of reasons.

First, Kenya's experience with the consolidation of democracy reflects that of many countries on the continent. Kenya has made several successful steps in the democratization process, which have been followed by an equal, if not greater, number of reversals. It was the reversals, most recently witnessed by deadly politically-instigated ethnic violence during the 2005 constitutional referendum and 2007 election that have caused many, both scholars and Kenyans alike, to question whether Kenya is in the process of transitioning to or consolidating democracy.

Second, an evaluation of the role of missionaries in the context of the civil society debate is critical given their large presence in Africa. Contrary to popular perceptions, the presence and role of Christian missionaries has grown, not decreased. Although the number of Catholic missionaries from the traditional European congregations diminished appreciably in the 1970s and 1980s, they were replaced by a surge of missioners from India, the Philippines, Latin America and other African countries. By 2002, it was estimated that there were more than 200 different Catholic religious communities in Kenya.[10] In addition to the large number of Catholic missionaries, Kenya has the largest concentration of Protestant missionaries on the continent.[11]

Third, although this thesis is about the OHR specifically, its experience in promoting human rights was not out of step with the historical and contemporaneous experience of other civil society organizations working in slum areas. The slum dwellers and civil society actors involved with the Muungano faced most of the same challenges as the OHR in mobilizing slum dwellers, but on a larger city-wide scale. I have also alluded to several other groups, namely, the housing NGOs in Kibera whose experience mobilizing Kiberans, on the face of things, further corroborates the findings here.

Finally, the situation in Kibera slums reflects a continent-wide phenomenon with respect to slum growth. According to estimates of UN-Habitat, in 2001 sub-Saharan Africa had the highest percentage of urban slum dwellers in the world, with 80% of the urban population living in slums.[12] By that time, the slum population reached 116 million, nearly two-thirds more than in 1990 (101 million). According to UN-Habitat's projections, 27% of the world's slum dwellers will live in sub-Saharan Africa by 2020, almost double the percentage in 1990. In light of these projections, the urban slum will probably become one of, if not the most important, milieus for studying and understanding African society. The focus on the OHR during 2002-2005, therefore, has broad applicability to understanding the role and efficacy of civil society in the consolidation of democracy on the continent.

---

[10] See Gifford, *Christianity, Politics*, 63-70.
[11] Hearn, "The 'Invisible' NGO," 32.
[12] UN-Habitat, *The Second Urban World Forum, September 2004* (Nairobi: UN-Habitat, 2004), 61, 69.

BIBLIOGRAPHY

Aboum, Agnes. "The Churches' Involvement in the Democratisation Process in Kenya." In *Peacemaking and Democratisation in Africa*, edited by Hizkias Assefa, and George Wachira, 95-114. Nairobi: East African Educational Publishers, 1996).

Acacia Consultants. "Investigation of Actors Operating in Kibera." Report prepared for the Government of Kenya, and UN-Habitat, Nairobi, 2004.

Adar, Korwa. "Assessing Democratization Trends in Kenya: A Post-mortem of the Moi Regime." *Commonwealth & Comparative Politics* 38, no. 3 (2000): 103-30.

Africa Watch Committee. *Kenya, Taking Liberties, an African Watch Report*. New York: Human Rights Watch, 1991.

African Population and Health Center. *Population and Health Dynamics in Nairobi's Informal Settlements: Report of the Nairobi Cross-Sectional Slums Survey 2000*. Nairobi: African Population and Health Research, 2002.

AMECEA. *Small Christian Communities 20 Years Later*. Nairobi: Amecea Documentation Service, 1997.

Amis, Philip. "Commercialized Rental Housing in Nairobi, Kenya." In *Spontaneous Shelter: International Perspectives and Prospects*, edited by Carl Patton, 235-57. Philadelphia: Temple University Press, 1984.

—. "Squatters or Tenants: The Commercialization of Unauthorized Housing in Nairobi." *World Development* 12, no. 1 (1984): 87-96.

Anderson, David. "Briefing Kenya's Election in 2002." *African Affairs* 102, no. 407 (2003): 331-42.

—. "Corruption at City Hall: African Housing and Urban Development in Colonial Nairobi." In *The Urban Experience in Eastern Africa c. 1750-2000*, edited by Andrew Burton, and British Institute in Eastern Africa, 138-54. Nairobi: British Institute in Eastern Africa, 2002.

Archdiocese of Nairobi. *Strategic Plan 2003-2008*. Nairobi: Archdiocese of Nairobi, 2002.

Atieno-Odhiambo, Elisha S. "Hegemonic Enterprises and Instrumentalities of Survival: Ethnicity and Democracy in Kenya." *African Studies* 61, no. 2 (2002): 223-49.

Azarya, Victor. "Civil Society and Disengagement in Africa." In *Civil Society and the State in Africa*, edited by John W. Harbeson, Donald S. Rothchild, and Naomi Chazan, 83-102. Boulder, CO: L. Reinner Publishers, 1994.

Badejo, Babafemi A. *Raila Odinga: An Enigma in Kenyan Politics*. Lagos: Yintab Books, 2006.

Bannon, Alicia. "Designing a Constitution-Drafting Process: Lessons from Kenya." *Yale Law Journal* 116 (2007): 1824-72.

Barkan, Joel. "The Rise and Fall of a Governance Realm in Kenya." In *Governance and Politics in Africa*, edited by Goran Hyden, and Michael Bratton, 167-93. Boulder, CO: L. Reinner, 1992.

Baur, John. *The Catholic Church in Kenya: A Centenary History*. Nairobi: St. Paul's Publications, 1990.

Bayart, Jean François. "Civil Society in Africa." In *Political Domination in Africa: Reflections on the Limits of Power*, edited by Patrick Chabal, 109-25. Cambridge: Cambridge University Press, 1986.

Bebbington, Anthony, and Roger Riddell. "Heavy Hands, Hidden Hands, Holding Hands? Donors, Intermediary NGOs and Civil Society Organizations." In *NGOs, States and Donors: Too Close for Comfort*, edited by David Hulme, and Michael Edwards, 107-27. New York: St. Martin's Press, 1997.

Becker, Kristina Flodman. "Follow-up Mission on Program Management Collaborative Nairobi Slum-upgrading Program." Report prepared for SIDA, Nairobi, 2002.

Beetham, David. *Democracy and Human Rights*. Cambridge: Polity Press in association with Blackwell, 1999.

Belshaw, D., Robert Calderisi, and Chris Sugden. *Faith in Development: Partnership between the World Bank and the Churches of Africa*. Oxford: Regnum Books, 2001.

Benson, Paddy. "Faith Engaging Politics: the Preaching of the Kingdom of God." In *Religion and Politics in Kenya* edited by Ben Knighton, 96-120. New York: Palgrave Macmillan, 2009.

Berger, Julia. "Religious Nongovernmental Organizations: An Exploratory Analysis." *Voluntas: International Journal of Voluntary and Nonprofit Organizations* 14, no. 1 (2003): 15-39.

Berman, Bruce. "Ethnicity, Bureaucracy & Democracy: The Politics of Trust." In *Ethnicity & Democracy in Africa*, edited by Bruce Berman, Dickson Eyoh, and Will Kymlicka, 38-53. Oxford: James Currey, 2002.

Biau, Daniel. "Three Things We Should Know about Slums." *Habitat Debate* (March 2007): 6.

Bodewes, Christine. "Can the Pastoral Circle Transform a Parish?" In *The Pastoral Circle Revisited: a Critical Quest for Truth and Transformation*, edited by Frans Wijsen, Peter Henriot, and Rodrigo Mejia, 56-72. Maryknoll, NY: Orbis Books, 2005.

—. "The Catholic Church and Civic Education in the Slums of Nairobi." In *Jesus and Ubuntu: Exploring the Social Impact of Christianity in Africa*, edited by Mwenda Ntarangwi, 147-74. Trenton, NJ: Africa World Press, 2011.

—. "Chang'aa Drinking in a Kibera Slum: The Harmful Effects of Contemporary Changes in the Production and Consumption of Traditional Spirits." *African Journal of Drug and Alcohol Studies* 9, no. 1 (2010): 49-56.

—. "Civil Society and the Consolidation of Democracy in Kenya: An Analysis of a Catholic Parish's Efforts in Kibera Slum," *The Journal of Modern African Studies* 48, no. 4 (2010): 547-72.

—. *Parish Transformation in Urban Slums: Voices of Kibera, Kenya.* Nairobi: Paulines Publications Africa, 2005.

Bodewes, Christine, and Ndaisi Kwinga. "Kenyan Perspective on Housing Rights." In *National Perspectives on Housing Rights*, edited by Scott Leckie, 221-40. The Hague: Martinus Nijhoff, 2003.

Branch, Daniel. *Kenya: Between Hope and Despair, 1963-2011*. New Haven, CT: Yale University Press, 2011.

Bratton, Michael. "Beyond the State: Civil Society and Associational Life in Africa." *World Politics* (1989): 407-30.

—. "Civil Society and Political Transitions in Africa." In *Civil Society and the State in Africa*, edited by John W. Harbeson, Donald S. Rothchild, and Naomi Chazan, 51-77. Boulder, CO: L. Reinner Publishers, 1994.

Bratton, Michael, and Nicolas Van de Walle. *Democratic Experiments in Africa: Regime Transitions in Comparative Perspective*. Cambridge: Cambridge University Press, 1997.

Brown, Stephen. "Theorising Kenya's Protracted Transition to Democracy." *Journal of Contemporary African Studies* 22, no. 3 (2004): 69-100.

Burgeap, Seueca and Runji and Partners. "Kibera Urban Environnemental Sanitation Project." Report prepared for the Ministry of Local Government, and Nairobi City Council, Nairobi, 2002.

Burton, Andrew, and the British Institute in Eastern Africa, ed. *The Urban Experience in Eastern Africa c. 1750-2000*, Nairobi: British Institute in Eastern Africa, 2002.

Callaghy, Thomas. "Civil Society, Democracy, and Economic Change in Africa: A Dissenting Opinion about Resurgent Societies." In *Civil*

Society and the State in Africa, edited by John W. Harbeson, Donald S. Rothchild, and Naomi Chazan, 231-57. Boulder, CO: L. Reinner Publishers, 1994.

Center on Housing Rights and Evictions. *Listening to the Poor? Housing Rights in Nairobi*. Geneva: COHRE, 2005.

—. "Civil and Political Rights in Kenyan Informal Settlements." Submission to Human Rights Committee, New York, February 2005.

Chabal, Patrick, ed. *Political Domination in Africa: Reflections on the Limits of Power*. Cambridge: Cambridge University Press, 1986.

Chabal, Patrick, and Jean-Pascal Daloz. *Africa Works: Disorder as Political Instrument*. Oxford: James Currey, 1999.

Chazan, Naomi. "Africa's Democratic Challenge." *World Policy Journal* 9, no. 2 (1992):279-307.

Clark, John. *Democratizing Development: The Role of Voluntary Organizations*. West Hartford, CT: Kumarian Press, 1991.

Clayton, Andrew, ed. *NGOs, Civil Society and the State: Building Democracy in Transitional Societies.* Oxford: INTRAC, 1996.

Committee of Eminent Persons on the Constitution Review Process, and B.A. Kiplagat. *Report of the Committee of Eminent Persons on the Constitution Review Process*. Nairobi: Government of Kenya, 2006.

Constitution and Reform Education Consortium and Institute for Education in Democracy. *Kenya Civil Society Observation Program (KCSOP), Report on the Referendum on the Proposed New Constitution of Kenya, 21st November 2005*. Nairobi: CRECO and IED, 2006.

Cottrell, Jill, and Yash Ghai. "Constitution Making and Democratization in Kenya, (2000-2005)." *Democratization* 14, no. 1 (2007):1-25.

Crowley, Jerry. *Go to the People: An African Experience in Education for Development*. Eldoret, Kenya: Gaba Publications, 1985.

da Cruz, Fernando, Kerstin Sommer, and Ombretta Tempra. *Nairobi Urban Sector Profile*. Nairobi: UN-Habitat, 2006.

Davis, Mike. *Planet of Slums*. London: Verso, 2006.

de Gruchy, John W. *Christianity and Democracy: A Theology for a Just World Order*. Cambridge: Cambridge University Press, 1995.

de Smedt, Johan. "Kill me Quick: a History of Nubian Gin in Kibera." *International Journal of African Historical Studies* 42, no. 2 (2009): 201-20.

—. "'No Raila, No Peace!' Big Man Politics and Election Violence at the Kibera Grassroots." *African Affairs* 108, no. 433 (2009): 581-98.

de Tocqueville, Alexis. *Democracy in America*. Edited by Phillips Bradley. Translated by Henry Reene. New York: Alfred Knopf, 1945.

Diamond, Larry. "Beyond Autocracy: Prospect for Democracy in Africa." Paper presented at the inaugural seminar of the governance program, Carter Center, Emory University, Atlanta, 1989.

—. "Civil Society and Democratic Consolidation: Building a Culture of Compromise and Reconciliation in a New South Africa." Paper presented at conference on Consolidating a Democracy in South Africa, Johannesburg, undated.

—. *The Democratic Revolution: Struggles for Freedom and Pluralism in the Developing World, Perspectives on Freedom*. New York: Freedom House, 1992.

—. *Developing Democracy: Toward Consolidation*. Baltimore: Johns Hopkins University Press, 1999.

—. "Toward Democratic Consolidation." *Journal of Democracy* 5, no. 3 (1994): 4-17.

Diamond, Larry, Juan Linz, and Seymour Lipset. *Democracy in Developing Countries*. Boulder, CO: L. Reinner Publishers, 1988.

Diamond, Larry, Leonardo Morlino, and American Political Science Association Meeting, ed. *Assessing the Quality of Democracy*. Baltimore: Johns Hopkins University Press, 2005.

Diamond, Larry, and Center for Democratic Studies (Nigeria). *Globalization of Democracy: Trends, Types, Causes, and Prospects*. Abuja, Nigeria: C.D.S. Occasional Publications, 1992.

Dicklitch, Susan. *The Elusive Promise of NGOs in Africa: Lessons from Uganda*. New York: St. Martin's Press, 1998.

Doepp, Peter Von. "Liberal Visions and Actual Power in Grassroots Civil Society: Local Churches and Women's Empowerment in Rural Malawi." *Journal of Modern African Studies* 40, no. 2 (2002): 273-301.

Edwards, Michael. *Civil Society*. Oxford: Polity Press, 2004.

Ehresmann, Peter. "Nairobi's Housing Crisis: An Analysis of the Kenya Slum Upgrading Program." BA thesis, College of St. Benedict/St. John's University, Minneapolis, May 2004.

Fatton, Robert. "Africa in the Age of Discrimination: The Civic Limitations of Civil Society." *African Studies Review* 38, no. 2 (1995): 67-99.

—. *Predatory Rule, State and Civil Society in Africa*. Boulder, CO: L. Reinner, 1992.

Fernandes, Edésio, and Ann Varley. *Illegal Cities: Law and Urban Change in Developing Countries*. London: Zed Books, 1998.

Finkel, Steven. "The Impact of the Kenyan National Civic Education Program on Democratic Attitudes, Knowledge, Values and Behavior."

Report prepared for U.S. Agency for International Development, Nairobi, AEP-I-00-0001800-00, December 2003.

Fisher, William. "Doing Good? The Politics and Antipolitics of NGO Practices." *Annual Review of Anthropology* 26 (1997): 439-64.

Foley, Michael, and Bob Edwards. "The Paradox of Civil Society." *Journal of Democracy* 7, no. 3 (1996): 38-50.

"*Forced Evictions –Toward Solutions?*" Report of the Advisory Group on Forced Evictions to the Executive Director of UN-Habitat, Nairobi: UN-Habitat, 2005.

Gellner, Ernest. *Conditions of Liberty: Civil Society and Its Rivals*. London: Penguin Press, 1996.

Gerard, Clarke. "Faith Matters: Faith-Based Organizations, Civil Society and International Development." *Journal of International Development* 18 (2006): 835-48.

Gibbon, Peter, ed. S*ocial Change and Economic Reform in Africa*. Nordiska Afrikainstitutet, 1995.

Gifford, Paul. *African Christianity: Its Public Role*. London: Hurst & Co., 1998.

—. "Africa's Churches and the 'Second Liberation Struggle,' of 1989-93," In *The Years 1989-90: Turning Point in European and Non-European Christian History*, edited by Klaus Koschorke, 136-55. Wiesbaden: Harrassowitz Verlag, 2008.

—. ed. *The Christian Churches and the Democratization of Africa*. Leiden: E.J. Brill, 1995.

—. *Christianity, Politics and Public Life in Kenya*. London: Hurst & Co., 2008.

Githiga, Gideon G. *The Church as the Bulwark against Authoritarianism: Development of Church and State Relations in Kenya with Particular Reference to the Years after Political Independence 1963-1992*. Oxford: Regnum, 2001.

Goux, Marie-Ange. "Consultancy on the Habitat Project: Sustainable Neighborhood Program Kenya Pilot Project: Preliminary Studies." Report provided to the Embassy of Finland, Nairobi, 2003.

Gramsci, Antonio. *Selections from the Prison Notebooks*. Edited and translated by Quintin Hoare, and Geoffrey Nowell Smith. New York: International Publishers, 1971.

Gulyani, Sumila, and Debabrata Talukdar. "Slum Real Estate: The Low-Quality High-Price Puzzle in Nairobi's Slum Rental Market and its Implications for Theory and Practice." *World Development* 36, no.10 (2008): 1916-37.

Hadenius, Alex, and Frederick Uggla. "Making Civil Society Work, Promoting Democratic Development: What can Donors Do?" *World Development* 24, no. 10 (1996): 1621-39.

Hake A. *African Metropolis: Nairobi's Self-Help City*. London: Chatto and Windus for Sussex University Press, 1977.

Hansen, Holger Bernt, and Michael Twaddle Throup, ed. *Religion & Politics in East Africa: The Period since Independence*. London: James Currey, 1995.

Harbeson, John W. "Civil Society and Political Renaissance in Africa." In *Civil Society and the State in Africa*, edited by John W. Harbeson, Donald S. 1994.

Hardoy, Jorge E., and David Satterthwaite. *Squatter Citizen: Life in the Urban Third World*. London: Earthscan, 1989.

Healey, Joseph, and Jeanne Hinton, ed. *Small Christian Communities Today: Capturing the New Moment*. Maryknoll, NY: Orbis Books, 2006.

Hearn, Julie. "The 'Invisible' NGO: US Evangelical Missions in Kenya." *Journal of Religions in Africa* 32, no. 1 (2002): 32-60.

Hegel, G. *Philosophy of Right*. Translated by T. M. Knox. Oxford: Clarendon Press, 1942.

Herr, Harvey, and Karl Guenter. "Estimating Global Slum Dwellers: Monitoring the Millennium Development Goal 7, Target 11." Working paper presented to UN-Habitat Nairobi, 2003.

Hirst, Terry, and Davinder Lamba. *The Struggle for Nairobi, the Story of an Urban Environment Built at the Place of Cold Waters*. Nairobi: Mazingira Institute, 1994.

Holland, Joe, and Peter Henriot. *Social Analysis: Linking Faith and Justice*. Maryknoll, NY: Orbis Books, 1983.

Hope, Anne, and Sally Timmel. "A Kenyan Experience for Faith-Based Transformative Action." *Development* 46, no. 4 (2003): 93-99.

Huchzermeyer, Marie. "Slum Upgrading Initiatives in Kenya within the Basic Services and Wider Housing Market." Discussion Paper No. 1/2006 presented to Center for Housing Rights and Evictions, Geneva, 2006.

Hulme, David, and Michael Edwards. *NGOs, States and Donors: Too Close for Comfort?* New York: St. Martin's Press, 1997.

Human Rights Watch, Africa Watch. *Kenya: Taking Liberties: An Africa Watch Report*. New York: Africa Watch, 1991.

Huntington, Samuel P. *The Third Wave: Democratization in the Late Twentieth Century*. Norman, OK: University of Oklahoma Press, 1991.

Hyden, Goran and Michael Bratton, ed. *Governance and Politics in Africa*. Boulder, CO: L. Reinner, 1992.

Igoe, Jim, and Tim Kelsall. *Between a Rock and a Hard Place: African NGOs, Donors and the State.* Durham, NC: Carolina Academic Press, 2005.

Joireman, Sandra F. *Where There is No Government: Enforcing Property Rights in Common Law Africa*. Oxford: Oxford University Press, 2011.

Juma, Lawrence. "Ethnic Politics and the Constitution Review Process in Kenya." *Tulsa Journal of Comparative and International Law* 9 (Spring 2002): 471-532.

Kabagambe, Denis, and Cliff Moughtin. "Housing the Poor: A Case Study in Nairobi." *Third World Planning Review* 5, no. 3 (1983): 227-48.

Kamande, Mugane. "Microbiological, Physical and Chemical Analysis of Local Alcoholic Brews in Korogocho (Nairobi)." Report prepared for St. John's Catholic Church, Nairobi, 2000.

Kanji, Nazneen, Carla Braga, and Winnie Mittulah. *Promoting Land Rights in Africa: How do NGOs Make a Difference?* London: International Institute for Environment and Development, 2002.

Kanyinga, Karuti. "Civil Society Formations in Kenya: A Growing Role in Development and Democracy." In *Civil Society in the Third Republic*, edited by Duncan Okello, and National Council of NGOs (Kenya), 9-24. Nairobi: National Council of NGOs, 2004.

—. "The Social-Political Context of the Growth of Non-Governmental Organizations in Kenya." In *Social Change and Economic Reform in Africa*, edited by Peter Gibbon, 53-77. Uppsala: Nordiska Afrikainstitutet, 1995.

Kanyinga, Karuiti, and Carl Wesselink. *Transition to Democracy-The Role of Civic Education in Kenya*. Phatlaslatsa Newsletter, December 2002.

Kasfir, Nelson, ed. "Civil Society, the State and Democracy in Africa." In *Civil Society and Democracy in Africa: Critical Perspectives,* edited by Nelson Kasfir, 123-49. London: Frank Cass, 1998.

Kassimir, Ronald. "The Social Power of Religious Organization and Civil Society: The Catholic Church in Uganda." In *Civil Society and Democracy in Africa Critical Perspectives*, edited by Nelson Kasfir, 54-83. London: Frank Cass, 1998.

Keane, John. *Civil Society and the State: New European Perspectives*. London: Verso, 1988.

Keengwe, Maina, Fiona Percy, Orito Mageka, and Muhamud Sheik Adan. *NGO Roles and Relationships: Partnership Dilemmas for International and Local NGOs (in Kenya).* Nairobi: International Institute for Environment and Development, 1998.

Kenya Colony and Protectorate. *Report of the Kenyan Lands Commission*. Nairobi: Kenya Colony and Protectorate, 1933.

Kenya Shadow Justice. London: Africa Rights, 1996.

Kenyan Human Rights Commission. *Behind the Curtain: A study on Squatters, Slums and Slum Dwellers*. Nairobi: Kenya Human Rights Commission, 1996.

Kinuthia, Macharia. "Slum Clearance and the Informal Economy in Nairobi." *The Journal of Modern African Studies* 30, no. 2 (1992): 221-36.

—. "Tensions Created by the Formal and Informal Use of Urban Space: The Case of Nairobi, Kenya." *Journal of Third World Studies* 24, no. 2 (2007): 145-62.

Kirii, Mugo P. *The Nairobi Basic Needs Basket: Cost of Basic Needs Basket in Twelve Informal Settlements, Nairobi-Kenya, 2004*. Nairobi: Paulines Publications Africa, 2004.

Kithari, Miloon. "Addendum Mission to Kenya." Report presented to the 61st Session of the Commission on Human Rights, Geneva, February 2004.

Klopp, Jacqueline M. "Pilfering the Public: The Problem of Land Grabbing in Contemporary Kenya." *Africa Today* 47, no. 1 (2000): 7-26.

Knighton, Ben, ed. *Religion and Politics in Kenya: Essays in Honor of a Meddlesome Priest*. New York: Palgrave Macmillan, 2009.

Koschorke, Klaus. *The Years 1989-90: Turning Point in European and Non-European Christian History*. Wiesbaden: Harrassowitz Verlag, 2008.

Kuhn, Marko. *Prophetic Christianity in Western Kenya: Political, Cultural and Theological Aspects of African Independent Churches*. Frankfurt: P. Lang, 2008.

Kuperus, Tracy. "Building Democracy: An Examination of Religious Associations in South Africa and Zimbabwe." *The Journal of Modern Africa Studies* 37, no. 4 (1999): 643-68.

Kurtz, John R. *Urban Obsessions, Urban Fears: The Postcolonial Kenyan Novel*. Trenton, NJ: Africa World Press, 1998.

Langford, Malcolm, Leslie Quitzow, and Virginia Roaf. *Human Rights and Slum-Upgrading: General Introduction and Compilation of Case Studies*. Geneva: COHRE, 2005.

Law Society of Kenya. *Report: A Mission to Kibera*. Nairobi: Law Society of Kenya Land Reform Program, 2002.

Leo, Christopher. *Land and Class in Kenya*. Toronto: University of Toronto Press, 1984.

Lewis, David. "Civil Society in African Contexts: Reflections on the Usefulness of a Concept." *Development and Change* 33, no. 4 (2002): 569-86.

Lonsdale, John. "Compromised Critics: Religion in Kenya's Politics." In *Religion and Politics in Kenya*, edited by Ben Knighton, 58-94. New York: Palgrave Macmillan, 2009.

Lukudu, Caesar, Catholic University of Eastern Africa, and Konrad-Adenauer-Stiftung. *Alienation of Public Land in Kenya*. Nairobi: Catholic University of Eastern Africa, 2000.

Lynch, Gabrielle. "The Fruits of Perception: 'Ethnic Politics' and the Case of Kenya's Constitutional Referendum." *African Studies* 65, no. 2 (2006): 233-69.

Macoloo, Gervase C. "The State and Low-income Urban Housing Production and Consumption in Kenya." In *Issues in Resource Management and Development in Kenya: Essays in Memory of Professor Simeon H. Ominde*, edited by Robert A. Obudho, and J.B. Ojwang, 247-70. Nairobi: East African Educational Publishers, 2000.

Magesa, Laurenti. "The Church in Eastern Africa: Retrospect and Prospect." In *How Local Is the Local Church? Small Christian Communities and Church in Eastern Africa*, edited by Agatha Radoli, 3-35. Eldoret, Kenya: AMECEA Gaba Publications, 1993.

Makoloo, Maurice O., Yash Ghai, Minority Rights Group International, and CEMIRIDE (Kenya). *Kenya: Minorities, Indigenous Peoples and Ethnic Diversity*. London: Minority Rights Group International; CEMIRIDE, 2005.

Makumbe, John. "Is there a Civil Society?" *International Affairs* 74, no. 2 (1998): 305-17.

Marx, Karl. *Critique of 'Philosophy of Right.'* Edited by Joseph O'Malley. Cambridge: University Press, 1970.

Matanga, Frank. "Kenya: A Chequered Path to Democracy." *African Journal on Human Rights & Democracy* 31 (2003): 31-41.

Maupeu, Herve. "The Churches and the Polls." In *Out for the Count: The 1997 General Elections and Prospects for Democracy in Kenya*, edited by Marcel Rutten, Ali Al Mazrui, and François Grignon, 50-71. Kampala: Fountain, 2001.

—. "Religion and the Elections." In *The Moi Succession: Elections 2002*, edited by Herve Maupeu, Musambayi Katumanga, and Winnie Mitullah, 33-68. Nairobi: Transafrica Press, 2005.

Mbithi, P. M. *The Spontaneous Settlement Problem in Kenya*. Kampala: East African Literature Bureau, 1975.

Mejia, Rodrigo, ed. *The Social Teaching of the Catholic Bishops of Kenya 1960-1995: The Conscience of Society*. Nairobi: Paulines Publication Africa, 1995.

Ministry of Local Government, Urban Development Department, and Nairobi City Council Water and Sewage Department. "Kibera Urban Environmental Sanitation Project: Consultancy Services for Identification, Preparation and Implementation." Report prepared for Government of Kenya, Nairobi, 2002.

Mitullah, Winnie. "Civic Elections in Nairobi." In *The Moi Succession: Elections 2002*, edited by Herve Maupeu, Musambayi Katumanga, and Winnie Mitullah, 375-90. Nairobi: Transafrica Press, 2005.

—. "Towards a Policy of Upgrading Informal Settlements and Site and Service Schemes in the City of Nairobi, Kenya." *African Urban Quarterly* 7, nos. 1 and 2 (1992): 186-97.

Mitullah, Winnie, and Kivutha Kibwana. "A Tale of Two Cities: Policy, Law and Illegal Settlements in Kenya." In *Illegal Cities: Law and Urban Change in Developing Countries*, edited by Edesio Fernandes, and Ann Varley, 210-21. London: Zed Books, 1998.

Moreno, Antonio F. *Church, State, and Civil Society in Postauthoritarian Philippines: Narratives of Engaged Citizenship*. Manila: Ateneo de Manila University Press, 2006.

Moschetti, Daniel. *Urban Ministry in Africa: Need for New Models*. Eldoret, Kenya: AMECEA Gaba Publications, 1997.

Mugai, Githu. "Jomo Kenyatta and the Rise of the Ethno-Nationalist State in Kenya." In *Ethnicity & Democracy in Africa*, edited by Bruce Berman, Dickson Eyoh, and Will Kymlicka, 200-17. Oxford: James Currey, 2002.

Mugambi, J. N. K. *From Liberation to Reconstruction: African Christian Theology after the Cold War*. Nairobi: East African Educational Publishers, 1995.

Mugisha, Frederick, Jacqueline Arinaitwe-Mugisha, and Bilhah Hagembe. "Alcohol, Substance and Drug use among Urban Slum Adolescents in Nairobi, Kenya." *Cities* 20, no. 4 (2003): 231-40.

Munene, Macharia. "Kibaki's Moment in History: The Election of 2002 and its Aftermath." *East African Journal of Human Rights and Democracy* 71 (2003): 71-89.

Murithi, Joseph, and Stella Nzoi. "Mathare 4A: The True Story." *Mwananchi* 274 (April 1999): 1-2.

Murunga, Godwin R. "Governance and the Politics of Structural Adjustment in Kenya." In *Kenya: The Struggle for Democracy*, edited by Godwin R. Murunga, and Shadrack W. Nasong'o, 263-300. London: Zed Books, 2007.

—. "The State, Its Reform and the Question of Legitimacy in Kenya." *Identity, Culture and Politics* 5, nos. 1 and 2 (2004): 179-206.

Murunga, Godwin R., and Shadrack W. Nasong'o. Murunga."Prospects for Democracy in Kenya." In *Kenya: The Struggle for Democracy*, edited by Godwin R. Murunga, and Shadrack W. Nasong'o, 3-18. London: Zed Books, 2007.

Mute, Lawrence. "Legal-political Transition in Kenya: The Role of Civic Education." In *Building an Open Society: the Politics of Transition in Kenya* edited by Wanza Kioko, Lawrence Mute, and S. Kichamu Akivaga, 126-56. Nairobi: Claripress, 2002.

Mutua, Makau, ed. *Human Rights NGOs in East Africa: Political and Normative Tensions*. Philadelphia: University of Pennsylvania Press, 2009.

—. *Kenya's Quest for Democracy, Taming Leviathan*. Boulder, CO: L. Reinner Publishers, 2008.

Mutunga, Willy. *Constitution-Making from the Middle: Civil Society and Transition Politics in Kenya, 1992-1997*. Nairobi: SAREAT, 1999.

Muyebe, Stanslaus C., and Alexander Muyebe. *The African Bishops on Human Rights: A Resource Book.* Nairobi: Paulines Publications Africa, 2001.

Mwangi, Issac. "The Nature of Rental Housing in Kenya,' *Environment & Urbanization* 9, no. 2 (1997): 141-59.

Nasong'o, Shadrack W. *Contending Political Paradigms in Africa: Rationality and the Politics of Democratization in Kenya and Zambia*. London: Routledge, 2005.

—. "Negotiating New Rules of the Game: Social Movements, Civil Society and the Kenyan Transition." In *Kenya: The Struggle for Democracy*, edited by Godwin R. Murunga, and Shadrack W. Nasong'o, 19-57. London: Zed Books, 2007.

—. "Political Transition without Transformation: The Dialectic of Liberalization without Democratization in Kenya and Zambia." *African Studies Review* 50, no. 1 (2007): 83-107.

National Council of Churches of Kenya. *Nairobi Demolitions, What Next?* Nairobi: National Council of Churches of Kenya, 1991.

Ndegwa, Stephen N. *The Two Faces of Civil Society: NGOs and Politics in Africa*. West Hartford, CT: Kumarian Press, 1996.

Ndungo, Catherine. "Language, Gender, Political Participation and Democracy in Kenya." Paper presented to Language Project Conference, University of Maryland, November 2004.

Neuwirth, Robert. *Shadow Cities: A Billion Squatters, a New Urban World*. New York: Routledge, 2005.

Nge'ethe, Njuguna, and M. Katumanga. "Transition and the Politics of Constitution-Making: A Comparative Study of Uganda, South Africa and Kenya." In *The Politics of Transition in Kenya: From Kanu to Narc*, edited by Walter Oyugi, Peter Wanyande, and C. Odhiambo-Mbai, 303-42. Nairobi: Heinrich Boll Foundation, 2003.

Ngunjiri, Njuguna, and William Ong'aro. *Raila Odinga, the Unbwogable*. Nairobi: Immediate Media Services, 2003.

Ngunyi, Mutahi. "Religious Institutions and Political Liberalization in Kenya." In *Markets, Civil Society and Democracy in Kenya*, edited by Peter Gibbon, 121-77. Uppsala: Nordiska Afrikainstitutet, 1995.

Njogu, Kimani. "Ahadi ni Deni, The Aftermath of the Elections." In *The Moi Succession: Elections 2002*, edited by Herve Maupeu, Musambayi Katumanga, and Winnie Mitullah, 401-32. Nairobi: Transafrica Press, 2005.

Nyanjom, Othieno, and Kenya Human Rights Commission. *The State and Land: Case Studies in Corruption and Mismanagement*. Nairobi: Kenya Human Rights Commission, 2000.

Nyinguro, Philip O., and Eric E. Otenyo. "Social Movements and Democratic Transitions in Kenya." *Journal of Asian and African Studies* 42, no. 5 (2007): 5-24.

Nzomo, Maria. "Civil Society in the Kenyan Political Transition: 1992-2002." In *The Politics of Transition in Kenya: From Kanu to Narc*, edited by Walter Oyugi, Peter Wanyande, and C. Odhiambo-Mbai. Nairobi: Heinrich Boll Foundation, 2003.

Obudho, R.A. "Nairobi, National Capital and Regional Hub." In *The Urban Challenge in Africa: Growth and Management of its Large Cities*, edited by Carole Rakodi, 292-334. Tokyo: United Nations University Press, 1997.

Obudho, R.A., and J.B. Ojwang, ed. *Issues in Resource Management and Development in Kenya: Essays in Memory of Professor Simeon H. Ominde*, Nairobi: East African Educational Publishers, 2000.

O'Donnell, Guillermo. "Why the Rule of Law Matters." In *Assessing the Quality of Democracy*, edited by Larry Diamond, Leonardo Morlino, and American Political Science Association, 3-17. Baltimore: Johns Hopkins University Press, 2005.

Office of Human Rights. "Kibera East Baseline Survey." Report submitted to Christ the King Catholic Church, Nairobi, 2008.

Okech, Owiti, Kivutha Kibwana, Smokin Wanjala, and Center for Law and Research International. *The Anatomy of Corruption in Kenya:*

Legal, Political and Socio-Economic Perspectives. Nairobi: Claripress, 1996.

Okello, Duncan, and National Council of NGOs (Kenya), ed. *Civil Society in the Third Republic*. Nairobi: National Council of NGOs, 2004.

Okuku, Juma A. "Civil Society and the Democratization Processes in Kenya and Uganda: a Comparative Analysis of the Contribution of the Church and NGOs." *Politikon* 30, no. 1 (2003): 51-63.

Olima, Washington. "The Dynamics and Implications of Sustaining Urban Spatial Segregation in Kenya: Experiences from Nairobi Metropolis." Paper presented to Lincoln Institute of Land Policy, Nairobi, 2001.

Orvis, Stephen. "Civil Society in Africa or African Civil Society?" *African and Asian Studies* 36, no. 1 (2001): 17-38.

—. "Conclusion: Bringing Institutions Back into the Study of Kenya and Africa." *Africa Today* 53, no. 2 (2006): 95-100.

—. "Kenyan Civil Society: Bridging the Urban-rural Divide?" *Journal of Modern African Studies* 41, no. 2 (2003): 247-68.

Osborn, Michelle. "Fueling the Flames: Rumor and Politics in Kenya." *Journal of Eastern African Studies* 2, no. 2 (2008): 315-27.

Ottaway, Marina, Thomas Carothers, and the Carnegie Endowment for International Peace, ed. *Funding Virtue: Civil Society Aid and Democracy Promotion*. Washington, D.C.: Carnegie Endowment For International Peace, 2000.

Otiso, Kefa. "Colonial Urbanization and Urban Management in Kenya." In *African Urban Spaces in Historical Perspective*, edited by Steven J. Salm, and Toyin Falola, 73-97. Rochester, NY: University of Rochester Press, 2005.

—. "Forced Evictions in Kenyan Cities." *Singapore Journal of Tropical Geography* 23, no. 3 (2002): 252-67.

—. "State, Voluntary and Private Sector Partnerships for Slum Upgrading and Basic Service Delivery in Nairobi, Kenya." *Cities* 20, no. 4 (2003): 221-29.

Outreach Development Services. "Participatory Urban Appraisal Study of Mashimoni, Kambi Muru, Lindi and Silanga Villages–Kibera Informal Settlement." Report prepared for Oxfam GB, Nairobi, 2001.

Owiti, Jeremiah, Otieno Aluoka, and Adams Oloo. "Civil Society in the New Dispensation: Prospects and Challenges." In *Civil Society in the Third Republic*, edited by Duncan Okello, and National Council of NGOs (Kenya), 71-86. Nairobi: National Council of NGOs, 2004.

Oyugi, Maurice O., and Owiti A. K'Akumu. "Land Management Challenges for the City of Nairobi." *Urban Forum* 18, no. 1 (2007): 94-113.

Oyugi, Walter. "The Role of NGOs in Fostering Development and Good Governance at the Local Level in Africa with a Focus on Kenya." *African Development* 24, no. 4 (2004): 19-55.

Oyugi, Walter, Peter Wanyande, and C. Odhiambo-Mbai, ed. *The Politics of Transition in Kenya: From Kanu to Narc*. Nairobi: Heinrich Boll Foundation, 2003.

Pamoja Trust, and Tecta Consultants. "Relocation Action Plan for Improving the Safety Along Kenya Railway Line." Report prepared for the Government of Kenya, Ministry of Transport and Communication and Kenya Railways Corporation, Nairobi, October 2005.

Parsons, Timothy. "Kibra is our Blood: the Sudanese Military Legacy in Nairobi's Kibera, Location, 1902-1968." *The International Journal of African Historical Studies* 30, no. 1 (1997): 87-122.

Partanen, Juha. *Sociability and Intoxication: Alcohol Drinking in Kenya, Africa, and the Modern World*. Helsinki: The Finnish Foundation for Alcohol Studies, 1991.

Patel, Sheila, Sunda Burra, and Celine de'Cruz. "Shack/Slum Dwellers International: Foundations to Treetops." *Environment & Urbanization* 13, no. 1 (2001): 45-59.

Pierli, Francesco. "The Church and the Slums: 50 Years of a Painful and Yet Fruitful Journey." In *The Slums: A Challenge to Evangelization*, edited by Francesco Pierli, and Yago Abeledo, 133-41. Nairobi: Paulines Publications Africa, 2002.

Pirouet, M. Louise. "The Churches and Human Rights in Kenya and Uganda since Independence." In *Religion and Politics in East Africa: The Period since Independence*, edited by Holger Bernt Hansen, and Michael Twaddle, 247-59. London: Frank Cass, 2002.

Political Patronage, Access to Entitlements and Poverty in Kenya, Final Report of Findings of a National Survey. Nairobi: KEC-CJPC and Dan Church Aid, 2007.

Press, Robert M. *Peaceful Resistance: Advancing Human Rights and Democratic Freedoms, Ethics and Global Politics*. Aldershot, England: Ashgate, 2006.

Putnam, Robert D. *Bowling Alone: The Collapse and Revival of American Community*. New York: Simon & Schuster, 2000.

Putnam, Robert D., Robert Leonardi, and Raffaella Nanetti. *Making Democracy Work: Civic Traditions in Modern Italy*. Princeton, NJ: Princeton University Press, 1993.

Radoli, Agatha, ed. *How Local Is the Local Church? Small Christian Communities and Church in Eastern Africa*. Eldoret, Kenya: AMECEA Gaba Publications, 1993.

Rakodi, Carole, ed. *The Urban Challenge in Africa: Growth and Management of its Large Cities*. Tokyo: United Nations University Press, 1997.

Research International. "Kibera Social and Economic Mapping: Household Survey." Report prepared for Government of Kenya, and UN-Habitat, Nairobi, 2005.

Ruteer, Mutuma, and the Kenya Human Rights Commission. *Mission to Repress: Torture, Illegal Detentions and Extra Judicial Killings by the Kenyan Police*. Nairobi: Kenyan Human Rights Commission, 1998.

—. *Shackled Messengers: The Media in Multiparty Kenya*. Nairobi: Kenyan Human Rights Commission, 1997.

Rutten, Marcel, Ali Al Mazrui, and François Grignon, ed. *Out for the Count: The 1997 General Elections and Prospects for Democracy in Kenya.* Kampala: Fountain, 2001.

Sabar-Friedman, Galia. *Church, State, and Society in Kenya: From Mediation to Opposition, 1963-1993*. London: Frank Cass, 2002.

—. "Church and State in Kenya, 1986-1992: The Churches' Involvement in the 'Game of Change.'" *African Affairs* 96 (1997): 25-52.

Salm, Steven J., and Toyin Falola Otiso, ed. *African Urban Spaces in Historical Perspective*. Rochester, NY: University of Rochester Press, 2005.

Schwartz-Barcott, Rye. "Youth Culture, NGO Involvement, and Collective Violence in Kibera, Nairobi–East Africa's Largest Slum." Master's thesis, University of North Carolina at Chapel Hill, 2001.

Seligman, A. *The Idea of Civil Society*. New York: Free Press; Maxwell Macmillan International, 1992.

Shorter, Aylward. *The Church in the African City*. Maryknoll, NY: Orbis Books, 1991.

Smith, Colin. "A Missiological Study of Pentecostal Churches in an Informal Settlement in Nairobi, Kenya." PhD diss., University of South Africa, 2007.

Society for International Development Eastern Africa Office. *Pulling Apart: Facts and Figures in Inequality in Kenya*. Nairobi: Society for International Development Eastern Africa Office, 2004.

Southall, Roger. "The Ndungu Report: Land and Graft in Kenya." *Review of African Political Economy* 103 (2005): 142-51.

Steeves, Jeffrey. "Presidential Succession in Kenya: The Transition from Moi to Kibaki." *Commonwealth & Comparative Politics* 44, no. 2 (2006): 211-33.

Stren, Richard. "Urban Policy and Performance in Kenya and Tanzania." *The Journal of Modern African Studies* 13, no. 2 (1975): 267-94.

Syagga, Paul, Winnie Mitullah, and Sarah K. Gitau. *Nairobi Situation Analysis; Consultative Report*. Nairobi: Government of Kenya, and UN-Habitat, 2001.

—. *Nairobi Situation Analysis Supplementary Study: A Rapid Appraisal of Rents in Slums and Informal Settlements*. Nairobi: Government of Kenya, and UN-Habitat, 2002.

Thobhani, Akbarali. "Political Developments During the 1990's." In *Modern Kenya: Social Issues and Perspectives*, edited by Mary Ann Watson, 1-21. Lanham, MD: University Press of America, 2001.

Throup, David W. "Render unto Caesar the Things that are Caesar's: The Politics of Church-State Conflict in Kenya1978-1990." In *Religion and Politics in East Africa: The Period since Independence*, edited by Holger Bernt Hansen, and Michael Twaddle, 143-76. London: James Currey, 1995.

Throup, David W., and Charles Hornsby. *Multi-Party Politics in Kenya: The Kenyatta and Moi States & the Triumph of the System in the 1992 Election*. Oxford: James Currey, 1998.

Umoja wa Kupigania Demokrasia Kenya. *Moi's Reign of Terror: A Decade of Nyayo Crimes against the People of Kenya*. London: Umoja Secretariat, Editorial and Publications Department, 1989.

UN-Habitat. *The Challenge of Slums: Global Report on Human Settlements*. London: Earthscan, 2003.

—. *Rental Housing: An Essential Option for the Urban Poor in Developing Countries*. Nairobi: UN-Habitat, 2003.

—. *The Second Urban World Forum, September 13-17, 2004*. Nairobi: UN-Habitat, 2004.

VeneKlasen, Lisa. "The Challenge of Democracy-Building: Practical Lessons on NGO Advocacy and Political Change." In *NGOs, Civil Society and the State: Building Democracy in Transitional Societies*, edited by Andrew Clayton, 219-40. Oxford: INTRAC, 1996.

Waliggo, John Mary. "Urbanization in Africa: Challenges for the Church." Mimeo, Nairobi, April 1994.

Wambuii, Henry K. "*The Politics of HIV/AIDS and Implications for Democracy in Kenya*." Lewiston, NY: Edwin Mellen Press, 2006.

Wanjohi, Nick. *Modern Local Government in Kenya*. Nairobi: Konrad Adenauer Stiftung Agency for Development Education and Communication, 2003.

Wanyama, Fredrick. "The Third Sector and the Transformation of Governance in Africa: The Case of Community-Based Organizations." Paper presented to the International Society for Third-Sector Research, University of Cape Town, 2002.

Watson, Mary Ann, ed. *Modern Kenya: Social Issues and Perspectives*. Lanham, MD: University Press of America, 2001.

Werlin, Herbert H. *Governing an African City: A Study of Nairobi*. New York: Africana Publishing Co., 1974.

Weru, Jane. "Community Federations and City Upgrading: the Work of Pamoja Trust and Muungano in Kenya." *Environment & Urbanization* 16, no. 1 (2004): 47-61.

Widner, Jennifer A. *The Rise of a Party-State in Kenya: From "Harambee!" To "Nyayo!"* Berkeley: University of California Press, 1993.

Wijsen, Frans, Peter Henriot, and Rodrigo Mejia, ed. *The Pastoral Circle Revisited: a Critical Quest for Truth and Transformation*. Maryknoll, NY: Orbis Books, 2005.

Willis, Justin. "Drinking Crisis? Change and Continuity in Cultures of Drinking in Sub-Saharan Africa." *African Journal of Drug and Alcohol Studies* 5, no. 1 (2006): 1-15.

—. "New Generation Drinking: The Uncertain Boundaries of Criminal Enterprise in Modern Kenya." *African Affairs* 102 (2003): 241-60.

—. *Potent Brews, a Social History of Alcohol in East Africa 1850-1999*. Nairobi: The British Institute in Eastern Africa, 2002.

Zalot, Jozef D. *The Roman Catholic Church and Economic Development in Sub Saharan Africa: Voices yet Unheard in a Listening World*. Lanham, MD: University Press of America, 2002.

INDEX

AA (Alcoholics Anonymous), 109, 119, 130
abortion, 93, 103
Aboum, Agnes, 22n109
Adar, Korwa, 27n15
AICs (African Independent Churches): ethnicity within, 172; in Kibera, 53-54; and housing NGOs, 145; and Soweto upgrade, 147, 159-60
AMECEA (Association of Member Episcopal Conferences of East Africa), 56
Amis, Philip, 48n86
Anglicanism: support for democratic reform, 22, 28n19; in Kibera, 53; response to 2004 eviction threat, 179, 185, 199; and Soweto upgrade, 142
ANPPCAN (African Network for the Prevention and Protection against Child Abuse and Neglect), 53; and 2004 eviction threat; 164, 181-83, 195; and Soweto upgrade, 144-46
Administrative Police, 49-50, 120-22
Archdiocese of Nairobi, 56-59, 215, 232; and civic education, 66, 87; conflicts with housing NGOs, 233-34; conflicts with missionaries, 34, 228; funding pressures on, 66; and the JPC, 58, 153-56; limited focus on slums, 35-36, 40, 153, 227-28; and peace building project, 152-54; response to slum demolitions, 37-38; 40; restrictive protocols within, 227-29, 235; and Soweto upgrade, 153, 156, 170. *See also* Ndingi, Archbishop Mwana a'Nzeki, Rafael
Aristotle, 3
Athi River, 140-41, 158
Atieno-Odhiambo, Elisha, 25n3
Awori, Moody, 118, 188, 193, 195
Azarya, Victor, 3n6

Bakalutu, 113
Baptist Church, 53n101
Basic Rights Campaign, 183, 196
Bayart, Jean-Francois, 5
Bebbington, Anthony, 2
Becker, Kristina Flodman, 137n3
Beetham, David, 8n40
Benson, Paddy, 22n110
Berman, Bruce, 25n2
Biau, Daniel, 45n76
Bratton, Michael, 5n24, 6, 9n43
Brazil, 59, 62, 78, 191
Britain. *See* United Kingdom
British High Commission, 193. *See also* Clay, Sir Edward
Burra, Sunda, 43n72

Catholicism, 23; and civic education, 62-63, 66; and constitutional reform 28-29, 65, 69, 87; and DELTA, 62; hierarchal structures in, 28-29; and human rights, 28; opposition to one-party state, 28-29, 69; repression by Moi, 27. *See also* AMECEA; Archdiocese of Nairobi; CTK; KEC; missionaries; SCCs
changáa, 102-03; chief's role in, 103, 105, 108; history of in

Kibera, 102-03; Moi's prohibition of, 103, 105; negative impact of, 103-07; police involvement in, 103-05, 108, 111-18, 120-22, 125-26; as priority issue for Soweto sub-parish, 112, 122-32; societal attitudes toward, 103-06. *See also* OHR: campaign against chang'aa
Chabal, Patrick, 13
Chazan, Naomi, 6, 14
chiefs, 12; abuse of power by, 51, 88, 92-93, 217, 224; and corruption, 105; and demolition of slums, 37; and illegal land allocations, 33, 48; opposition to civic education, 69-70, 77, 96; opposition to community organization, 39, 41, 96; political manipulation of, 37, 121-22; retaliation by, fear of, 179-80, 182, 185-86, 194, 199-200, 217; use of force by, 179-80, 186, 200. *See also* PA
Christian churches: as members of civil society, 1, 7, 22-23, 213, 227; divisions among, 142-43, 171-72, 226-27; and civic education, 62-63; opposition to by Moi, 28; support for constitutional reform, 29; support for multi-party democracy, 28-30; and social justice, 142, 227. *See also* AICs; Anglicans; Catholicism; Pentecostals; Protestants
civic education, 61-62; allowances paid, 74-75, 80; Catholic Church's provision of, 62-65; and the CRKC, 61, 65, 80; impact of, 64, limitations of 63-65; and the NCEP; 64-65; donor support for, 63; opposition by Moi, 63; NGO provision of, 63. *See also* constitutional reform; elections; OHR: civic education programme
civil society,1-6; and Christian churches, 22-23; criticisms of, 13-14, and democratization, 6-7; functions of, 9-13; as government watchdogs, 6, 13; in Kenya, 16-22; and NGOs, 6-7; suppression of by Moi, 26-27; under Kenyatta, 25. *See also* Christian churches; housing NGOs; human rights NGOs
CJPC (Catholic Justice and Peace Commission), 58; and civic education, 63, 65. *See also* Catholicism
CKRC (Constitution of Kenya Review Commission), 62, 65, 68, 80. *See also* constitutional reform
CLAN (Children's Legal Action Network), 52-53
Clark, John, 15
Clay, Sir Edward, 176, 195, 201, 233. *See also* British High Commission
clientelism, 12, 25. *See also* patronage
COHRE (Centre for Housing Rights and Evictions), 169, 191, 193, 197, 201-02, 206. *See also* eviction threat of 2004
colonialism, 25, 31; housing policies 31-32; and land allocations, 31-32; and the PA, 50; and slum demolitions, 32
Comboni missionaries, 36, 38
community-based organizations (CBOs), 146, 152, 158, 164, 181-82; and democratization, 20; in Kibera, 54; and Soweto upgrade, 159, 167
community organizing: and eviction threat of 2004, 203-04; in Nairobi slums, 38; opposition to by Catholic Church, 37; opposition to by Moi, 38-39; support for by some missionaries, 37
Consolata Catholic Church, 118

Constitution of Kenya: amendments to, 25, 27; under Kenyatta, 25; under Moi, 27. *See also* constitutional reform
constitutional reform, 29, 64-66, 68; and 2005 referendum, 87; Catholic Church's role in, 65-66, 70; Christian churches support for, 28-29, 87; civic education on, 61, 65, 80, 87-88; civil society's support for, 29; NGO role in, 86. *See also* CKRC; IPPG, NCEC; Ufungamano Initiative
corruption, 2, 21, 51, 61, 99, 133, 174; in the changáa trade, 104, in the judiciary, 39; 219 under Kenyatta, 25-26; under Moi, 26-30, 65, 89; and NGOs, 189; in the PA, 51, 92, 96, 101, 103-04, 121, 159; in Soweto upgrade, 135, 159; 167-70, 172. *See also* clientelism
Carothers, Thomas, 7n34, 15-16
Cottrell, Jill, 27n10, 29n25, 86n35
Crowley, Jerry, 62n3
CRS (Catholic Relief Services), 153
CTK (Christ the King Catholic Church), 55-58; ethnicity within, 94, 150, 225, 231; focus on pastoral activities, 216-17; influence of missionaries, 56, 58, 60, 217, 232-33; and the JPC, 59, 66, 68, 74, 77, 84, 110; and leadership structures, 58, 73, 90-92, 95; limited group formation in, 146, 151; and the pastoral team, 59, 67, 74, 85, 111, 149, 179; parish groups, 70n18, 83; relationship with other churches, 142, 161, 227; planning and restructuring of, 123-24, 131-32; restrictive protocols in, 62, 95, 97-98, 107, 151. *See also* OHR; pastoral circle; PPC; SCCs; social analysis
Daloz, Jean-Pascal, 13n65
Dandora, 118
Davis, Mike, 31n31
da Cruz, Fernando, 35n50
de'Cruz, Celine, 43n72
de Gruchy, John, 1n3, 22n109
de Smedt, Johan, 46n81, 48n87, 103n7
de Tocqueville, Alexis, 3, 5, 10
Deep Sea, 157
DELTA (Development Education Leadership Teams in Action), 62, 84
democratization,1-2; civil society's role in promoting, 6-9; as a civic education topic, 70, 82; consolidation of, 8; movement for, 16, 64-65, 231; within parish structures, 73-74; values and behavior of, 8-10, 13. *See also* multi-party elections
Diamond, Larry, 4-6, 7n35, 8-10, 11n52, 12n58, 13n62, 15
Dicklitch, Susan, 1n1, 10n50
Diocese of Nakuru, 41
DO (District Officer), 50, 69, 95-96, 185; limitations of authority, 122; response to eviction threat, 176-77, 185-86; relationship with OHR, 216, 233; role in Soweto upgrade, 159, 161, 169; support for campaign against changáa, 119-22. *See also* Administrative Police; PA
Doepp, von Peter, 13n64, 23n112
donors: competition among NGOs for funds, 147, 158, 172, 202, 205, 226; criticism of civil society, 15-16; and democracy agenda, 2; dependency on, 19-21; influence of, 43, 204, 214; lack of linkages to communities, 205, 223; manipulation of, 44, 75, 184; and the OHR, 83, 85, 111, 113, 115, 133; preference for NGOs, 6, 15-16; role in Soweto upgrade,

157, 162, 168; support for Catholic development projects, 57-58, 66, 119, 148, 153; support for civil society, 6-7; support for multi-party state, 28

Edwards, Bob, 13n63
Edwards, Michael, 2n4, 7n29, 15
Egypt, 191
elections: 1992 general election, 28, 68; 1997 general election, 29, 68; 2002 general election, 65, 68, 71; 2007 general election, 86, 235; and civic education, 63-64, 68, 70-71; and corruption, 28n17, 28; and ethnicity, 68, 220; and multi-party, 8, 17, 28; and OHR: civic education programme, 70-71, 76-77, 79-80; and violence, 28, 68, 70, 76. *See also* vote buying
ethnicity, 86-87; in CTK, 72, 81, 98, 103, 158, 231; in Kibera community, 47-49, 95, 103, 146, 159, 171, 222, 225; in churches, 145, 150, 160, 186, 226; in housing NGOs, 145, 226; political manipulation of, 171, 220, 225; related to structure owner and tenant, 140, 151, 181; in Soweto upgrade, 135, 137, 152-53, 157-58, 160-61; under Kenyatta, 25-26; and violence, 28, 137, 142, 235
EU (European Union), 157, 193
eviction threat of 2004, 173-74; as a breach of international law, 175n2; consequences of, 175-77, 189; demolition of Raila village, 174-75; diplomatic opposition to, 193, 201; ethnic divisions over, 180; fears related to, 173, 177-79, 185-86, 196; housing NGOs' response, 175, 182-84, 196-99, 203-08; and the Muungano, 182, 204-05; and the NARC government, 174-76, 186, 195, 204-05, 209; and railway relocation plan, 198-99, 207-08; response of other religious groups, 173, 179, 184-87, 208; support for by Raila, 174, 177, 180-81, 192; suspension of, 195-96, 206; and NDP youth wingers, 199, 207; UN-Habitat's response, 192. *See also* COHRE; HakiJamii; NGO Coalition against Evictions; OHR: response to eviction threat of 2004
evictions: during colonialism, 32; effects of, 36-37, 174-75; response of Catholic Church, 37-38; 40; response of human rights NGOs, 38-44; response of some missionaries, 38, 40-44; under Kenyatta, 33; under Kibaki, 173-74, 221; under Moi, 37; strategies to resist, 38-39. *See also* Kibagare; Land Caucus; Muoroto; Muungano wana Vijiji; Raila village; Slums Committee

Fatton, Robert, 14, 98
Finkel, Steven, 64
Finland, 140, 157-58, 215. *See also* Soweto upgrade
Fisher, William, 15n76
Foley, Michael, 13n63
Freire, Paul, 62
Friends Church, 53n101

Gellner, Ernest, 3
Ghai, Yash, 27n10, 29n25, 86n35
Gifford, Paul, ix; 1n3, 22n109, 23n111, 53n100, 235n10
Gitari, Bishop David, 28n19
Gitau, Sarah, 33n42, 34n45, 49n89, 52n99, 54n105
Githiga, Gideon, 22n110
Goux, Marie-Ange, 136n2, 139n8
Gramsci, Antonio, 4
Green Belt Movement, 17
Grignon, Francois, 63n5

Guadalupe Missionaries, 36, 56-57, 59, 116
Guenter, Karl, 35n51
Gulyani, Sumila, 221n5

Hadenius, Axel, 5n21
HakiJamii, 206
Harbeson, John, 6
health, 66; in Kibera, 52, 57, 66. *See also* HIV and AIDS
Healey, Joseph, 57n107
Hearn, Julie, 7n29, 235n11
Hegel, George, 2-4
Henriot, Peter, 60n109
Herr, Harvey, 35n51
Hindu, 30
Hinton, Jeanne, 57n107
HIV and AIDS, 54; and changáa, 106-07, 117; impact on parish activities, 73, 150; response of CTK, 58, 75, 84, 93, 102. *See also* health
Hobbes, Thomas, 3
Holland, Joe, 60n109
Hope, Anne, 62n2
housing NGOs, 143; competition among, 145-47, 183, 202-05; co-option by NARC, 173, 183, 205, 208, 225; distrust of, 168, 144, 172, 184; ethnicity within, 145, 226; lack of connection to slums, 144-45, 183, 198, 203-05; lack of unity, 145-46, 163, 172, 183, 202, 205-06; limitations of, 143-46, 168, 183-85, 202-06, 226; opposition to by Moi, 26, 39, 183; response to 2004 eviction threat, 182-84, 194-99, 207-08; role in Soweto upgrade, 143-44, 162-63, 167-69. *See also* human rights NGOs, KCS, Maji na Ufanisi, NGO Coalition against Evictions; Pamoja Trust, Shelter Forum
human rights NGOs, 7,; criticisms of, 15-16; and democratization, 7; donor influence on, 15-16; fear of deregistration 38, 40; in Kenya, 16-22; limitations of, 17-20; response to slum evictions, 38-44. *See also* housing NGOs; KCS; NGO Coalition against Evictions
Huchzermeyer, Marie, 35n49
Hulme, David, 2n4, 7n29, 15
Huntington, Samuel, 22n109
Huruma, 136-37, 143, 157
Hussein, Saddam, 118

IFC (International Finance Corporation), 207
Igoe, Jim, 7n31
informal settlements. *See* slum settlements
IJM (International Justice Mission), 193
ILO (International Labor Organization), 34
India, 43, 191, 198, 235
IPPG (Inter-Parties Parliamentary Group), 30, 105. *See also* constitutional reform
Islam. *See* Muslims
Italy, 4, 38, 118, 193
Jesuits, 67
John Paul II (pope), 190
Joint Project Planning Team, 137, 163. *See also* Soweto upgrade
Joireman, Sandra, 50n91
judiciary, 8; corruption within, 27, 39, 50

Kaiser, John, 229n8
Kalejin, 25, 26n4, 27
Kamande, Mugane, 102n2, 104n8
Kamba, 26n4, 47-48, 50, 159-60
Kambi Muru, 46
Kangemi: opposition to chang'aa, 104-05, 109, 117-19
KANU (Kenya African National Union), 27, 51-52, 65, 73, 136. *See also* Moi, Daniel arap
Kanyinga, Karuti, 18-20, 26n8, 63n6

Kasfir, Nelson, 13n63, 14-15

Kassimir, Ronald, 23n112, 218
Kawangware, 34
Kayamba Africa, 113
KCS (Kituo cha Sheria), vii, 39-40, 43, 67, 69, 111, 149; government opposition to, 39; limitations of, 39, 42-43, 146; response to 2004 eviction threat, 183-84, 194-97, 202, 206; response to Soweto upgrade, 144, 169. *See also* housing NGOs; Muungano wana Vijiji
Keane, John, 3n5
KEC (Kenya Episcopal Conference): opposition to one-party state, 29, 227. *See also* Catholicism
Keengwe, Maina, 20n96
Kelsall, Tim, 7n31
KENSUP (Kenya Slum Upgrading Program), 137, 139-40, 144, 147; access to officials of, 139; and Soweto enumeration, 162; failure to inform community, 149, 157; inaction of, 152-53, 157, 159; interaction with churches, 160-61; NGO representative of, 144, 162-63. *See also* UN-Habitat; Soweto upgrade
Kenya Human Rights Commission, 183
Kenya Land Commission, 48
Kenyatta, Jomo, 25, 51; and authoritarianism, 25; and corruption, 26; and ethnicity, 25-26; human rights abuses by, 25; and illegal land allocation, 48; and Moi, 25; manipulation of PA by, 33; slum policy, 33-34; support for NGOs, 26; and urbanization, 33
Kenyatta, Uhuru, 65
Kibagare, 37
Kibaki, Mwai, 65, 71, 77, 173; and changáa, 122; constitutional reform, 86; policy on slums, 220-21; position on forced evictions 141, 173-74, 195-96, 201; and the PA, 219; and Soweto upgrade, 137, 191. *See also* NARC
Kibera, 44-45, 47; and CBOs, 53-54, 181-82; and Christian churches in, 53, 142, 226-27; conflict between landlords and tenants, 47-49, 138-39, 146, 181, 220; and corruption of local governance, 49-50, 76, 105, 133, 166-70, 172, 218, 222-23; education levels in, 45, 222; ethnicity within, 45-48, 68, 76, 121, 137-38, 146-47, 159, 222, 224; and housing, 45-46, 48; lack of community groups, 147, 223-24; lack of rule of law, 93, 219; limited knowledge of laws and rights, 67; land ownership of, 46-48, 222; NGOs in, 52-53, 68; political manipulation in, 51-52, 68, 96, 219-20, 224; religious leaders' weaknesses, 116-17, 142-43, 160-62, 171-72, 226-27; religious polarization in, 142, 160; and rent clashes, 49, 51, 69, 224; threats by NDP youth wingers, 69, 96, 99, 109, 151, 164, 171, 182, 200, 223; under Kibaki, 220. *See also* chiefs; OHR; PA; Raila, Odinga
Kibwana, Kivutha, 25n1, 27n14
Kikuyu, 26n4, 150, 159, 177, 182; displacement by colonials, 32; as Kibera structure owners, 46-49, 136, 140, 147, 180-81; Kibaki as one, 141; under Kenyatta, 25-26; under Moi, 27
Kimondo, George Kanyi, 25n1, 29n24
King's African Rifles, 48
Kirii, Mugo, 45n80

Kisii, 26n4, 50, 140
Kithari, Miloon (Special Rapporteur on Adequate Housing to the UN Commission on Human Rights), 192, 195, 206, 221. *See also* eviction threat of 2004
KPLC (Kenya Power and Light Company), 176-77. *See also* eviction threat of 2004
Korogocho, 36, 38, 141, 153; dependency on NGOs, 180; and campaign against chang'aa, 118-19; response to 2004 eviction threat, 176, 189, 193, 195, 200-01
Klopp, Jacqueline, 37n59
KRC (Kenya Railways Corporation), 47, 176, 197-98, 203, 207. *See also* eviction threat of 2004
Kuperus, Tracy, 23n112
Kutoka network, 44, 190; access to finances, 233; access to diplomats, 192, 212, 217; and campaign against changáa, 116-18; and civic education, 66; limitations of, 118, 208, 229; response to 2004 eviction threat, 187-190, 196-97, 201, 212; response to Soweto upgrade, 153, 156. *See also* Land Caucus; Muungano wana Vijiji

land: conflicts over, 31-32; ownership of in Kibera, 48-49; and land grabbing, 37-39; illegal allocation of, 32, 49, 221; and landlessness, 31-33
Land Caucus, vii, 40-41, 149, 156, 217; conflict with NGOs, 43-44, 145, 183, 189; response to slum evictions, 40-41. *See also* Kutoka network; Muungano wana Vijiji
Landlords Multi-Purpose Cooperative Society, 141, 148. *See also* Soweto upgrade
Langford, Malcolm, 149n27
Latin America, 56-57, 59, 227, 230, 235
Lebeaupin, Archbishop Alain Paul, 167, 170
Leo, Christopher, 32n35
Legio Maria Church, 28n19
Lewis, David, 3n6
liberation theology, 56-57
Lindi, 46, 57, 117; conflicts with PA, 122, 169; demographics of, 47; and 2004 eviction threat, 185; SCCs in, 68, 74, as a sub-parish, 91, 123n24. *See also* Kibera
Line Saba, 56; demographics of, 46; and 2004 eviction threat, 179, 184; SCCs in, 67; as a sub-parish, 123n24. *See also* Kibera
Locke, Johne, 3
Lonsdale, John, 23n111
LSK (Law Society of Kenya), 28
Lukudu, Caesar, 31n34
Luo, 26n4, 108, 121, 148; and church affiliations, 159; conflicts with other ethnic groups, 135, 148, 155, 160, 166; in Kibera, 47; political allegiance to Raila, 52, 136-38, 220; as parish leaders, 148, 166; as tenants, 47, 51, 121, 136, 140-41, 159, 220. *See also* NDP; NDP youth wingers; Raila, Odinga
Lutheran Church, 53n101
Lynch, Gabrielle, 30n27

Maasai, 26n4, 32, 49
Macharia, Kenneth, 33n39
Macharia, Kinutha, 37n58
Macoloo, Gervase, 32n38
Magesa, Laurenti, 57n106
Maji na Ufanisi (Water Aid): limitations of, 144, 146, 163-64; presence in Kibera, 53, 144, 184; as SEC representative, 163, 166; response to 2004 eviction threat, 182-84. *See also* housing NGOs;

NGO Coalition against Evictions; SEC
Makumbe, John, 19n95
Mandela, Nelson, 1
Marcos, Ferdinand, 38
Marx, Karl, 2-4
Maryknoll Missionaries, vii, 38
Mashimoni, 46-47. *See also* Kibera
Mathare 4A slum upgrade, 148-50, 156-57, 161, 170. *See also* Soweto upgrade
Mathare Valley, 34, 103
Mau Mau Emergency, 48, 141
Maupeu, Herve, 28n20
Mazrui, Ali, 63n5
media, 68, 111, 152, 205; and campaign against changáa, 105, 115, 118; in Kibera, 54, 115; and 2004 eviction threat, 187, 191, 197, 201-02, 208
Mexico, 56-57, 132, 193, 234
Misereor, 40n65
missionaries, 62, 67, 110, 116, 174, 234; access to finances, 67, 83, 110, 118-19, 142, 172, 212, 227, 232; in CTK, 59, 74, 78; civic education promoted by, 66-67; collaboration with NGOs, 39-40, 233; conflict with local church, 172, 228-29; conflict with NGOs, 42-43, 145, 148, 229; development role of, 26, 56; growth of, 234; immunity to state retaliation, 101, 158, 188, 229, 232; and the Land Caucus, 39; limitations of, 119, 171, 188, 198, 200, 209, 228-29, 233; links to diplomats, 155, 171, 173, 190, 193, 201-02, 216, 232-33; support for human rights, 149, 213, 232-33; role in slum parishes, 35-36, 148, 153-54; transient nature of, 43, 172, 233. *See also* Catholicism; Comboni Fathers; CTK; Guadalupe Missionaries; Kutoka network; Maryknoll
Mitullah, Winnie, 33n42, 34n44, 49n89, 52n99, 54n105
Moi, Daniel arap, 16, 25, 175; and authoritarianism, 26-28,73; and changáa prohibition, 103, 105; civil society repressed by, 16, 26, 28, 34, 37, 62, 68, 183; and corruption, 26-29, 65; and constitutional reform, 29-30, 80n29; and ethnicity, 25-26; human rights abuses by, 26-30; land grabbing by, 37, 48,174, 209; and the PA, 219, opposition to by some churches, 28-30; repression of civic education, 63, 68; slum policy of, 34, 37; and Soweto upgrade, 136-37. *See also* KANU
Mombasa-Uganda railway, 47
Moreno, Antonio, 8n36
Mountain View, 41n67
Mugai, Githu, 25n2
Muge, Bishop Alexander, 28n19
Mugisha, Frederick, 106n16
Mukuru kwa Njenga, 118, 176, 180, 187, 192
Multi-Stakeholder Support Group, 137, 163. *See also* Soweto upgrade
Muoroto, 37
Muslims: conflict over land, 47-48, 142; and constitutional reform, 30; the DO as one, 120; and Nubians, 48; response to 2004 eviction threat, 185
Mutua, Makau, 65n12
Mutunga, Willy, 30n26
Muungano wana Vijij (Federation of the Urban Poor), 40-41, 53, 151, 204, 235; financial support for, 40, 42; government repression of, 40, 42; impact of, 41-42; in Kibera, 164, 168, 226; opposition to by Moi, 41-42; relationship to Catholic Church, 41; as savings groups, 43. 182; strategies of, 40;

weakness of, 41-42. *See also* KCS; Land Caucus; Pamoja Trust
Muyebe, Alex, 228n7
Muyebe, Stanlaus, 228n7

Nairobi, vii, x, 30, 34, 45, 49, 104, 231; and slum growth, 31-32
NARC (National Alliance Rainbow Coalition), 65, 68, 79, 121, 173, 186; cooption of housing NGOs, 173, 183, 205, 208, 213, 225-26; eviction policies of, 173-75; and house demolitions, 174. *See also* Kibaki, Mwai; Odinga, Raila
Nasong'o, Shadrack, 17-20, 30n28
National Alliance Party, 65
NCC (Nairobi City Council), 37, 45; and Department of Housing, 160; and Department of Physical Planning, 143; and Director of Housing, 139, 152, 170, 184; role in slum upgrading, 164; and the Soweto upgrade, 137, 143, 160
NCCK (National Council of Churches Kenya), 35, 63
NCEC (National Convention Executive Council), 29-30. *See also* constitutional reform
NCEP (National Civic Education Programme), 64-65. *See also* constitutional reform
Ndegwa, Stephen, 1n2, 17-19
Ndingi, Archbishop Mwana a'Nzeki, Rafael, 58, 97, 195, 228; and the 2004 eviction threat, 187; and human rights, 41, 58, 66, 195; and Mathare 4A slum upgrade, 148-49, 156; opposition to changáa by, 104, 118; position on slums, 41; and Soweto upgrade, 153, 156; support for multi-party democracy, 28n19. *See also* Archdiocese of Nairobi
NDP (National Development Party), 52. *See also* NDP youth wingers; Odinga, Raila
NDP youth wingers, 37, 217; corruption of enumeration process, 199, 207; enforcement of Raila agenda, 52, 68-69, 138, 141, 159, 185, 220; retaliation by, fears of, 70, 96, 99, 109, 151, 164, 170, 182, 186, 199, 224; harassment of civic educators, 70, 77, 96; use of force by, 96, 108-09, 121-22, 146, 164, 168. *See also* NDP; Odinga, Raila
Ndungo, Catherine, 64n8
Netherlands, 193
Neuwirth, Rob, 139n11, 165n37
New Policy Agenda, 7
NGOs (non-governmental agencies): as civic education providers, 63; as civil society actors, 6; criticisms of, 15-22; and democracy building, 7; and donor agendas, 20-22; and dependency on, 81, 180; and development, 7, 25, 38; financial allowances paid by, 75, 114, 226; in Kibera, 52-54; leadership challenges of, 17-19; undemocratic structures in, 19; under Kenyatta, 26; and urban bias, 64. *See also* housing NGOs; human rights NGOs
NGO Coalition against Evictions, 196; strategies of, 197, 200, 202; and Soweto upgrade, 146; weaknesses of, 202-06, 225-26. *See also* eviction threat of 2004; housing NGOs
Nge'ethe, Njuguna, 31n30
Ngunyi, Mutahi, 28n19
NHC (National Housing Corporation), 137, 139
Nigeria, 197
Njoya, Rev. Timothy, 28n19
Njugunjiri, Njuguna, 51n93
Nubians, 185; and changáa trade, 102-03; and conflicts over land and rent, 51, 141-42, 148; and

eviction threat of 2004, 178, 185; history in Kibera, 47-48
Nyayo Highrise, 46, 139
Nzomo, Maria, 63n7

Odinga, Raila, 52, 68, 140, 144; and constitutional reform, 86; defections to opposition parties, 65; and ethnicity, 52, 68, 86, 136-140, 220; and Kibaki, 220; influence in Kibera, 137-38, 181, 220; and Moi, 220; as Minister of Roads, Public Works and Housing, 136-37, 140, 174, 220; political manipulation of Soweto upgrade by, 135-36, 138-140, 151, 156, 158, 168, 170, 192; support for 2004 slum evictions, 174-76, 195; use of force by, 51-52. *See also* NDP; NDP youth wingers
Odinga, Jaramogi Oginga, 51
OHR (Office of Human Rights), vii, ix, 56, 59; access to funds, 67, 81, 85, 110, 115, 132, 213; as a parish ministry, 59-60; conflict with JPC, 59-60, 74, 82; international networks of, 156, 173, 187, 208; limitations of, 133, 208-09. *See also* CTK; Kibera; OHR: campaign against changáa; OHR: civic education programme; OHR: response to 2004 eviction threat; OHR: response to Soweto upgrade
OHR: campaign against changáa, 101; advocacy strategies of, 101, 110-11, 113, 117-20; allowances demanded, 114; and awareness raising, 110-16; conclusions on, 211-12; fears related to, 103, 108, 112, 115-16, 124-26, 133; funding for, 110-115; impact of, 113, 117, 120, 131; limitations of, 111-13, 115, 117-21, 125-28, 130, 132; religious groups' response to, 115-19; and social analysis findings on, 105-08, 111, 131; support for by Archbishop Ndingi, 104, 118; violence related to, 112, 115, 118, 121-22, 125. *See also* changáa; CTK; DO; Kutoka network; PA
OHR: civic education programme, 62; and allowances, 74-76, 80, 83- 84; apathy toward, 61, 80, 99; and Catholic social teaching, 67, 70, 82, 88; challenges of, 72-80, 99; collaboration with Kutoka network, 66, 87; conclusions on, 211-13; and constitutional review, 86-87; and curriculum, 70, 81, 83-86; fears related to, 68-69, 77; funding for, 81, 83, 85; harassment by PA, 68-69, 77, 95-96; and HIV and AIDS, 73, 75, 84; impact of, 61-62, 71, 80-85, 88-100, 211, 213-15; and the JPC, 68, 74, 77, 84; knowledge of rights by parishioners, 67-68, 222-23; and legal cases, 92; limitations of, 95-100; opposition to within parish, 74, 84-85; pedagogy of, 69-71, 80, 83, 85-86; and restrictive church protocols, 95, 97, 99; and Sunday Christians, 70, 76-77, 81; and threats by NDP youth wingers, 68-70, 93, 96; and women, 68-69, 71, 77-79, 81, 84, 86-88, 90-91; and youth, 70, 76-78. *See also* civic education; constitutional reform
OHR: response to eviction threat of 2004, 173-74; and advocacy efforts, 173, 175-76, 187-88, 201-02; apathy towards, 179-80, 199-201, 208; awareness raising on, 178-79, 185-86, 199-200, and Archbishop Ndingi, 187, 195; and collaboration with housing NGOs, 175, 183-84, 191, 194-96; and

collaboration with religious leaders, 184-87, 190, 199-200; conclusions on, 211, 217; conflicts with housing NGOs, 199, 201-05; and ethnicity, 177-78, 180-81; fears related to, 173, 177-80, 182, 185-86, 199, 208; impact of, 191, 193-95, 2007; and Kutoka network, 187-88, 192, 201, 208; and lawsuit filed, 193-95, 197; limitations of, 181-82, 185-87, 200-01, 208-09; lobbying by the Catholic Church officials, 190-91, 193, 195, 201; lobbying by diplomats, 193, 201; and UN-Habitat's response, 191-92; strategies of, 178-79, 184-85, 190-91, 193-94, 196, 199-203. *See also* CTK; evictions; NGO Coalition against Evictions
OHR: response to Soweto upgrade, 135; advocacy efforts by, 147-48, 156-59; and Archbishop Ndingi, 155; awareness raising on; 149, 151, 158; and collaboration with Catholic Church officials, 156, 167, 170; conclusions on, 212; collaboration with religious leaders, 160-63, 167; and the Kutoka network, 153-54; limitations of, 146-47, 150-51, 160, 167-69, 171; links with housing NGOs, 143-46, 163; lobbying of diplomatic missions, 156-58; lobbying of UN-Habitat, 152, 156, 168-70; coordinator's role in the SEC, 159, 166-67; and the peace building project, 153-155; response to councilor's corruption, 166-67, 169-70; role of CTK in, 147-49; strategies of, 148, 151-52, 156-57, 161-62, 169-71. *See also* KENSUP; Mathare 4a slum upgrade; Soweto upgrade; UN-Habitat
Okech, Owiti, 27n14
Okullo, Henry, 28n19
Oloo, Adams, 26n7
Orvis, Stephen, 4n14, 21, 30n29, 66
Otiso, Kefa, 32n36, 148n24
Ottaway, Marina, 7n34, 15-16
Otunga, Cardinal Maurice, 35-36, 41; policy on slums, 36; response to slum demolitions, 37
Our Lady of Guadalupe Catholic Church, 116, 190
Owiti, Jeremiah, 26n7
Owiyo, Suzanna, 113
Oxfam GB, 40n65
Oyugi, Walter, 18-20

PA (Provincial Administration), 104, 119-20, 176, 185, 201, 216; abuse of power by, 96,179-80; corruption within, 108, 141, 159, 219; retaliation by, fear of, 77, 132, 224 in Kibera, 50-51; limited authority of, 121-22; repression of civic education, 63, 78; under Kibaki, 219; use of force by, 96, 219. *See also* Administrative Police; chiefs; DO; PC
Pamoja Trust, vii, 43, 80, 150, in Kibera, 53; and 2004 eviction threat, 180, 182-84, 196-99, 207; and slum upgrading, 136; and the Soweto upgrade, 144-45, 162-63, 168
papal nuncio. *See* Tonucci, Archbishop Giovanni; Lebeaupin, Archbishop Alain Paul
Parsons, Timothy, 48n84, 103n5
pastoral circle, 60, 102. *See also* CTK; social analysis
pastoral letters, 29, 66, 228. *See also* KEC
pastoral team, 58-60, 177-79, 216; and campaign against changáa, 110, 127-28; opposition to OHR by some, 74, 85; and the social analysis, 102, 123-24; and Soweto upgrade, 150. *See also* CTK

Patel, Sheila, 43n72
patronage, 49, 76, 103, 143, 229; under Kenyatta, 25, under Moi, 26-27, 36; and Raila, 138, 220
PC (Provincial Commissioner), 50, 104-05; support for campaign against changáa, 119-21. *See also* PA
Pentecostals, 107, 126, 160; and campaign against changáa, 117; collaboration with other churches, 142, 159; in Kibera, 53; response to 2004 eviction threat, 185-86, 199; response to Soweto upgrade, 142, 159
Percy, Fiona, 20n96
Permanent Observer of the Holy See to UN-Habitat, 156. *See also* Tonucci, Archbishop Giovanni
Philippines, 38, 191, 227
Pierli, Francesco, 36n54
Pioneer Abstinence Movement, 109, 123
police, 94,114-15, 169, 185; abuse of power by, 27, 37, 38- 41, 219, 221; corruption within, 70, 76, 88, 219; role in changáa trade, 101, 103-05, 108, 110-12, 117-21, 125-26, 130, 211. *See also* Administrative Police
politics: creation of patrimonial state, 25; and democracy movement, 16, 28-30, 64-65; as a one-party state, 25-26, 29. *See also* Kenyatta, Jomo; Kibaki, Mwai; Moi, Daniel Arap
poverty, 1-2, 25, 27; as a result of changáa, 106; in Kibera, 45; NGO response to, 15; in rural areas, 34, 78; under Moi, 27
PPC (Parish Pastoral Council), 58; ethnicity within, 148, 155, 166; impact of civic education on, 90; and the peace building project, 155; protocols within, 97; role in parish planning, 123; weaknesses of, 148, 155, 232. *See also* CTK
press. *See* media
Press, Robert, 28n18
Presbyterian Church, 53n101
prostitution, 36, 46, 102-03, 106
Protestants; 142, 235; in Kibera, 53; opposition to one-party state, 28; opposition to slum evictions, 35; support for constitutional reform, 28
Putnam, Robert, 4

Raila village: demolition of, 174-76; and eviction threat of 2004, 181, 192; response by OHR, 175. *See also* Kibera
Redeemed Gospel Church, 28n19
Renato, Cardinal Martino, 190-91, 195, 228
Roughtone, 113
Rutten, Marcel, 63n5
Sabar-Friedman, Galia, 28n21, 63n4

SCCs (small Christian communities), 56-60; civic education classes in, 70-74, 81-86, 88; function of, 57; impact of civic education in, 89-95, 101, 113, 115, 123; leadership problems in, 73-74, 108; weaknesses of, 68-69, 77-79, 99, 113, 123, 147, 151, 182, 230-32. *See also* Catholicism; CTK
SDI (Slum Dwellers International), 43n72, 198
SEC (Settlement Executive Committee), 137, 163-64; corruption within 164-170; limitations of, 159, 163. *See also* KENSUP; Soweto slum upgrade
Seventh Day Adventists, 28n19
Shelter Forum, 137, 196-97; and response to slum evictions, 183, 197; and role in Soweto upgrade, 144, 163

Shilanga: challenges for civic education in, 72, 79; demographics, 46; response to 2004 eviction threat, 199; SCCs in, 68; as a sub-parish, 57. *See also* Kibera

slum settlements, 31; Catholic church's response to, 35-38, 40-42; civil society's response to, 35-44; during colonialism, 31-33; growth post-independence, 33; as income source, 221; Kibaki's policy on, 221; living conditions in, 34-35; growth in sub-Saharan Africa, 235. *See also* Kawangware; Kibagare; Kibera; Korogocho; Mathare Valley; Mukuru kwa Njenga; Muroto

slum upgrading, 95, 131, 143, 233; as a civic education topic, 80, 86; historically in Kibera, 159; and housing NGOs, 163-64. *See also* Huruma; Mathare 4A slum upgrade; Nyayo Highrise; Soweto upgrade

Slums Committee, 38-39

Smith, Colin, 53n102

social analysis: input on changáa, 102, 105-08, 110-11, 131-32; methodology of, 60; and parish restructuring, 123-24. *See also* CTK; pastoral circle

Sommer, Kirsten, 35n50

South Africa, 191, 227

Soviet Union, 1

Soweto: and the changáa trade, 105, 107-08, 115, 120-21; changáa as priority for sub-parish, 102-03, 111-12, 122-23, 126-33; effect of 2004 eviction threat in, 177-78, 181-82, 199. *See also* changáa; Kibera; Soweto upgrade

Soweto upgrade, 135-40; apathy toward, 164; and Athi River, 140, 158; consequences of, 137-38; co-option of by councilor, 138, 151, 159, 165-171; and corruption within, 135, 141, 158, 166-71, 220; and enumeration process, 161-63, 170; ethnic manipulation of, 136-41, 146-47; fears related to, 137-39, 142, 147, 150, 158, 160, 169-171; and the Finnish government, 140, 158; manipulation of by Raila, 135-40, 146, 170; opposition to by structure owners, 139-41; response by housing NGOs, 143-46, 163, 167-68; response by religious leaders, 142, 160-61; and violence, 138, 140-42, 145, 164. *See also* KENSUP; OHR: response to Soweto upgrade; SEC; UN-Habitat

Special Rapporteur on Adequate Housing to the UN Commission on Human Rights, 192-93. *See also* Kithari, Miloon; eviction threat of 2004

St. Jerome's Church, 53

St. Mary's Catholic Church, 187

St. Michael's Catholic Church, 56, 116

Sunday Christians, 70, 102, 108, 127, 232; disinterest in civic education, 76, 81. *See also* CTK

Sweden, 193

Syagga, Paul, 33n42, 34n45, 52n99, 54n105

Talukdar, Debabrata, 221n5

Tangaza College, 83, 190

Tempra, Ombretta, 35n50

Teyie, Andrew, 87n37

Tibaijuka, Anna, 136; and Cardinal Martino, 190-91; lobbying by papal nuncio, 156-57, 170; OHR lobbying of, 156, 170-71; position on Soweto upgrade, 136-37, 152, 168, 192. *See also* Soweto upgrade, UN-Habitat

Timmel, Sally, 62n2

Toi Market, 41n67, 184
Tonucci, Archbishop Giovanni, 156-57, 233; advocacy related to 2004 eviction threat, 189-90, 193, 195; limited impact on local church, 228; response to Soweto upgrade, 156-57, 167
Trocaire, 85, 110, 129, 132
Turkey, 191

Ufungamano Initiative, 30. *See also* constitutional reform
Uganda, 218
Uggla, Frederick, 5n21
UN Commission on Human Rights, 192
UN Human Rights Committee, 201
UN-Habitat, 164, 168; failure to inform community, 135, 152, 156, 168, 170; and housing NGOs, 168; lack of response by, 152, 156, 161; limitations of, 136, 156, 161, 168; limited access to officials, 140, 143, 152, 168, 170-71; lobbying of by diplomats, 157, 169-70; lobbying of by OHR, 161, 170; lobbying of by Catholic Church officials, 157, 170; position on FBOs, 159; relationship with Raila, 168. *See also* KENSUP; Multi-Stakeholder Support Group; NHC; OHR: response to Soweto upgrade; Soweto Upgrade
UN-Habitat Advisory Group on Forced Evictions, 192, 197, 202. *See also* eviction threat of 2004; UN-Habitat
United Kingdom, 31, 193
Undungu Society of Kenya, 17
United States, 4, 14, 67, 153
upgrading. *See* slum upgrading; Soweto upgrade

VeneKlasen, Lisa, 16n79
village elders, 50, 219, 224. *See also* PA
violence, 8, 36, 76, 99, 220; against the parish, 156, 170; of a domestic nature, 104, 107; election-related, 28-30, 68, 70, 76, 90; ethnically provoked, 152, 235; in Kibera, 49, 54, 68, 76; politically provoked, 54, 68, 70; related to rent conflicts, 49, 141; resulting from eviction threat, 177-78, 185; and Soweto upgrade, 141, 147-48, 150
Viva Nairobi, 189
vote buying, 69, 76-77. *See also* elections
voter education, 7, 63. *See also* civic education

Wainaina, Eric, 113
Waliggo, John Mary, 228n6
Wambuii, Henry, 21-22
Wanjala, Smokin, 27n14
Wanjohi, Nick, 50n91
Wanyama, Frederick, 20
Wasonga, Bishop Otieno, 105
Werlin, Herbert, 33n41
Weru, Jane, 136n1
Wesselink, Carl, 63n6
Westlands Market, 40n64, 41n67
Widner, Jennifer, 27n9
Willis, Justin, 102n4, 103n6
women: challenges facing, 73, 79, 84, 231; fears of PA, 69; limited knowledge of rights, 68; impact of civic education on, 71, 78, 81-82, 86-88, 90-91; and single mothers, 72, 78-79, 175
women's groups: as CBOs, 54; in the parish, 58; as savings groups, 182; under Moi, 28n17
World Bank, 159; and slum upgrading in Kibera, 165, 177, 207
World Urban Forum, 201
World War II, 32

youth: and campaign against changáa, 110-14, 118; challenges facing, 106-07, 224; in the parish, 58-59, 81, 155, 176; participation in OHR civic education, 70, 77-78, 83, 151; and violence, 49

Zambia, 17
Zimbabwe, 197